$10.95

Crisis in the Philippines

The preparation of this book has been made possible by The Asia Society, New York as part of a project on the Philippines and Philippine-American relations.

CRISIS IN THE PHILIPPINES

The Marcos Era and Beyond

EDITED BY

JOHN BRESNAN

PRINCETON UNIVERSITY PRESS

PRINCETON, NEW JERSEY

Copyright © 1986 by Princeton University Press
Published by Princeton University Press, 41 William Street,
Princeton, New Jersey 08540
In the United Kingdom: Princeton University Press, Guildford, Surrey

All Rights Reserved

Library of Congress Cataloging in Publication Data will be
found on the last printed page of this book

ISBN 0-691-05490-8 (cloth)
ISBN 0-691-00810-8 (pbk.)

This book has been composed in Linotron Sabon

Clothbound editions of Princeton University Press books
are printed on acid-free paper, and binding materials are
chosen for strength and durability. Paperbacks, although satisfactory
for personal collections, are not usually suitable for library rebinding

Printed in the United States of America by Princeton University Press
Princeton, New Jersey

CONTENTS

FOREWORD

DAVID D. NEWSOM

This volume by the Asia Society takes a close look at the Philippines today through both Philippine and American eyes. It explores the status and the importance of the relationship between these two nations, and in the process, examines the disturbing political and economic issues confronting the Philippines and its friends. The essays of this volume were written in large part before the dramatic events in the Philippines of February 1986. It is the more remarkable that they presaged so accurately the circumstances that precipitated those events, and required so little change in the light of them.

The signs of impending trouble were apparent even at the time of my own short term as ambassador in Manila, from November 1977 to April 1978. I went with a mixture of emotions and impressions. Coming from another post in Asia, as I did, an American diplomat is already impressed with the talent, the dynamism, and the identity with the United States of the many Filipinos living in other parts of that continent. They are managers, technicians, musicians, teachers—each one testifying to a special national heritage and to the advantages of one of the more advanced educational systems in Asia.

To an American who has spent many years in the former colonies of other powers, it is a rare experience to sense in the Philippines the same complex of post-colonial feelings that one has observed elsewhere—except that this time it is your country that has been the colonist. It is the diplomat of the United States who must deal with the pressure for immigration, the residual problems of veterans, pensions, and family reunification, the inevitable question of the nationalization of property, and the more basic challenge of maintaining a fruitful relationship.

No U.S. diplomat who has served in a country bordering on the Indian Ocean or who has faced the problems of global strategy and fleet deployments can come to Manila without a consciousness of the worldwide significance for the United States of the bases in the Philippines and, in particular, Subic Bay.

But I came to the Philippines with two other sets of experiences.

An uncle of mine, John W. Dunlop, had gone to Cebu as a missionary in 1919. With a fondness for the people and the hills of Cebu that he never lost, he retired to the Philippines and died there in 1977. I had the opportunity to visit with him from my post in Jakarta shortly before he died. We visited farmers he had helped in the interior of Cebu. We visited his parishioners in the city, the poor and the lower middle-class. When I subsequently was appointed to Manila and lived in the ostentatious surroundings of Forbes Park, I could never forget that other Philippines that I had seen in the barrios and farms of Cebu. I could never quit myself of the feeling that the gap was too great—dangerously great—between those people in Cebu and those isolated wealthy who lived in a different world in Manila.

Five times in my foreign service career, I had responsibilities relating to countries where violent revolutions occurred, revolutions detrimental to the interests of the United States: in Iraq, Libya, Ethiopia, Iran, and Nicaragua. In each case, in varying degrees, the elements were present that I detected upon coming to the Philippines in 1977: the gap between the poor and the rich, the corruption in high places, the ruler protecting his family and friends and unwilling to face the realities of an ultimate transition of authority to someone else. In each case, the United States had been unable to influence events or protect its interests.

Fortunately for us, the situation turned out differently in the Philippines. The strength and courage of the Filipino people, their faith in democracy, and the vital roles of the middle class and the Church turned the tide against Marcos and his rule. The United States, even though there were moments of uncertain signals, was seen to be on the right side.

It is to be hoped that there was another result from these

events: that the people of the United States have seen the relationship with the Philippines in broader terms than before.

Until now, the importance of the Philippines to the United States has been seen almost totally in terms of the continued use of the two bases at Clark Field and Subic Bay. Debates in Washington on how to deal with the Philippines in both the executive and legislative branches have tended to revolve around this issue.

Filipinos have both resented and regretted this. They have seen other advantages to the United States in the relationship. They have believed that the United States should be proud of much that it did in the development of the Philippines and of the Filipino people. They have looked for a greater recognition of the sacrifices of the Filipinos in the common cause with Americans during World War II. In no other Asian country has there been such a deep feeling of friendship toward the United States, solidified by the countless family ties with relatives in America; not too many years ago, six million Filipinos signed a petition for statehood within the United States. Instead of a recognition of these ties, the Filipinos have seen what they regard as a neglect of the basic needs of the island republic and a concentraton solely on the issue of the bases.

Undoubtedly, the Filipinos now hope that the reports of their country and its people on television, the extensive visits by prominent Americans, and the identity with the success of Mrs. Aquino will lead the people of the United States and the U.S. government to a deeper appreciation of the full measure of this relationship.

The political changes in the Philippines have not resolved its deep problems, many of which are discussed in this volume. One hopes that they have given the people and the government opportunities to deal with the problems, free of the burdens of a corrupt and authoritarian regime. The Filipinos will hope that the United States will continue to be interested and involved.

With their national pride and sensitivity over sovereignty, the Filipinos wish the Americans to be interested and concerned in their affairs, but not to interfere. The distinction, never very clear, is spelled out only in reaction to individual

acts of the United States or, occasionally, in opportunistic political rhetoric. Much of that will, in the years immediately to
come, revolve around the issue of the bases.

In 1991, the agreement between the United States and the
Philippines over the use of the two major bases will expire.
There are those who, ignoring the realities of Philippine politics and trends, insist that the Filipinos will always want the
bases because of their security implications and economic benefits. Others feel this is a dangerous assumption and that a prudent view of both U.S. interests and the possible future course
of events in the Philippines should lead us to examine alternative arrangements. President Aquino has insisted that the issue
be left open until 1991.

Our long-term relationship with the Philippines will depend
on how we deal not only with the bases issue but with the other
problems facing the islands. The concern over how much the
United States is interested in Philippine affairs may, in the
longer term, be a passing issue. A new generation growing in
the islands, where 50 percent of the population is under
twenty, may be less interested in the historic American tie.
These years ahead will be times of difficult choices for both Filipinos and Americans. Those who have tasted, even briefly,
the uniqueness of this relationship hope for wisdom and the
maintenance of mutual respect and interests on both sides. The
foundation of such a relationship is a knowledge of the issues.
We hope this book will help to contribute some of that knowledge.

PREFACE

JOHN BRESNAN

At nine o'clock in the evening of February 27, 1986, Ferdinand Marcos fled the presidential palace of Malacañang in Manila, crossed the Pasig River at its rear, and from the opposite shore took a United States air force helicopter to Clark Field. His long domination of his nation was over. Corazon Aquino, the widow of his assassinated rival, Benigno Aquino, acceded to power as the new president of the Philippines.

This book describes the rise and fall of Ferdinand Marcos. It assesses the impact of his regime on the political, economic, and social life of the Philippine people. And it considers the implications of this experience for the United States. The book does so in the light of history and from the perspectives of ten Philippine and American scholars.

The book had its origin in the assassination of Benigno Aquino on August 21, 1983. The event triggered an immediate reaction of shock and dismay, not only in the Philippines, but also in the United States. In Manila, millions watched his funeral cortege pass, and the central bank reported massive capital flight from the country. In Washington, the House of Representatives passed a resolution by a vote of 413 to 3, deploring the killing, calling for "a thorough, independent, and impartial" investigation, and giving its support to "genuine, free and fair" elections in the Philippines. It was evident that the Philippines and Philippine-American relations had entered a period of trial and testing.

The officers of The Asia Society invited me in the fall of 1983 to advise them as to how the Society should respond to these developments. The Society is a private, nonprofit, nonpartisan educational institution that has its principal offices in New York. For more than a quarter century the Society had acted to increase American understanding of Asia through programs of education focused on Asian history, culture, and art. The Society was in 1983 beginning to give equal attention to the political and economic life of contemporary Asia and to issues in the current relations of Asian countries with the United States. But it was not immediately clear what the Society could usefully do in the widening Philippine crisis.

The Society made it possible for me to consult widely in the Philippines and in the United States. I heard a good deal of opinion in both countries that a serious problem existed in the level of American knowledge and understanding of the Philippines. The situation was in some respects predictable: the United States tended to have a considerable impact on the Philippines, much of it unintended, while the Philippines had great difficulty even gaining American attention. But this could be said of many countries. The Philippines, I was told by many I consulted, was different in two respects.

First, the impact of the United States on the Philippines has been unlike that on any other. It has been much greater than the impact of the United States on Mexico, for example, where the United States has been much more proximate but where it has never been a colonial power. The impact of the United States on the Philippines has been truly enormous, extending not only to political and economic values and institutions, but also to language, literature, the graphic and performing arts, even religion. There has thus been a tendency for Americans to see Filipinos as being rather like themselves, and to fail to appreciate the great differences that continue to exist within the familiar outer forms of Filipino life.

Second, the number of Americans who have a continuing interest in and familiarity with the Philippines is very small. Except for a few scholars, government officials, bankers, and investors, Americans did not follow the affairs of the Philippines at all closely until the dramatic events of February 1986. The community of Filipino-Americans, although growing rapidly, was still too new to be a significant factor in American opinion. There is thus nothing like the wider constituency of interested and informed citizens who thicken the American relationship with some other societies and who provide a balance to the rise and fall of official relations.

In these circumstances, The Asia Society was urged to try to do two things: to broaden the unofficial community of Americans with an interest in the Philippines, and to help those who did know the country well to communicate their views to a wider American public.

The Society accepted this advice. Under its auspices, a group of ten leading Americans from a variety of walks of life visited the Philippines in January 1986; their findings have since been published by the Society under the title *The Philippines: Facing the Future*. A similar group of Filipinos was scheduled to visit the United States in June 1986.

To serve the wider public, the Society commissioned me to plan and edit for publication a book on the crisis precipitated by the Aquino death and its aftermath. It was agreed that the book should be relevant to the issues of the moment, and several chapters have been revised just prior to publication in order to take into account the further crisis occasioned by the fraudulent election of February 7, 1986, and the swift fall of Mr. Marcos thereafter. But it also was agreed that the opportunity should be taken to explore, for the benefit of readers coming new to a book about the Philippines, the deeper origins of these crises in the social, economic, and political history of the country.

Beyond that, the Society left me free to proceed. In an early communication to prospective contributors to the book, I explained that it was my aim to produce a book for the serious general reader, someone who had an interest in foreign affairs, but who probably had no special knowledge of the Philippines. I also outlined the scope of each chapter. Subsequently, with the help of outside readers, I also exercised a fairly strong hand in the revision of some, though not all, of the chapters. Any shortcomings with respect to the scope, balance, and coherence of the book are therefore fairly laid at my feet, as are any failings in regard to the text's accessibility to the general reader.

The book is, however, chiefly what the chapter writers have made it. All are established authorities on the subjects about which they write; the reader is invited to consult the section

"About the Authors" in the rear of the book for further information about them. Because of the emotionally charged nature of some of the subject matter, the chapter writers also were selected with an eye to their ability to maintain some emotional distance between themselves and their subject.

The Asia Society is grateful to a number of individuals and foundations whose support for the Philippines project made this book possible. Mr. David Rockefeller and Mr. and Mrs. George O'Neill provided generous and timely support that enabled the Society to undertake the project. Grants from the Ford, Henry Luce, Andrew W. Mellon, and Rockefeller foundations and the Rockefeller Brothers Fund have supported the development of the Society's contemporary affairs programs, including the Philippines project. The Society is grateful for their early and continuing support.

The editor of such a book as this has many people to thank. The contributors have been generous and patient in meeting the demands we have placed upon them. My colleagues on the staff of The Asia Society, including Robert Oxnam, David Timberman, Emily Collins, and particularly Marshall Bouton, Eileen D. Chang, and Sara Robertson, were unfailing in their assistance and support during the two years in which the book has been in preparation. James W. Morley and my other colleagues in the East Asian Institute of Columbia University have been especially generous and supportive in making my time free over the same period. Finally, I wish to thank my wife, Barbara, and my son, Mark, for the personal sacrifices they have made in order to make work on the book possible.

March 1986

Crisis in the Philippines

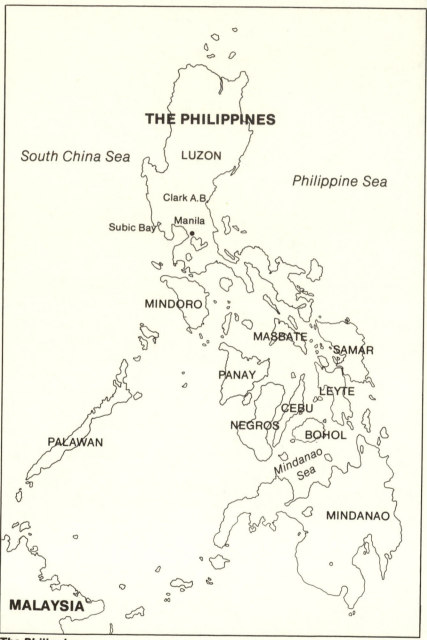

The Philippines

CHAPTER I

PHILIPPINE-AMERICAN TENSIONS IN HISTORY

THEODORE FRIEND

For many Filipinos the United States continues to have almost magical power as benefactor and exploiter. In popular mentality many Filipinos ascribe to America a nearly limitless capacity to shape and resolve, for good or for evil, Philippine destiny.

In fact, the United States that once enjoyed nearly half the world's gross national product now accounts for about one-fifth. And whereas a series of victories in wars, 1846 to 1945, tempted Americans to think of themselves as invincible, Vietnam changed that. We have learned caution about the tactical applicability of power in distant situations. The rise of the Soviet Union to strategic parity in military power has intensified this new realism.

Although the United States is a presumably chastened and ordinarily cautious world power, with limits to its capabilities and intentions regarding the Philippines, Filipinos correctly note that massive differences in scale have indeed determined much of the history between the two nations. But America's raw military and economic power are not sufficient to explain the fond dependence and acute resentment that mark the Philippine side of the relationship. These conflicted feelings derive from the cumulative impact of American social models, cultural standards, and political perspectives, all of which are remarkably deep—and extraordinary for being largely unconscious and unintended by policy.

When other Southeast Asians look at the Philippines, they tend to feel that their own historical permeability to colonial influence was much less; and that they operate now out of

stronger traditions and more genuine autonomy than the Philippines. That may be objectively true. Close inspection of the
Philippine-American relationship, however, will not make ob-
jectivity easy for the key parties involved. Filipinos have
tended to mirror American styles even while resisting American presences. And Americans have tended to look at the Philippines through a one-way glass so darkened with their own
preoccupations that they can hardly see through it.

Conquest and Response

The United States did not plan the conquest of the Philippines.
Neither did it sidestep the opportunity. In the century after the
Northwest Ordinance, the young republic had raced across the
continent, absorbing sparsely settled land into its constitutional framework as states. Still filling its land with diverse
peoples, mainly European, America began to realize its capacity to express itself as an extra-continental power. Like other
nation-states, it found an occasion where will joined capacity.

The last outposts of the Spanish empire, Cuba and the Philippines, had erupted in simultaneous turmoil in 1896-1898.
Each threw its own revolutionary dynamic against the arthritic
rule of Spain. The events that drew the United States into
Cuba—most notably the destruction of the battleship
Maine—drew it also into the Philippines. Why the far Pacific
in addition to the near Caribbean? Chance favors the prepared
mind. One of the best prepared, Theodore Roosevelt, saw the
opportunity to realize the strategic imperialism theorized by
Captain Alfred Thayer Mahan. As Assistant Secretary of the
Navy, Roosevelt sent Commodore Dewey steaming to Manila.
There American forces overpowered the Spanish. Roosevelt
himself resigned his office to lead volunteers into Cuba.

Roosevelt's triumphant gallop up San Juan Hill was eu-
phoric for him, and John Hay called the whole thing a "splen-
did little war." In the Philippine theater, however, easy defeat
of the Spanish was followed by a terrible struggle against Filipinos. The nationalist army led by Aguinaldo and diffusely

captained guerrilla forces held out staunchly. American-declared martial law was not lifted until 1901.

The United States had stepped into the last Latin American revolution against Spain and simultaneously the first Asian revolution against Western power. In the Philippines, America prevailed in savage fighting; then had to take responsibility for the squalid deprivation that followed.

An imperial sense of triumph among some was countered by anti-imperial dismay among others. William Graham Sumner, who wrote of "the conquest of the United States by Spain," foresaw the dangers of becoming a surrogate imperial power. Those errors and terrors the United States would later repeat on a larger, more anachronistic scale: by trying to stand in for the French in Vietnam.

What tilted the United States against its anti-imperial instincts in the Philippine case? The American nation was moved by the logic of expansion that drives most political entities to grow until checked. The United States grasped a strategic opportunity in the Philippines to equip itself as a world military power with a major Asian base; as an economic power, with a tutorial ward to fulfill its democratic-religious mission. Power, profit, and prophecy here converged.

The treaty to annex the Philippines almost failed of passage, nonetheless, in the Senate. New imperial responsibilities never moved the American public to a rage of pride comparable to European cases. The summons in Kipling's exhortation to "take up the White Man's Burden" went against much in the American grain. American energies for Philippine annexation were neither conspiratorial nor inevitable; once provoked, to be sure, they were powerfully confluent with the forces of the age. But after the initial convulsion, basic policies for the Filipinos were defined by Elihu Root (secretary of war, 1899-1904) "to conform to their customs, their habits, and even their prejudices." Practices of rapid Filipinization of all branches and levels of government followed, especially under Francis Burton Harrison (governor-general, 1913-1921).

Hostilities subsided, sympathies arose. Filipinos over time settled into a nationwide pattern of assimilation to the conqueror's style, in harmony with the imperial ruler's accommodations of local interests and aspirations. But that took time. The fact of superior American power was hard to swallow; the realization that Americans were there to stay was hard to digest. Six men summarized the range of responses:

Felipe Salvador, who had fought against the Spanish and the Americans as a guerrilla officer, came forth in 1903 as the "pope" of the Santa Iglesia, a mystical and militant conspiracy that contended for some years against the new regime. He was hanged for murder and sedition in 1911. Having drawn upon a legacy of peasant rebellion, he left it further enriched.

General Artemio Ricarte, though captured in 1900, refused to take an oath of allegiance to the new regime; was deported; returned illegally and was jailed; was deported again in 1910; took root in Japan; returned to the Philippines with Japanese forces in 1942, and died with them in 1945.

General Emilio Aguinaldo, after capture, took the oath of allegiance; ran for President of the Commonwealth in 1935 with weak results; cooperated fully with the Japanese; survived to advanced old age, archaic in his views.

Manuel Quezon, a young guerrilla captain, surrendered only after he saw Aguinaldo in comfortable detention; rose to the presidency of the Senate in 1916; was elected president of the Commonwealth in 1935; died in Washington in 1944, head of the Commonwealth government-in-exile, after two decades at the top of the Philippine political scramble.

Trinidad H. Pardo de Tavera, a Hispanic Filipino, a Europeanized nineteenth-century liberal, supported the Revolution; was appointed by Governor-General Taft to the Philippine Commission, an early colonial governing council; moved on to become a pamphleteer for public secular education, and against church and superstition.

Sergio Osmeña, a young Chinese mestizo from Cebu, rose as a lawyer to become the majority leader among Filipino legislators from 1907 to 1922; after that, second in command to Quezon until 1944, when he succeeded to the presidency of the Commonwealth until just short of independence, 1944 to 1946.

These six men may be arrayed in a continuum of declining

hostility and ascending plasticity to the American imperial presence: Salvador, the irreconcilable guerrilla-pope; Ricarte, the unreconstructable exile; Aguinaldo, the domesticated rebel; Quezon, the conservative dissident; Pardo, the cooperating aristocrat; Osmeña, the constitutional technician. The first three were resisters. The last three represent cooperation in high degree with the new regime. Quezon was the most effective of all, because he projected to the Philippine electorate his guerrilla sense of affronted national pride, even as he learned the English language and American manners to charm American investors and officials.

Although these six can be said collectively to characterize the Filipino responses to American rule in the first part of the twentieth century, none of them epitomizes Philippine character as well as another, who died in 1896, before the Americans arrived. The Spanish executed Jose Rizal as a revolutionary, and thereby made him a national hero and martyr. Even had they not, he would have earned an elevated place in his people's memory as searcher for the lost Filipino past, loving analyst of the national character, and sublime propagandist. He continues still to endear himself to his people as novelist and physician, adventurer and healer, romantic secular saint.

The American-dominated Philippine Commission chose Rizal to honor with statues and celebrations rather than Andres Bonifacio, a more radical revolutionary, or Apolinario Mabini, a pre-Marxian theorist of class struggle. But imperial sponsorship did not besmirch Rizal in the eyes of his people. Even now, with nearly forty years of sovereignty behind them, Filipinos still look to Rizal as their prime exemplar, and their supreme educator. For some, devotion becomes worship. Numerous cults and sects among peasants and urban laborers elevate Rizal to divine status: the word become flesh in the Philippines; one man standing for liberated nation, autonomous culture, and free individual spirit.

The Philippine-American Amalgam, 1901-1941

The United States remained in the Philippines despite three major frustrations. First, the colony did not prove valuable as a jumping-off place to the China trade, and that trade itself, in relation to the visions of vast wealth in 1898-1900, proved to be a mirage. Second, the colony itself could not be deemed a significant economic asset. Private investment returns were small. The United States bought more protected agricultural products from the Philippines than it sold manufactured goods there. The costs of administration were not fully covered by insular taxes, and were enlarged by defense costs met by the United States Treasury. In sum, the Philippines could be considered a significant net economic liability. Third, United States military and naval installations in the Philippines were not developed adequately to meet the potential threat of Japan. Instead of becoming part of the globe-circling power desired by Theodore Roosevelt, they constituted what he feared would be an American "Achilles' heel."

Although Spain had also clung to the Philippines despite its financial losses, it did so because of its territorial imperatives, Christianizing mission, and imperial nostalgia. The United States held on far less tenaciously. The liabilities were analogous, but the motivations to cut loose were much stronger. As early as 1916, a bill for Philippine independence almost passed the American Congress. The act that did pass contained a promise of eventual independence, the first such to arise amid the neomercantilist wave of imperialism that had swept over Asia and Africa from 1870 to 1900.

By 1933 the American forces for independence were strong enough to prevail. These included American beet and sugar lobbies opposed to Philippine sugar, dairy lobbies opposed to coconut oil, and labor lobbies opposed to Filipino immigrant labor. Such economic factions could not have prevailed without the isolationists and the power realists (the latter concerned about exposure vis-à-vis Japan), a new generation of anti-imperialists by party or by principle, and others who might be called emancipatory gradualists, disinterested persons who simply believed that "the time had come" for an independent Philippines.

The time was scheduled for 1946. During this period, a semi-autonomous Commonwealth was headed by a nationally elected Filipino president. Quezon won more than two-thirds of the vote. But nearly one-third of the vote was split between General Aguinaldo and Bishop Gregorio Aglipay of the Philippine Independent Church. Together, the two minority candidates might be said to represent the nativist, provincial, traditional side of nationalism. Judge Juan Sumulong continued as a critic of Quezon, and precursor of the socially conscious, programmatic nationalism of Claro Recto in the 1950s, Jose Diokno in the 1970s and 1980s, and Lorenzo Tañada spanning both periods.

The Commonwealth period was the peaceful apex of Philippine-American cooperation. A constitutional representative system was functioning effectively with a native chief executive. The style that went with this structure was one of shifting, personally based coalitions, with strong familial and provincial ties determining allegiances. Concepts of the debt of honor and of in-group togetherness and trustworthiness were pronouncedly important in a bilaterally extended family system. They produced angles of discourse and axes of alliance too fluid to be called feudal, but certainly regional and factional, bound by personal, authoritarian, and charismatic values.

Two quotations by Manuel Quezon suggest the dynamics and dilemmas of the system in which he flourished: "Better a government run like hell by Filipinos than one run like heaven by Americans" and "Damn the Americans! Why don't they tyrannize us more?" The first, a classic anti-colonial slogan, might have been invented anywhere; but it was earliest said in the Philippines, and easier to say there than anywhere else in Southeast Asia. The second was the frustrated statement of a leader in need of a foreign antagonist and issues of imperial injustice, but not finding them.

Politically conscious Filipinos looked about them and realized, with gratitude toward the Americans, that they had the highest literacy rate in Southeast Asia, even though that was partly owed to a foundation in Spanish times. They saw expenditures on health unrivaled as a proportion of government budget throughout the region. The infrastructure of roads, bridges, and communications lagged behind the Netherlands East Indies, and in agricultural development the Japanese were doing far better in Formosa. What came through to the average Filipino, however—often more forcibly to the minimally educated peasant than to the analytical urban dweller—was that the aim of the United States was to help the Philippines evolve to a scheduled independence, and that its policies with regard to education, health, and welfare were in accord with that aim.

Some other realities clouded the picture. Part of American motivation was negative self-interest, to get rid of the Philippines as a responsibility. The absolute expenditures of the insular government per capita were dramatically small, even if relatively great compared to other imperial powers. American racial attitudes tended to cluster in the range from condescension to bigotry. Even so, the Fil-American colonial skies were fundamentally sunny, whereas stormy overcasts were gathering in Indochina and Indonesia.

With political development toward independence, however, there also proceeded economic development toward dependency. The United States avoided some errors of European empires, such as the plantation systems in Sumatra, Malaya, and Indochina, and the government opium monopolies operated by the Dutch, the French, and the British. The American Congress in the Progressive Era passed landholding and corporation laws that made it extremely difficult for American investors to wrest away "the patrimony" (as Filipino politicians called the land) or to control industrial growth. Meantime the trade patterns fostered by American legislation pushed the external economy into further dependence upon sugar and coconut exports, while allowing preference for American manufactured goods.

What alternative vision of an independently vigorous Philippine economy was there? None was forthcoming from Filipino political leaders, preoccupied as they were with husbanding power or reaching for it. None had yet arisen from the nascent entrepreneurial class—men like Vicente Madrigal, Leopoldo Aguinaldo, and Toribio Teodoro. Their companies borrowed American techniques of organization and styles of marketing, but persisted in spirit as Philippine-style family enterprises.

Central to the Philippine-American bond was the cultural affinity that had arisen. Whereas some of the mandarinate in Vietnam became genuinely enamored of things French, and some of the *pangreh pradja* (native civil service) in Indonesia felt devoted to things Dutch, such influences went little further. In contrast, the Philippine population in general was swayed, even captivated, by American culture. Rotarian civics and optimism in business, Madison Avenue slickness in advertising, Hollywood B (or C) heroes and heroines in the theaters, and Hit Parade stars in wave after wave of music swept into Philippine urban life to enthusiastic response. These may not constitute a worthy complex; but to take a highbrow stance on the question would make understanding the Philippines impossible.

Carmen Guerrero-Nakpil has often reflected since the 1950s on the Philippine experience of "falling in love with" American culture. Her tone, when not bitter, is rueful and amused: what a strange thing to do; what commonplaces and mischances it leads to; are we not deserving of a better fate? N.V.M. Gonzalez goes further, and explores the rootlessness that results from America having become for many Filipinos their promised land, their dream of heaven.

How could it have been otherwise? The indigenous "high tradition" of the Philippines was Hispano-Catholic as distinct from, say, Burma's Buddhistic national identity, or Java's proud syncretism of several Asian elements. To the degree that the Philippines was already partly "Western," American concepts of individual freedom grafted easily upon Catholic notions of the value of the individual soul. And to the degree that the Spanish had been anti-developmental, and an ecclesiastical bureaucracy had helped provoke the Revolution of 1896, an American secular religion of democracy and progress found it easy to slip in sideways and steal over the whole country. Further, to the extent that the Philippines (in contrast to Thailand and Indonesia) lacked an elaborate indigenous tradition in the arts, there were few bulwarks of resistance and canons of criticism by which foreign elements could be held at bay and local imitations effectually derided.

The Philippines of the late 1930s had some painting—superficially Spanish in character—and a good symphony orchestra in Manila, vaguely Germanic. Of its cultural phenomena, however, the most notable was the florescence of writing in English. An early generation, already schooled in Spanish, reeducated themselves to eloquence in English. Only a few, like Don Claro Recto, scathingly noted concurrent losses in Spanish-Filipino culture. A next group, converted early, produced in Carlos P. Romulo a Pulitzer prize-winning journalist. Now another generation was rising, educated from the beginning in English. They wrote short stories, poems, novels, essays, political journalism, business and legal journalism, with a conscientious sense of craft. They thought and felt in English. Some of them saw injustice and told of it; saw revolt simmering in Central Luzon and sympathized with it; participated in the women's movement and youth movement of the late 1930s and helped articulate both. They felt independence coming and yearned for it. So completely and so comfortably were they Americanized that they did all this without questioning English—rather than Tagalog or Visayan or Ilocano—as their most intimate language. Then came the war.

The Second World War as Revelation

The World War of 1939-1945 was on one front the Second War of European Suicide; on the other, the First Pacific War of Identity. For the first time, modern technology, economics, and politics embraced in war everything from the eastern borders of India through the innards of China to the fringe of Alaska; it seared the islands of the South Pacific and all the countries of insular and marshland Southeast Asia, until it concluded with nuclear bombing and occupation of Japan, both unique in history.

The Japanese, whose initiative created these vast theaters, saw the region as Greater East Asia, and the battle as the Holy

War for Asian Liberation. But freeing Asian peoples from the yoke of the Europeans and Americans had as its immediate sequel imposing the yoke of the Japanese. The "Co-Prosperity Sphere" that the Japanese established was focused upon Japan as its industrial hub, and the rest of Asia as supplier of raw goods and markets. A bitter Filipino joke had it as "Ako-Prosperity": or "me-first-prosperity."

What Theodore Roosevelt had foreseen had come true: American armaments were far from equal to the American commitment to defend the Philippines. American air power was destroyed on the ground at Clark Field hours after the disaster at Pearl Harbor. The American naval detachment withdrew before Christmas to fight another time. MacArthur, as the local American commander and Field Marshal of the Philippine Army, had been preparing against Japanese attack for six years. Immediate loss of control of air and sea now put his greatly superior numbers on the defensive. Philippine-American land forces yielded to the much smaller Japanese expeditionary force and were rapidly driven back to Bataan and Corregidor. There they managed to hold out for six months.

The truly remarkable factor was not generalship. Any luster that attaches to the name of Bataan belongs to the ordinary soldiers, American and Filipino, who stuck it out. They did not delay the Japanese from any other immediately scheduled strategic target, but they were the only force that stood up effectively to them in Southeast Asia. The Dutch surrendered Java within ten days; the British, Singapore, within weeks; and the French, under Vichyite orders, puppeteered themselves to Japanese power in Vietnam. Fil-American forces, however, resisted the Japanese for half a year, the only significant instance in Asia of a colonized people siding clearly with their white colonizer, and making mortal sacrifices in the name of a shared history.

During the Japanese occupation, guerrilla resistance sprang up. At first it did little but harass local Japanese patrols or gather information, if connected to the rudimentary intelligence network left behind by MacArthur's forces. By September 1943, when an occupation republic was proclaimed by the

Japanese, one of Jose Laurel's early acts as president was a declaration of amnesty to resisters. The gesture netted few who repented or feared enough of their activity to give it up. As American forces approached the Philippines, the intelligence network elaborated, and guerrilla action accelerated. Following the invasion of Leyte in October 1944, recruitment of auxiliaries by the Japanese grew extremely difficult; enlistment of guerrillas against them was easy. After the war, over a quarter of a million Filipinos were awarded back pay for fighting on the American side. Even if that number contained a certain proportion of opportunists and frauds, there were a great number who fought from conviction and valiantly. At the end of the war in 1945, 118,000 Filipinos were officially under arms fighting with Americans—perhaps double the number that MacArthur had effectively ready by 1941. The Makapili and other Filipino auxiliary forces drummed up and supplied by the Japanese probably never equaled one-tenth of that strength, and stood ground in no significant conflict.

Some of those fighting on the side of America were professionals, former members of MacArthur's forces. At the other extreme were Hukbalahaps fighting for revolution, in parallel with the Americans but separate from them, against the greater evil, Japan. In between, and by far the greatest number, were those guerrillas whose sense of the future was colored by a desire for independence under American auspices. They were moved to fight for reasons similar to those Dwight Eisenhower ascribed to ordinary American and British soldiers, each "to preserve his freedom of worship, his equality before law, his liberty to speak and act as he sees fit." There was also an impulsive, trusting quality to many Filipino commitments, such as the band called Hunter's ROTC Guerrillas, many of them collegians from the University of the Philippines, who fought out of a sense of shared destiny with America. Within twenty years of the war, three former guerrillas were elected president. Magsaysay, Garcia, and Marcos each found their wartime activity helpful to their political careers. Marcos made the most of it, including some decorations bestowed an unusually long number of years after events difficult to document.

To have fought with the Americans was clearly the popular thing to have done. In 1949, nonetheless, Jose Laurel, the president under Japanese occupation, was almost elected president of the postwar republic. Many voters perceived him as having done his best to defend their interests against the Japanese, and even his critics conceded that his courage was real. Among Laurel's many acts of clearly nationalistic impact during the war was encouragement of Tagalog/Pilipino as the national language. He very likely would have done so even without the Japanese insistence upon replacing Western languages wherever they went.

Encouraging native culture, particularly in its analogues to values held by the Japanese, was part of the "Holy War for the Liberation of Asia." In Java, the *jiwa ksatriya*, or warrior spirit, could be encouraged in line with samurai values and *bushido* spirit as a spiritual resource against the return of the Allies. In the Philippines it was much harder to strike such harmonies. The Japanese nevertheless laid open new layers of nationalist consciousness, not as much by the dexterity of their propaganda as by the sheer aggravating, provocative fact of their presence. Essayists for the wartime *Philippine Review*, such as S. P. Lopez, reached beyond the accommodation to Americanism that had been the prevailing norm of the 1930s to conceive of Philippine culture as developing strength through synthesis. In such a manner one could recognize the vitality of Japan's own adaptive culture as being of inspiring value to Filipinos, without any demeaning concession to Japanese presence. An Asian counterweight could be poised against the tremendous pull—or drag?—of American culture without betrayal of past associations or future hopes.

The Binational Restoration

Other regions of Southeast Asia were freed suddenly and bloodlessly by Japanese surrender in August 1945, except for Burma, where light fighting had occurred earlier in the year. Throughout the Philippine archipelago, however, beginning in October 1944, the Japanese were beaten island by island,

beach by beach, city by city, mountain by mountain, by combined Filipino and American forces. When the Allies returned
to Burma, Malaysia, Indonesia, and Vietnam, it was the "reoc-
cupation." But in the Philippines the arrival of the Americans
was called "the liberation." Years of wartime deprivation had
brought grim conditions; malnutrition in some areas was approaching starvation; and Japanese repression had become
still more brutal in retreat. Now the Filipinos were freed, and
they rejoiced. The Commonwealth and its constitution were
restored; independence was around the corner.

Euphoria, however, is a transient condition for individuals,
and more so for collectivities. Humans cannot live at the peaks
of experience; history seeks the plains of the normal to play itself out. The postwar norm for Filipinos, like the prewar norm,
was a willingly cultivated dependence on the United States,
blended with what might be called compadre anti-colonialism.
American policy and practice in the immediate postwar period
strategically echoed Admiral Mahan, economically proceeded
from the mercantilist assumptions of the turn of the century,
and culturally resumed a benign tutorship, distant and indifferent.

The American expansionary surge took shape in the Bell
Trade Act of 1946 and the Military Bases Agreement of 1947.
The trade legislation tied rehabilitation funds for the Philippines to the passage of an amendment to the Philippine constitution that gave American investors parity rights with Filipinos. At the same time the tight bonds of tariff preference for
Filipino goods in the United States, and vice versa, an arrangement that was to have been terminated in 1946, was prolonged
to 1974. The rationale—that a devastated Philippines needed
American rehabilitation funds *and* American capital for new
initiatives, *and* trade preference for a stabilized recovery—was
plausible. But it was also clearly a recipe for prolonged semi-
colonial association, and an independence confined to the sovereign legal sense of the word. Even that sovereignty was in-
fringed by asking that Filipinos grant Americans investment
rights equal to that of nationals, and by the extra-territorial jurisdiction granted in the bases agreement of 1947. Not only

were the major bases—Subic Bay for the Navy, Clark Field for the Air Force—secured, but many smaller sites, some already developed, some not, were identified for ninety-nine-year leases.

The astonishing thing, taking a worldwide view of the matter, is the degree of Filipino assent to these developments. The plebiscite to insert the parity provision in the constitution passed by a 4 to 1 ratio. Even allowing for lack of interest among the electorate for issues (as distinct from personal contests); even noting low voter turnout; even acknowledging a certain, not unusual, level of fraud, vote-buying, and intimidation, the results may be taken as a referendum on American colonial rule. It was O.K. Filipinos in general liked it rather more than they disliked it. The benefits in health, literacy, and democracy were not forgotten. And if the cost of recovery after the war was to give back some of the independence at last achieved, then that could be justified either on grounds of clear necessity or even by *utang na loob*—paying a debt of honor to a patron and protector. The protection factor was not inconsiderable. Quezon and Osmeña during the war had not merely conceded, but had sought, a continuing American military-naval presence; and Roxas, after the war, tempered the discussions only with sensitivity about probable racial incidents and opposition to any bases close to the city of Manila.

By 1974 the termination of the trade agreement and by 1979 multiple amendments to the bases agreement left the Philippines free of presumptive diminutions of sovereignty. But the pull of history and forces of political gravity kept the nation in the American orbit. In 1955, when Sukarno had engineered the Bandung Conference, the first great gathering of Afro-Asian nations, the Philippines was seen as a satellite, and her spokesman, Carlos Romulo, was heard as a voice of America. Over time both the reality and the international perception have softened. American officials like to think of themselves as partners, not as patrons. But the special relationship remains—a relationship described by one eminent and moderate Filipino as too special for self-respect and too close for comfort.

Philippine Nationalism and National Development

A peculiar amalgam of Filipino and American elements exists in Philippine political culture. One may accurately speak of Filipino "binationalism," but that ought not obscure and must not inhibit understanding of Philippine nationalism per se. The revolution of 1896 against Spain is the basic orientation point of that nationalism, and fierce resistance against the Japanese is a more modern and secondary source of pride. Because opposition to imperial power is so fundamental to Philippine nationalism, the question arises: is it already, and will it become further, anti-American? Binationalism, with its pro-American element, is still vigorous, but increasing criticism of, reaction against, and resistance to the United States are and will be only natural in the foreseeable future.

Not long after the concessions of the restoration period of 1945-1947, Philippine economic nationalism began to come into clear focus. Arguments sharpened for limiting American penetration into the economy, reducing dependence on bilateral trade, and invigorating indigenous industry, commerce, finance, and entrepreneurship. By the late 1950s, the Laurel-Langley agreement set renegotiated trade terms, and waves of legislation and regulation were helping Filipinos strengthen their position vis-à-vis foreign, and especially American, business.

A quarter of a century later, what are the consequences? The bilateral economic relationship must be seen in its overall proportions, and then broken down into investment, trade, and finance. A clear case exists for stating that American economic influence is diminishing while the Japanese is rising and the indigenous is strengthening. The fact remains that the United States, with a gross domestic product more than eighty times as great as that of the Philippines, and with a trade volume forty times as great, will influence the Philippines heavily without planning, without trying, without even wanting to do so.

Within the disproportionate relationship of a great (and generally uncaring) large mass to a small (and sometimes ultrasensitive) small one, there have been some notable changes.

Whereas in the mid-1930s a careful estimate of Philippine capital stock represented by American investment was 6.8 percent, that proportion in 1977, based on NEDA figures, had diminished to 2.4 percent. American colonial-era ownership was small, and has since become slight. And whereas American direct investment in the Philippines of $414 million in 1960 represented 1.26 percent of its worldwide total, American direct investment of $913 million in 1977 accounted for only 0.61 percent thereof. American investment in the Philippines increased more in dollar terms in the 1960s than under martial law, and has been steadily declining as a percentage of an American global sum for over twenty years.

As for trade: the United States in the 1930s accounted for about 70 percent of all the foreign trade of the Philippines; in the 1950s, 60 percent; and by 1982, according to American Embassy data released by the Department of Commerce, about 27 percent, barely ahead of Japan.

If American investment and trade have been steadily and significantly declining, the factor of foreign private borrowing has been clearly rising. The debt peril in which the Philippines found itself beginning about 1979, and which rose to critical urgency in 1983-1984, included a component of 483 mainly American commercial banks that held a large part of the Philippines' total foreign debt of about $26 billion. Whatever the relative roles of unfavorable worldwide economic trends, Philippine government mismanagement, oligarchic plunder, and shoddy foreign lending practices in contributing to these debt problems, the United States publicly and privately continues to own a significant share of them.

All told, the United States still leads Japan as the Philippines' major economic partner. America's investment stake and trade share in the Philippines, however, have sharply declined in the last quarter century, while at the same time rising in Hong Kong, Indonesia, Singapore, Malaysia, and Taiwan.

If the economic component of the Philippine-American tie is absolutely small and relatively diminishing, what accounts for the intensity of discussion of Fil-American relations? That intensity is a factor both of affinities based on popular culture and of political ties pivoting on the existence of military bases.

Politico-cultural nationalism critical of the United States emerged early in the twentieth century. A famous editorial in 1908, "Aves de Rapina" ("Birds of Prey"), attacked Commissioner Dean C. Worcester for using official position for private gain. Worcester sued for libel and won; this official victory led naturally to bitter attacks upon the libel law. Over time, however, the burning nationalism of the turn of the century grew tempered, and Spanish as a language of opposition petered out.

After President Ramon Magsaysay, with American aid and advice, quelled the Huk rebellion in the mid-1950s, a new wave of nationalism began to take place. The appearance of biting articles by Filipino journalists was a sign of cultural self-respect edged with self-critique, of confidence in fluent command of English, and of a people sovereign within their own system of law. They felt no need to go to libelous lengths. The caustic articles of Carmen Guerrero-Nakpil in the late 1950s and of J. V. Cruz in the late 1960s signified a daily willingness to twit or roast a chosen target—American if judged insensitive to Philippine identity and prerogatives, Filipino if judged undignified in imitation of American styles or policies. Cruz was particularly scathing in his attacks on "Little Brown Americans." William Howard Taft at the turn of the century had referred to Filipinos as "little brown brothers," and his son, Senator Robert Taft, had condescendingly repeated the phrase in 1946. Now Filipinos were transforming the phrase into an insult, and using it to ridicule those among themselves who yielded to excessive dependence, consciously or unconsciously.

The obstacles, however, to a relaxed and confident cultural nationalism still remained great. In movies, television, popular music, pulp fiction and comics, American influence has been and remains overpowering. By the late 1960s a thriving Philippine movie industry ranked fifth in the world in volume of production, ahead even of Great Britain. But its themes were thin on Filipino content and its standards were far from the highest in a Third World context, let alone by any global criterion. The sharpest critic of the American movie industry, Renato Constantino, sees it as an omnipresent ideological force, cudgeling and subverting Filipinos of all kinds, cheating them of their heritage and substituting American ways and outlook.

His criticism is flawed, however, in not distinguishing between American policy intentions and American individual hopes for the Philippines on the one hand, and the systematic effect of American cultural impact on the other. Neither does it sufficiently acknowledge weaknesses in Philippine taste (who buys bad stuff, and why?) as distinct from the American product (where the percentage of trash is indefensibly high). Nor does it consider the best of American movies and wonder why they draw so poorly in the Philippines, in contrast to horror movies, mindless comedies, and superficial romances. Constantino has his own battering-ram style—a humorless neo-Marxist didacticism.

Also critical of American impact, but more courageous in confronting particulars and more subtle in analysis, is Doreen Fernandez. If American popular songs, radio, and film drove the *kundiman* and the *zarzuela* into different and smaller compartments of people's lives, it was not the triumphant result of a planned cultural struggle, but evidence of a sad and inevitable overshadowing. Noel Coward once observed, "Strange how potent cheap music is." The remark applies to the seduction of all Philippine popular culture by the gods and goddesses of Hollywood and Tin Pan Alley.

The writer Nick Joaquin sympathizes with the "anti-Saxons" in twentieth-century Philippine history, and warns that to give up one's native heroes, myths, and archetypes is to surrender the soul. Some younger scholars try to go behind even Spanish culture to identify and prize things indigenously Filipino. The effort tends to play out early, and to revert to observations on American popular culture: its conquest by sheer potency, by substitution, and by imitation. Even when Filipinos do not buy American products they build and produce their own on American designs: blue jeans, gadgets, sports, furniture, Christmases; values and aspirations; images of self and society.

To call this "manipulation" or "aggression" by the United States is to weaken the meaning of those words. Filipino critics, however, do observers in both nations a service by pointing to collusion between the two in popular culture, not necessarily to the credit of either. They help us see the anomaly of entertainment becoming big business in a poor country; that the Filipino entertainment industry supplies a false reality for those seeking escape from harsh existence; that it calls attention to a vacuum of noble aspirations; and that in the absence of farsighted educational and cultural policies, the residual effect will be regressive at best, rotten at worst. Can the movie director, Lina Brocka, become to the Philippines what Kurosawa is to Japan? The struggle of such spirits is not only one against local limitations, but a struggle to go beyond imitation of America, beyond adaptation of its standards, toward innovation upon native themes.

While modern economic and cultural nationalism were developing in the Philippines, political nationalism was both leaping ahead and dragging behind. It was out front, because political nationalism represents a power of will that fuels other forms of nationalism. And it was lagging because of the strange form of protectionism practiced in their hearts by many Filipinos. The first aim of the restoration period was not "protect our markets against your goods" but "protect our shores with your forces." The means was not raising tariffs against American products but raising a shield against any imaginary enemy by preserving American bases. The more sophisticated Filipino nationalists, first Recto, later Tañada and Diokno, saw American installations as a possible magnet for attack rather than a bulwark of defense. Many ordinary people became irritated or exasperated by special American rights, the misbehavior of some American military personnel, the undesirable subcultures of Angeles and Olangapo. The bases remained a prominent issue through numerous renegotiations. Even when in 1979 they were to be renegotiated on a regular five-year basis, their preserve held the potential for enduring differences, no matter how many ways Philippine sentiment was accommodated.

Meanwhile, however, between 1946 and 1972, the Philippines continued to pay the United States the compliment of adapting its two-party system for the working purposes of a factional familistic polity. Roxas over Osmeña (1946); Quirino over Laurel (1949); Magsaysay over Quirino (1953); Garcia over Yulo (1957); Macapagal over Garcia (1961); Marcos over Macapagal (1965), were presidential contests won by undramatic margins. The two-party pattern persisted despite fraud and the possibility of attempted coup in 1949, when Laurel abided Osmeña's peaceful example of 1946 rather than forcefully challenge election results; despite the Huk rebellion successfully seething not far from Manila in 1953; despite occasional public ruminations on the need for military or authoritative efficiency in the late 1950s and the early 1960s.

Marcos came through with enough rice, roads, and schoolhouses after his first victory to earn a second in 1969. But the constitution denied him a third. Believing that the nation needed his charisma (even if that were not always attached to far-seeing vision), his powers of organization (even if there were familistic fissures in his style), and the putative progress of his regime (even though Philippine indices of forward momentum were lagging behind other Pacific nations, which had begun to move faster), Marcos staged a constitutional coup in 1972. Under a decree of martial law, he made himself president without term.

The rationale for Marcos' coup was political/military in pointing at the Communist New People's Army (NPA) as an imminent threat; developmental in the sense that free discussion was submerged in the interest of restoring the people's welfare; and legal in the sense that it relied on an obscure American colonial statute in order to justify the action. Marcos' foremost opponent, Senator Benigno Aquino, Jr., was immediately arrested on dubious charges of treason and murder. And other critics, such as Senator Salvador Laurel, were for a long while rendered powerless by Marcos' momentum, or maneuvered into isolation.

Thus three generations of Philippine history came into sudden sharp focus. Marcos liked to claim descent from General Antonio Luna, his grandfather. Both Aquino and Laurel were also grandsons of revolutionary generals who had fought Spaniards and Americans. Both were sons of Nacionalista politicians with a strong pro-Asian identity who had cooperated prominently with the Japanese in 1942-1945. Both had been provincial governors, of Tarlac and Batangas, respectively; each had a strong regional base and a significant national following as a senator. Both wished to become president. Aquino was clearly the more likely to get to the top first out of proven popularity, evident decisiveness, and expressed social concern. Marcos, seeing that and not wishing the competition, recognized his nemesis by jailing him. Thus he made still more certain that Ninoy Aquino would be not only the leader of the opposition, but the symbol of suppressed Filipino rights.

Some in power feared Aquino even more than Marcos did. They had him murdered in 1983. The moment of Ninoy Aquino's return to native soil became a moment of martyrdom in Philippine political history surpassed only by the death of Rizal.

The Yellow Revolution, 1983-1986

The Aquino funeral, a mass expression of grief and longing for justice, was the beginning of an arousal of new Filipino energies. A prolonged series of demonstrations mixed the symbolic color yellow—from an American popular song about a returning prisoner—with elements of fiesta, remembrance of Ninoy, sacred mass, and civil disobedience. The Agrava Commission reports on the murder showed that the appetites for due process and public truth were still extraordinarily keen. Marcos retaliated with a pliable judicial panel that acquitted his military.

Whatever short-term gains the Marcos regime may have made through the earliest years of martial law had long since vanished by the mid-1980s. The Philippine economy was marked by inefficient industrial development, ineffective land reform, insufficient export agriculture, and declining competitiveness vis-à-vis ASEAN neighbors. Development increasingly depended on foreign borrowing. By the end of 1984, external debt equalled four-fifths of the GNP. By the end of 1985, real GNP itself had declined 9.5 percent (est.) over the two previous years. The failures of the Marcos government to undertake fundamental economic adjustment were threatening the credit on which rescheduling of debt depended, and eroding the already slender standard of living in a nation with a high percentage of malnourished people. At the same time, Paul Wolfowitz, assistant secretary of state for East Asia and the Pacific, said that the Communist Party of the Philippines and the New People's Army were already "meaningful" in two-thirds of the provinces of the Philippines. Both were clearly gaining adherents, confidence, and momentum, and thereby challenging the Marcos regime and threatening to create a strategic problem for the region.

Stagnant in economic and social development, corrupted, and nearly bankrupted; militarized and riven by insurgency; the Philippines by 1985 was in its greatest crisis since the Second World War. Marcos chose to navigate for power rather than lead for renewal. He called a snap election for February 1986, expecting to win another six-year mandate against a divided opposition.

But Corazon Aquino and Salvador Laurel managed to unite the opposition. The Catholic Church led by Cardinal Sin turned itself through pastoral letters into a medium of political conscience. The National Citizens Movement for Free Elections bravely monitored balloting and counting. The American and international press, and American and international observer teams, arrived to represent standards of truth and fairness. Against the tide, Marcos forces concocted and claimed election victory. But an aroused opposition rose up against them, halting tanks with their own prayerful massings, winning key defectors by the justice and momentum of their cause. They finally prevailed. Marcos accepted exile. Cory Aquino took office as president. And a moment of jubilation arrived after a political drama of nearly unbearable tension and danger.

Discernible Patterns, Unpredictable Events

The Philippines in the late twentieth century has been slowly emerging as more and more typical of Southeast Asia in pattern of development, less and less eccentric to the region. The insular Catholicism of the Spanish era and the hothouse democracy of the American period once seemed to mark it as exceptional. But the attrition of democracy under Marcos appeared to replicate processes in Indonesia and in other states. And the relative imperviousness to Marxist ideology that had previously marked the Philippines, even during the Huk rebellion, showed signs of giving way under conditions of political repression and social ossification.

Where Philippine history had been non-dynastic, the state never having had a line of sacral or kingly rulers, the government was showing signs of neo-dynastic pomp. Monuments to Marcos glorified him and political maneuvers attempted to prolong his rule and extend it through his family.

Where the Philippines had been minimally colonial in the period of American rule, 1901-1941, compared to colonies of other North Atlantic regimes, it was now neocolonial. American bases tied Philippine and American policy and destiny far more tightly than any post-colonial relationship in the region—the French were expelled, the Dutch a faint memory, the British at most a lingering influence.

Where Philippine thinking had been non-ideological and distinctly non-Marxist, now it was becoming, in urban chic and in rural catechism, increasingly accessible to neo-Marxism.

The intellectual tastes of the disoriented and the basic needs of the oppressed could no longer be fully met by the bread-and-butter unionism, Gompers style, of the United States, or the pragmatism and Rotarianism borrowed as American civic attitudes. Even the Catholic Church, once confident of its immunological power against Marxism in Philippine society, has become a carrier of new thinking. Which would prevail: the social conscience of papal encyclicals since Leo XIII, or the new strains of liberation theology from Latin America? The issue is joined, but far from resolution. To it have been added new questions of church-state relations, precipitated by Cardinal Sin's courageous defiance of Marcos, and his unique exhortations by radio to protect defectors from the government against Marcos' tanks and forces. The Vatican may treat the matter as a "local issue," but it may become central to the Philippine future.

Where will the Philippine party system go? Quezon's autocratic presidency of the Commonwealth, 1935-1941, and his "one-party democracy," were precursors of the 1970s. But the Marcos regime became rampantly corrupt in ways that an American high commissioner would not have permitted; and became thoroughly military in a manner Quezon never contemplated, insistent as he was on subordination of military to civic authority. Will the "Yellow Revolution" lead back to the two-party democracy of the Philippines, as in 1946 to 1972; and if so, can it avoid the lax economic discipline, the frivolous attitudinizings of that period? Or will the new regime move closer to something like the "one-and-a-half party" democracy of some other Pacific Rim states? And if so, will it choose to use the United States as a convenient antagonist and scapegoat, as the Nacionalista party did from 1907 to 1941, in the colonial period?

The peculiar confluence of forces in the Philippines deserves a fresh analysis. Native entrepreneurs, multinationals, and parastatals exist in profusion and variety. The native entrepreneurs have perhaps been overly praised as initiators of growth, but they include an element of tough, constructive, farsighted men, and their demands upon Marcos after 1983 revealed a previously hidden sensitivity to the political needs of the whole society. The multinationals are the natural target of the neo-Marxists. That brand of criticism, however, tends to be counterempirical and dogmatic, so that a net rendering of the true influence of the multinationals—for development or for exploitation?—is not readily available. The parastatal organizations are even less effectively analyzed. Those corporations, government-created, yet semi-independent of government, which could have provided drive to the Philippine economy and uplift to Philippine society, became, many of them, satrapies of Marcos' cronies, and instead retarded development. The International Monetary Fund and World Bank have implicitly noted their partly causal role in declining Philippine productivity. Other evidence suggests that they helped feed the gluttonous extravagance of the Marcos palace and family.

The Aquino-Laurel government thrown up by the Yellow Revolution faces enormous problems of unemployment and malnutrition; of dedicated armed rebellion; and of unrepentant Marcosites, holders of local power and even of private armies. In order to overcome the insurgent, the new government must help the indigent and nullify the intransigent. And these efforts must be systematic and unremitting.

There appears to be enough magnanimity and talent in the new government to make success possible. But the difficulties are great. An oligarchy of families has run the Philippines for decades. It has tended to transform new achievers into persons like themselves, insensitive to the poor. This oligarchy still leads, and must prove that crisis has purified and ennobled it, or deeper trouble lies ahead. Filipinos in the American census, between 1970 and 1980, increased from 343,000 to 775,000. A transformed leadership would attract many of those individuals to return, at the same time as generating new paths of upward mobility in Philippine society.

The late twentieth-century Philippines is not to be rescued by an American expeditionary force as against the Japanese, or by its politico-economic equivalent, as against the Huks. The United States, having lost the Vietnam War, knows limits to its capability to fight or even advise on Third World terrain. This United States generates a declining share of global GNP, and is far less inclined than it might once have been to throw money into others' problems. Meanwhile new generations have grown up in the Philippines to whom bloodshed in Bataan, tears of joy shed at liberation, are only their parents' history, or their grandparents'. That past matters little compared to the high unemployment, high inflation, sagging productivity, and low nutrition of current times.

Old habits in Fil-American relations will not suffice. The

Philippines cannot resort to a modern equivalent of crying for independence publicly while seeking, behind the scenes, as in 1916 and 1933, or openly, as in 1946, to prolong the security of dependence. The United States will not readily imagine that it can send a Lansdale into conference with a Magsaysay, as in the mid-1950s, and military advisers into the field with the Philippine army against the Huks. Philippine problems must have Philippine solutions: on that, leaders of both nations are likely to agree.

The danger remains, however, that the illusion of American omnipotence and the reality of Philippine oppression could fuse. American engagement in a Filipino civil war is a repellent idea. Because of the major American bases there, a creeping involvement in a deteriorating situation is imaginable, and could turn into a nightmare. Experience at working together must prevent it, and constructive action prevail.

The government of Aquino and Laurel, at its outset, is probably equipped with more collective hope and pride than at any juncture in modern Philippine history. The self-liberation it has achieved against an indigenous oppressor can free energies like those of earlier liberations from colonial powers in other Asian countries. But the Yellow Revolution must radiate far more beyond Manila than it has yet had a chance to do. And it must resist being tugged back into ignoble paths of the past.

On the means and style of maximizing Philippine freedom and development, there will be plenty of disagreement on both sides of the Pacific. But on a simply defined end all might agree: that the Philippines, within sovereign integrity, advance its society and economy by the best of its own cultural standards. The United States can contribute to that end, with continued long-term disengagement, and by the short-term acts of a supportive ally—no less, and no more.

CHAPTER II

TRADITION AND RESPONSE

DAVID STEINBERG

Recorded Philippine history has always taken place in the context of interaction with foreign peoples and cultures. Few countries have had the opportunity to draw upon so many wellsprings of culture—Chinese, Muslim, Spanish, Christian, American, Japanese. Yet in some ways the very richness of these sources has created a surfeit. The image of the melting pot is more attractive to Americans than to Filipinos still in search of a sense of peoplehood.

The ways in which Philippine society has decided what to retain and what to discard from abroad have been anything but stereotypical, however; certainly the process has not been a passive one. The Filipinos are the ones who have domesticated the initially foreign ideas, values, and institutions. Others may have brought these to the islands but, once there, it has been the natives, not the foreigners, who have decided what to keep. That is a truth all too easily forgotten by both Filipinos and foreigners, especially since the Filipinos have often kept the foreign shell, retaining form and nomenclature, while altering the inner reality.

Spanish-type Roman Catholicism, for example, has been dramatically altered in the Philippines as it has become an integral part of the indigenous culture. The Church is vibrant today in large measure because it has gone native, allowing local traditions and values to intermingle with foreign dogmas and alien institutions. It is not simply that there are folk elements present; it is a Philippine Church, with all that implies.

Roman Catholicism was adopted passionately but selectively. Filipino Catholics personalized God and domesticated their creed. The connection between man and God was widely understood in terms of the peasant family. God was the wise

Father; the Virgin was the devoted Mother; and Christ became the Filipino's savior, an older, ever-forgiving brother. Filipinos sought a kind of cosmic *compadrazgo*, a fictive kinship through which each Filipino became related to the Holy Family. Filipinos felt a debt of gratitude, *utang na loob*, to Christ for his sacrifice; Christ performed a set of favors, *puhunan*, that demanded every good Filipino to acknowledge his reciprocal burden through faith, sympathy, and charity. For many Filipinos, therefore, the death and resurrection of Jesus is not only an historical event that happened millennia ago but one relived today in the lives of the devout. The passion is endowed with a living remembrance in physical acts of flagellation and even crucifixion. Catholic "miracles" seem to resemble those of the *baylan*, the spirit medium. The pre-Christian blood compact that bound families to each other was absorbed into the ritual godparenthood of baptism. Artistic and iconographic images, especially of the Virgin, link Philippine Catholicism to earlier idol worship. Outside canonic authority, a local tradition also survives in millenial movements that have arisen over the centuries.

The persistent admixture of Catholic and indigenous values also has been reflected on the national political scene. Jose Rizal, the Filipino nationalist martyr of the late nineteenth century, is recalled today not only by political leaders as a precursor of contemporary nationalist values, but also by many of the pious faithful as a modern Filipino saint. In the same way, the martyrdom of Benigno Aquino, Jr., aroused religious as well as political passions, and the presidential campaign of his widow, Corazon, saw a powerful fusing of the two. Catholic masses became occasions for rousing political sermons, and Aquino rallies opportunities for partisan benedictions. Church and candidate became one in ritual as they were in policy.

The Tagalog word for independence is *kalayaan*. In today's secular, nationalist world, it is easy to assume that everybody means the same thing by independence. A national flag, a national anthem, and other such symbols seem to have a universal meaning, articulating the national dream of freedom and independence for a given country. Especially since the nationalist movement in the Philippines was articulated by a highly Westernized, sophisticated elite, it is easy for an outsider to assume that he or she understands what *kalayaan* means. And yet, as Reynaldo Ileto notes in his excellent study of peasant uprisings and popular movements, *Pasyon and Revolution*, the *pasyon* or passion, the folk liturgy recounting the death of Christ, "was freed from its officially sanctioned moorings in Holy Week and allowed to give form and meaning to the people's struggles for liberation."[1] This traditional vision of *kalayaan*, of independence as Redemption promised by Christ, enlarges and suffuses the modern, secular expression of freedom.

Among the many values embedded in Philippine social and cultural life, some are Western, some indigenous, some mixed. The average Filipino's loyalty to his immediate family is deep, and his or her sense of obligation to kin and fictive kin molds the social environment. The average Filipino knows far more about his extended family than does his American contemporary. Whereas Americans may form and break relationships casually and quickly, some barely remembering the injunction to honor their fathers and mothers, most Filipinos see themselves embedded in a plural and interlocking web of obligations in which individual desires and priorities are subservient to family and communal goals. Like ripples on a pond, Filipinos see these relationships radiating outward in concentric circles. Students of the culture have used the phrase "smooth interpersonal relationships" to describe the priority that Filipinos give to maintaining this social fabric. Just as one has an internal debt of gratitude or obligation to Christ, so too the burdens of *utang na loob* exist in daily life. To be accused of being insensitive or thoughtless is to violate a crucial social obligation.

Perhaps not unconnected with this, women have always had a special place in Philippine society, and pre-Spanish society was seemingly fairly free of discrimination. Children trace kinship bilaterally, and women have held power, and the purse

---

[1] Renaldo C. Ileto, *Pasyon and Revolution: Popular Movements in the Philippines, 1840-1910* (Quezon City: Ateneo de Manila, 1979), p. 316.

strings, throughout recorded Philippine history. From the female *baylan*, the traditional spirit medium, to Corazon Aquino and Imelda Marcos, women have been cloaked with authority and respect, with power and opportunity.

The interlocking of the extended family with the additional network of godparents and in-laws is tended, like the wet rice system of dikes and paddies, with exceptional care. As the ripples move out past these levels of association, Filipinos hold strong loyalties to others from their language group (there are some eighty-seven languages spoken in the Philippines), their region, and their island. Indeed, the interlocking of kinship extends to the symbolic tie, for example, between the Philippines and the United States. Filipinos took literally William Howard Taft's condescending phrase "little brown brothers." They have always seen the relationship with the Americans in kinship terms. They were recapitulating out of a collective past when they viewed the United States as big brothers who offered protection in exchange for loyalty. The reciprocity of that connection helps explain why Filipiinos fought so valiantly in 1942 with and for the United States—and why they were so angered by the behavior of postwar American governments, which bestowed far more aid on former enemies, Germany and Japan, than on them, devoted kin and loyal allies. The discussion of such values, therefore, is not an arcane subject for scholars. It is, rather, an important precondition to understanding the complexity of contemporary Philippine life or the Philippine-American experience.

To cite another example, Filipinos do not have the same sense of what is public and what is private as do Americans. To a Filipino, the space he or she is on becomes private property. Thus if a jeepney driver's jeep breaks down at an intersection, neither he nor other Filipinos rush to push him to the side of the road. The Western notion of right of way is subordinated by the bad luck of the individual driver's misfortune at having his engine fail. Anthropologist Richard L. Stone has described this phenomenon as "the private, transitory possession of public property." The public domain becomes private when a squatter builds his shack or when a street vendor sets up her stall. Those people see that space as theirs, and the line between what is public and what is personal blurs.

Similarly, Filipinos often see the opportunity of a career in government as fulfilling an obligation to improve the circumstances of the family. What in the West is called nepotism is softened in the Philippines by the blanket term "anomaly." The obligations of the civil servant to protect the public trust, as defined in America, are altered by the competing obligations to assure the well-being of your children, to help your kin get jobs, and to give contracts to those to whom you owe a debt of obligation. By Western criteria, such behavior smacks of corruption, a violation of the norms of public trust. And yet, in the Philippine context, and with Philippine values at play, the society sees far less transgression and judges that transgression far less harshly than do those in the West. Venality cannot be condoned and dishonesty explained in the name of social mores. But concepts of good and bad, public and private, honest and dishonest, are not universal in time or place. What America now defines as cruel and inhumane treatment of prisoners would have been considered lenient a century or two ago. The notion of throwing someone in jail for years because of his or her inability to pay a debt is alien but was once powerfully observed by Western societies. In this context of cultural relativism, it is possible to understand more fully the meaning of "corruption" in the Philippines.

The Philippines is also a conservative, capitalist society in which the value of private property is cherished and the importance of wealth is stressed. Visitors to the Philippines have always been puzzled by the seeming incompetence and inefficiency of the government alongside the vibrant efficiency of the private sector. The discrepancy, however, is not difficult to understand. Wealth is the social aribiter in the Philippines. After centuries of colonial rule in which social status was determined by country of origin, wealth became a way to identify where an individual fit. Moreover, the Spanish colonial regime, its successor the American administration, and the Roman Catholic Church all stressed the sanctity of private property and the very European values of land ownership. To be rich is to be powerful; to be powerful has been to own land. Today in Makati every residential subdivision has its rank in the hierarchy of socioeconomic status, with Forbes Park as the ultimate place to aspire to live. All the way through the society, therefore, runs a strong and passionate desire to "make it." People covet the good life, which today means a very material one of air-conditioned Mercedes cars and spectacular homes with swimming pools. They are willing to work hard to win these rewards for themselves and their families by their brains, entrepreneurial skills, contacts—or anomalies, if necessary. The dream of Horatio Alger is alive and well in the Philippines, and the society, especially its elite, has shown the flexibility to allow the newly rich an entree, a "piece of the action." Thus, people not only covet "making it" but can actually succeed in doing so. This upward mobility has been one of the key reasons why the Philippines has been able to relieve some of the social pressures of a developing nation with wide income disparities, pressures that might plunge another society into violent revolution.

The Mestizo-Shaped Culture

These observations about wealth and social status are linked in a complex way to the ethnic identity of the Filipinos. The single most important group within the archipelago is the racially mixed community of mestizos, many of whom today are only moderately aware of their mixed blood heritage. The term *mestizo* carries little of the negative connotation of Eurasian or half-caste in the Philippine case. Few countries of the world have an elite as diverse as the mestizos of the Philippines. The dominance by this group of the social life and political history of the past century makes it one of the most significant factors in any understanding of the Philippines today.

The Spanish empire of the sixteenth century was global, reaching from Europe through Latin America to the Far East. Spain saw itself as the temporal arm of the Roman Catholic Church, and the Philippines was to be the advance base from which missionaries would proselytize China and Japan. When it became impossible to fulfill that destiny, the missionaries turned their attention instead to the indigenous population of the Philippines, whom they called *indios*. All but a relatively small percentage, Muslims and hill tribes, were converted to Christianity within the first century of Spanish rule.

The economic lifeline of the colony was the Manila galleon linking it with Latin America. The Philippines was a colony of the New World as much as of Spain itself. Annually, the galleon carried Chinese silks, porcelain, and other items of value to Acapulco, and returned to Manila with a cargo of silver bullion, clerics, and civil servants. Chinese merchants, who had been trading for centuries in the archipelago, now came to Manila to become in effect the trading partners of the Spanish. And for these Chinese there were advantages in converting to Roman Catholicism. Residential restrictions that forced them to live in a ghetto, legal limitations that were imposed on the commerce of non-Catholics, and other exclusionary acts were partially mitigated by conversion. Some Chinese merchants spent much of their adult lives in the Philippines, marrying native women and raising families. Even if they returned to China to die, they left behind a community of mestizo children who were naturalized in the local Catholic environment by their *india* mothers.

The subculture that arose was neither native nor Chinese. These mestizos lived in their own section of Manila known as Binondo. By the middle of the nineteenth century, there were probably a quarter of a million Chinese mestizos out of a total population of four million in the Islands. Moreover, like the still ethnically pure Chinese themselves, these mestizos were concentrated in Manila and the other cities, where they engaged not only in trade and commerce but also in many of the service and artistic functions required by the Spanish authorities and the Roman Catholic Church. Most of the stone masons who built the churches and the sculptors who carved the ivory or wooden images were Chinese or Chinese mestizos, many of whom learned their trade as apprentices in Southern China. The mestizo community became not a subgroup of overseas Chinese, as in Malaysia and Java, but rather a special type of native.

There were other kinds of mestizos, as well. The Spanish empire was diverse, and many combinations of racial permutation occurred. The Philippines was halfway round the world from Spain, and most officials of the colonial service, tiny though it was, came from Mexico or other parts of Latin America. Especially at the lower ranks, these petty officers and bureaucrats often decided to settle in the Philippines in order to seek their fortunes. Whether these individuals were pure Caucasians or themselves Latin American mestizos, they either married or took concubines in the Philippines, often marrying the daughters of wealthy peasants, whose families were sometimes wealthier than their own in the Americas or Spain. For the native woman and her family, such a marriage substantially raised the status of the family, providing new-found social class and economic opportunity. By the middle of the nineteenth century, there were approximately 20,000 Spanish mestizos, many in the second or third generation, in the archipelago.

Technological developments, economic opportunity, and political events combined to make the nineteenth century a period of rapid change. A wave of Chinese migration into the Philippines at mid-century put pressure on the established Chinese mestizo community to reformulate its identity and develop alternate types of economic activity. There had earlier been a long period of Chinese exclusion, mandated by the Spanish, during which the mestizo community had prospered. The renewed arrival of mainland Chinese, with lines of credit in Hong Kong and Canton, a willingness to work for narrow profit margins, and a frugal work ethic, placed sharp pressure on the mestizo community. Some of these mestizos saw opportunity by shifting into land ownership and the newly emerging export crops, and by migrating to islands like Negros, for example. Some acquired land by becoming middlemen and lessees to the friars, subletting these tracts to *indio* farmers for a percentage of the crop yield. The practice became widespread, especially in the areas around Manila. Mestizos were also able

to acquire land through money lending. Both practices became
so common that one nineteenth-century observer warned that
"if no remedy is found, within a short time, the lords of the entire archipelago will be the Chinese mestizos."[2]

The new wave of Chinese immigration also placed the
Chinese mestizos under sociocultural pressure because to these
mainland Chinese the mestizos were apostates. The mestizos
themselves, being neither Chinese nor *indios*, felt adrift. The
Spanish mestizos also felt challenged after the Latin American
revolutions broke up the Spanish empire. The several kinds of
mestizos therefore began to forge a new identity for themselves
by reinterpreting the term "Filipino." In earlier centuries this
term had identified a Caucasian born in that part of the Spanish empire known as the Philippines. The mestizos now gave
new meaning to the name. A Filipino became anyone who was
born in and who chose to identify with the archipelago, whatever his or her race, creed, or national origin might have been.
These new Filipinos not only took the lead in forging a national identity and an anticolonial, nationalist movement; they
also created a pluralistic cultural definition for the nation.

Thus, status in the Philippines was not determined by ethnic
purity, family tree, or caste. Wealth and consumption came to
be a means to establish hierarchy. Land ownership has always
been a tangible symbol of success, conspicuous consumption a
way to trumpet status. Education has been the other way by
which this new elite has claimed authority. In most colonies in
Southeast Asia, education was carefully denied to the natives;
the imperial power limited access to education to preserve its
own control. In the Philippines, however, the situation was different, because it was the Roman Catholic Church that colonized and civilized. In the countryside, the priest was often the
only Caucasian the local *indio* population ever saw. To perform his ministry he needed to establish literacy, at least in the
vernacular. Each of the major orders of friars—the Augustinians, the Dominicans, the Jesuits, and the Franciscans—estab-

[2] Cited in Edgar Wickberg, "The Chinese Mestizo in the Philippines," *Journal of Southeast Asian History* 5:1 (March 1984), 75.

lished colleges, even seminaries, though until the late eighteenth century it was impossible for a native to be ordained as a priest.

Mestizo landlords and entrepreneurs sought for their children a Spanish education, often augmenting the education available locally by sending these young people abroad to Spain or elsewhere. Modern commerce, a growing bureaucratic and political infrastructure, and urbanization accelerated these trends. Jose Rizal, the great national hero of the nineteenth century, was a fifth-generation Chinese mestizo. He was a medical doctor, a brilliant linguist, a man of culture and letters. His educational achievement was a paradigm of the intellectual pursuits of this new class. These educated mestizos, known as the *ilustrados*, the enlightened ones, were the first "modern" Southeast Asians. They were empowered. There were 43 lawyers, 18 physicians, and numerous other professional people among the 110 constitutional delegates who came together in the city of Malolos in 1898 to draft a constitution. Not all of these *ilustrados* were wealthy, and not all were mestizo. But a sophisticated, modern education was increasingly the vehicle upward.

Americans saw democracy as resting on education, and American colonial administrators felt the greatest risk of social unrest would lie in a "vast mass of ignorant people easily and blindly led by the comparatively few."[3] Long after other government agencies had been turned over to Filipino management, the Americans retained control over the education ministry. But the mestizos had already gained the levers of power and had imposed their cultural stamp on the nation's culture, a stamp that remains strong to this day.

A Relevant Past

Perhaps the two most important facts of the pre-Spanish era were that an indigenous high culture did not exist prior to the arrival of the foreigners, and that there was relatively little to

[3] *Report of the Philippine Commission*, 1903, I, 59.

link the various islands, linguistic groups, and cultural sub-
units of the archipelago. Unlike Siam, Burma, Vietnam, or
Java, the Philippines did not have a great imperial past or sense
of self. It lacked a written history. Islam had arrived from Indonesia to the south fifty to a hundred years before the arrival
of the Christian Spanish in the sixteenth century. These two
competing world religions, which had struggled centuries before on the Spanish peninsula, thus continued their ancient
combat in this distant, tropical land.

The key institution in the pre-Spanish, pre-Islamic era was
the *barangay*, the village, which was rarely able to extend control to the next *barangay*. The indigenous elite, the hereditary
datu, were the village elders. In the Islamic south these *datu* became the rulers of the mini-sultanates that emerged out of the
barangay. When Magellan sailed to Cebu in 1521, there was
no central government anywhere, no sense of a larger identity,
and certainly no notion of a collective historical past. Philippine history, at least that which has survived in written form,
came with the foreigners—the Chinese, the Muslim Malays,
the Arab traders, and the Spaniards.

This reality has denied Filipinos the unifying advantages of
a glorious and indigenous heritage. It has given disproportionate significance to the role of foreigners. The foreigners themselves often saw the Philippines as a way-station to other more
interesting areas of Asia. The Spanish came hoping to find the
fabled new wealth of the Spice Islands and to gain a base to
convert China to Christianity. They were discouraged to learn
that there were no spices worth exporting in the Philippines
and that the Spice Islands they sought were thousands of miles
to the south—islands then in Portugese hands. After the defeat
of the Spanish Armada and the death of Philip II, Spain lacked
the money and human resources to develop an active policy in
Asia. The colony became a backwater.

Although it was relatively easy to sail from Spain to Latin
America, and possible, though risky, to sail directly from Latin
America to the Philippines, it was impossible to sail due east
from the Philippines back to the Pacific coast of Latin America,
because of prevailing winds. Initially Portugal and later Hol-

land blocked a route home around Asia. It took fifty years to discover that there was a way back via the Great Circle up around Japan and down along the California coast. The consequences of this discovery were enormous. The threat of the Spanish coming ashore on Japan was one factor that prompted the newly dominant Tokugawa family to isolate Japan for close to 250 years, because it feared that Spanish temporal and religious forces would upset the delicate balance of power that permitted it to sustain its position in Japan. The discovery also prompted the creation of a string of settlements along America's West coast, including San Francisco, Santa Barbara, and San Diego. Finally, the discovery linked the Philippines by communication and commerce to Spanish Latin America.

Spanish colonial control over the Philippines, which came after the discovery of the Great Circle route back to Mexico, was spearheaded by the religious orders, especially the Augustinians, Dominicans, Franciscans, and Jesuits. These friars were theoretically the shock troops who were to proselytize for the diocesan church and then move on to new frontiers. Since the Philippines proved to be the last stop in the line, however, these missionaries turned inward, devoting themselves to the *indios*. In the late sixteenth century, the orders of friars divided the Philippines into zones of influence that lasted for several centuries. The friars also made a critically important decision for the future life of the country—they decided to proselytize and to teach in the many vernaculars rather than in Spanish. Spanish never became the language of the great majority of the people, and among the Caucasians, only the priests usually had the capacity to communicate directly with the natives.

Inasmuch as Spain had colonized the Philippines in part as an act of devotion, the proselytizing zeal to make the islands a "showcase of the faith" placed ecclesiastical concerns at the center of colonial policy. To Philip II and his successors, there was no gap between the work of the state and that of the Church, and service to God and king created interpenetration of bureaucracies and functions. The Church became figuratively and literally the great structure dominating the Philippine landscape; the priest became judge, mentor, landlord, and symbol of foreign power.

The temporal Spanish authorities were thinly stretched across the archipelago. Few Spaniards or Latin American mestizos lived outside the main centers of power. In order to govern, therefore, the Spanish governor-general had to rely not only on the priests but also on the leaders of the local native gentry. These included the village headman, and at the township level a petty governor, who was the highest native official linking the Spaniards above with the *indios* below. This system of indirect rule generated a rural elite, the *principalia*, which like the urban mestizos became powerful and wealthy over time.

There was a long, sleepy era after the colony was established. The Spanish temporal authorities paid scant attention to what happened in the countryside, and focused almost exclusively on the opportunities to profit through the Manila galleon. This barely created sufficient revenue to fund the colony, however. So much Chinese silk was transshipped in the early years of the colony that the silk merchants in Spain forced the Madrid government to impose strict limits on the value and volume of the galleon trade. Each galleon, a great, unwieldy tub of a ship, was then permitted to sail only once or twice a year, and on its successful round trip rested the economic survival of the Spanish colony and of the satellite Chinese and mestizo urban enclaves. When a galleon was lost or captured, the residents of the colony were immediately in risk of individual and collective brankruptcy. Moreover, the galleon trade stultified other aspects of Philippine trade and economic growth, since the trade had very little to do with the Philippines beyond the building and outfitting of the ship and its capacity to carry from the New World the clerics and silver required to maintain the colony. The galleon trade drained hundreds of millions of silver pesos from the New World to China in exchange for silks, porcelains, and other Chinese finished goods. Moreover, this trade was a target of opportunity for those Chinese and the members of the tiny Spanish community who wanted to survive just long enough in the tropics to make a fortune before going home.

The governor-general and his staff were certainly no representatives of enlightened rule. The governor-general's appointment was strictly political and was usually a payoff for services rendered the Crown. It was understood, if rarely articulated, that the governor was to profit personally, provided he did not plunder too grossly. The whole system was based on a presumption of guilt. The first act of each incoming governor was to hold a formal trial, known as the *residencia*, of the outgoing governor. Bribery was endemic, and each outgoing governor understood that he needed to share a certain percentage of his profits with the incoming governor in order to take the rest home.

What might best be called a "colonial" era followed the brief British conquest of the archipelago from 1762 to 1764. This was an era characterized by a new attention to the Philippine interior and a rise in plantations. The hacienda came to dominate rice production. A landed native gentry arose and became the dominant group of the period. Some of the upwardly mobile mestizos married into these *cacique* families, injecting new blood, ideas, and values into their traditional, isolated societies, and in turn becoming domesticated and entrenched. Absentee ownership grew, and sharecropping created peasant penury. A social and economic gap opened between rich and poor that has yet to be closed.

The New World of the Nineteenth Century

The nineteenth century saw the Philippine colonial structure altered dramatically. Spain itself had become a sleepy backwater, geographically isolated. By the 1830s, the cataclysmic series of national wars of liberation in Latin America had reduced the Spanish empire from one of the greatest the world had ever seen to a few remnant colonies. Among these few remnants were Cuba, Puerto Rico, and the Philippines.

Steam power, meanwhile, altered the navigational patterns that had governed sailing for centuries, and the Suez Canal shortened the trip between Spain and the Philippines from three months to thirty days. Steam power was also introduced to drive mills, and sugar became a viable export commodity. The island of Negros in the central Philippines was virtually uninhabited until, in 1857, an Englishman working for Ker and Company brought the first sugar mill there. Whereas in 1856 only a half million pounds of sugar were produced, by 1864 some fourteen million pounds were exported. By the end of the century, 274 steam-operated sugar mills dotted Negros. The population grew tenfold. The number of municipalities expanded from six to thirty-four, and by the end of the century the island was divided into two provincial governments. Sugar became the largest business in the Philippines. In 1879 sugar exports totaled 47,025 tons; in 1910, 121,471 tons; and in 1932, 1,016,568 tons. Sugar dominated the life and the people of the archipelago.

The Philippines continued to fly the Spanish flag, but much of the capital for this development came from Chinese and English sources. The mestizos became guardians of a plantation culture, and Philippine peasants were uprooted in totally new ways. The development of sugar exports created an internal migration as the new technology brought the Philippines into the world marketplace. Public health programs and modern medicine led to an increase in population, creating a surplus labor force that ventured onto the rural frontier, a process as dramatic in many ways as the settlement of the American West or Russian Siberia.

As the cultivation of sugar and later coconut spread from one island to the other, lands that had previously been used for rice were converted to these export crops. The country lost its self-sufficiency in basic food production and became more dependent on a world marketplace over which it had little control. Markets in London, New York, and Paris had an impact on Filipinos that was both new and unpredictable, as Philippine crops competed with Indonesian, Cuban, and African products. Places like Negros, which previously had been unimportant politically and economically, assumed a status that challenged other regions and their leaders.

New ports, new cities, and new wealth all changed the islands. The changes put the mass of peasants under intense pressure. Landlord-tenant relationships were altered. Migration weakened traditional family patterns. Modern health care challenged the role of traditional mediums. Expectations of life and death changed. The peasantry turned increasingly inward to express its longings for an earlier, more stable world. Popular movements, often framed in religious rather than political terms, sought to synthesize the new and alien with the old and familiar. Peasant violence was another manifestation of frustration and aspiration.

There was meanwhile a growing assertion of Filipino national identity at other levels of society. Spain, buffeted by its own tensions of modernization, including a century-long struggle between secularism and Catholicism, viewed these stirrings within the Philippines with alarm. Spanish control depended upon repression, and as one observer, Sinibaldo de Mas, noted, it was a policy that was "suspicious and unenlightened but still useful for preserving the colony."[4] Between 1835 and 1898 there were fifty governors-general, and the Spanish governments rose and fell with such rapidity that coherent colonial policy was almost impossible. Increasingly the new Filipino elite saw the Spanish friars as the hated symbol of colonial repression, and one of the first goals of these nationalists was to achieve clerical equality. The upwardly mobile native elite demanded ordination and Filipinization of the Church. For decades they struggled to win appointments to a larger percentage of the parishes of the country and to tilt the balance away from the friars toward the then more liberal diocesan clerics. The Spanish priests responded with a mix of condescension and racism that further exacerbated a tense situation, especially since in some areas around Manila the friars owned more than 50 percent of the rice land under cultivation.

In 1872 three Filipino priests were executed on trumped-up charges. From then until 1896 there was a growing alienation

---

[4] Sinibaldo de Mas, *Report on the Conditions of the Philippines in 1842,* III (Manila: History Conservation Society, 1963), p. 169.

between Filipinos and Spaniards. During this same period, the number of Spanish civil servants and entrepreneurs increased dramatically as the greater ease of transportation and an improved quality of life encouraged Iberians to emigrate. In Manila, Andres Bonifacio, a lower-middle-class Filipino clerk, organized a secret society known as the Katipunan, a neo-masonic, revolutionary movement. Linked to a peasant tradition and using images of Christianity and the *pasyon*, Bonifacio tried to ally the *ilustrados* to his anti-clerical, anti-Spanish movement. Unsuccessful in these efforts, he plotted to implicate the *ilustrados* through forgery as supporters of his movement; he hoped that Spanish repression would cause the fundamentally conservative *ilustrados* to see the need for radical action. In particular, he tried to attract the most articulate of this group, Jose Rizal. In 1896 the Spanish moved to arrest the Katipunan leadership, after a clerical violation of confidentiality at the confessional confirmed Bonifacio's plans for a revolt. Bonifacio fled, beginning a war of national liberation that ultimately toppled Spanish power and led to American intervention.

Jose Rizal refused to be coopted by Bonifacio, and attempted to maintain a distance from his revolutionary movement. The Spanish, however, chose to implicate him as the source of rebellion. After a sham trial, Rizal was executed. Rizal's novels had been attacked as "heretical, impious, and scandalous in the religious order and anti-patriotic, subvervise of the public order [and] offensive" in the temporal sphere. Rizal was seen as "the principal organizer and the very soul of the Philippine insurrection."[5] And by his martyrdom the Spanish forged an alliance between the outraged *ilustrados* and other groups within Philippine society. Many years earlier, Rizal had written that "the day the Spanish inflict martyrdom . . . farewell, pro-friar government, and perhaps, farewell, Spanish government."[6] The Spanish fulfilled Rizal's prophecy.

[5] John N. Schumacher, "The Philippine Nationalists' Propaganda Campaign in Europe, 1880-1895," Ph.D. dissertation, Georgetown University, 1965, p. 191.

[6] Jose Rizal to Mariano Ponce, April 1889. Cited in Schumacher, "Propaganda Campaign," p. 547.

When he had to flee to the provinces, Bonifacio lost control of his movement to a young rural governor, Emilio Aguinaldo of Cavite. The ensuing internal struggles within the revolutionary group alienated the urbanized *ilustrados*. Aguinaldo was increasingly pursued by a reinforced Spanish military. The Spanish, eager to end this Philippine insurrection because of the Cuban revolution, struck a deal with Aguinaldo that sent him into exile and provided him with cash. It was a deal neither side honored.

American "Compadre Colonialism"

Aguinaldo was in Singapore when serendipity and American imperialism suddenly gave him an important chance. Admiral Dewey needed him. Although President McKinley, by his own admission, did not know within 2,000 miles where the archipelago was, he and his advisors were influenced by ideas of Manifest Destiny. The Americans brought Aguinaldo to Manila Bay, permitting him to organize an anti-Spanish government at the provincial city of Malolos. The situation had changed in the previous few years, and this government attracted *ilustrados*, who debated with lucidity and sophistication several models for their country.

Had the consensus between the *ilustrados* and the other groups at Malolos survived, the archipelago might have had a national movement of great strength. America might have tired of its imperial misadventure and followed William Jennings Bryan's urgings to grant the Filipinos their independence then and there. But because of class differences within the Philippine nationalist movement, and because of Aguinaldo's limitations as a leader, the Americans were able to offer the *ilustrados* a tacit deal: power and the fulfillment of their nineteenth-century dreams within a conservative, nonrevolutionary context. If that was the carrot offered, the American army acted as a powerful stick, chasing and harassing the fledgling Filipino government from place to place until finally it was isolated and Aguinaldo was himself captured. The mass of Filipinos nevertheless rallied to the fledgling government, waging a popular war of national liberation. The American commander, General Arthur MacArthur, noted in 1900, "This unique system of war depends on the almost complete unity of action of the entire native population."[7] It was a bitter and bloody struggle, one far more costly in lives and treasure for the United States than the Spanish-American war that had preceded it. But by 1902 it was over.

The American policy succeeded because it promised a government that would be structured "to satisfy the views and aspirations of the educated Filipinos."[8] American Progressives believed that these Filipinos would be of infinite value to the United States as leaders of the people. They saw these leaders as the chief agents of their people, securing their people's loyal obedience. It seemed common sense to secure their cordial attachment. The Americans intervened on socioeconomic issues: land distribution, the church's holdings, the rights of property holders, and the possession of the franchise—in each case supporting the existing elite. Rizal had written a "Manifesto to Certain Filipinos" in which he had noted some years earlier that "reforms, if they are to bear fruit, must come from above, for reforms that come from below are upheavals both violent and transitory."[9] The Americans saw that there were indeed "Filipinos of education, intelligence, and property," and that these conservative *ilustrados* were their natural allies.

The tacit deal shaped both the values of the society and the political process. It also left the inequities of the social system glaringly in place. By 1908, William Howard Taft, perhaps the key architect of American colonial policy, was afraid that American policy was "merely to await the organization of the Phillipine oligarchy or aristocracy competent to administer. . . ."[10] Taft's anxiety helps to explain the American emphasis on education as a vehicle to break "the feudal relation of de-

[7] As cited in Leon Wolff, *Little Brown Brother* (London: Longmans, 1961), p. 289.

[8] Senate Doc. 138, 56th Congress, 1st Session, 1899-1900, pp. 116-121.

[9] W. E. Retana's transcription of *The Trial of José Rizal*, translated and edited by H. de la Costa (Manila: Ateneo de Manila, 1961), pp. 102-103.

[10] Special Report of the Secretary of War William Howard Taft to President Theodore Roosevelt, January 23, 1908, III, 238-239.

pendence which so many of the common people now feel toward their wealthier, educated leaders." The central assumption of American colonial policy, however, was that the new government should "conform to the customs, habits, and even the prejudices" found in the Philippines. The oligarchy defined the nation's norms and prejudices; the *ilustrados* were firmly entrenched.

A political history would chronicle the evolution of successful nationalism from 1907 to the Commonwealth era to independence. A socioeconomic history must chronicle the hegemony of this oligarchy as it assumed the power rapidly abdicated by American colonialism. As early as 1903, the United States turned provincial affairs over to the Filipinos. Thereafter America lost its ability to influence, for better or for worse, the way in which the social fabric of the archipelago was structured.

Evidence of the dominance of the *ilustrado* elite was its capacity to collaborate with the Japanese in the Second World War, even though this put it at variance with the mass of the people who fought for and identified with Douglas MacArthur and the United States. The Japanese occupation divided the society between urban and rural, collaborators and guerrillas. It was a time of social distinction and savage physical destruction. It was not, however, a time in which a new elite emerged at the expense of the old. Indeed, the portrait of Jose Laurel, the wartime puppet president, hangs in Malacañang, the presidential palace, today. A few nonestablishment guerrilla leaders, most notably Ramon Magsaysay, did win entry into the postwar elite, but in the main, the prewar establishment survived, retained power, and passed that power on to its own children as the country moved through the first decades of independence.

The Continuities and Discontinuities of Independence

On July 4, 1946, formal independence was proclaimed with rhetoric as lofty as the rubble was deep. Some months earlier, Manuel Roxas, President Quezon's prewar heir presumptive, had defeated Sergio Osmeña, Quezon's successor to the presidency-in-exile, in the election to choose a president to lead the new Republic. Factional politics, which had swirled about these three men and their key supporters in the prewar and wartime eras, continued unabated. During the last days of the war, Douglas MacArthur had openly and problematically intervened by announcing that he had "liberated" Roxas, while capturing the other members of the prewar elite who had collaborated with the Japanese. By separating Roxas out and pardoning him by fiat, MacArthur lifted any taint of collaboration from Roxas, positioning him to challenge Osmeña successfully. The general's clear support for Roxas was typical of American behavior of the time. MacArthur not only influenced the political process, but he also helped to subvert the judicial process, since his intervention made moot the work of the People's Court, established to try the collaborators. The long-range consequence was to assure that the conservative *ilustrado* elite and their children, both literal and figurative, should remain the dominant power in the Philippines.

The country had been physically ravaged. Like Warsaw, Manila had been cruelly damaged, in part because MacArthur chose to reoccupy it, and in part because the Japanese had defended it house by house, room by room. The modern sector of the economy, concentrated in Manila, was destroyed. The task of rehabilitation seemed overwhelming, especially as the United States was focused on rehabilitating Germany and Japan, Europe and China. The painful fact was that the United States was disengaging rapidly from the Philippines, both emotionally and economically. Aid for rehabilitation was linked to concessions. Monetary arrangements, trade issues, access to natural resources, and land ownership were all decided in ways that were favorable to American economic interests, and the decisions to retain vast territories as military bases shattered the illusion that independence would usher in a golden era of Philippine-American partnership based on mutual respect.

In such a context, the Filipinos elected Manuel Roxas. That decision, by no means overwhelmingly ratified electorally, kept the trained technocrats, experienced bureaucrats, and self-promoting politicians in power. It linked what had happened in the Spanish, American, and Japanese colonial periods with what was to follow independence. It reaffirmed not only an oligarchy but also the *mestizo* culture that these oligarchs embodied. In sociocultural as well as political terms, the period from 1946 to 1972 was a continuation of the past, not a break with it. Compadre colonialism had worked. Unlike developments in Indonesia or Vietnam, for example, independence in the Philippines changed neither the players nor the system.

The institutions of government, modeled on their American counterparts, looked to outsiders very much like the originals. In reality, the external form masked other elements already strongly rooted. Factionalism, patron-client relationships built on reciprocal bonds of loyalty, regionalism, nepotism, violence at the lower levels, and a clubby old boy network at the top were the ingredients that produced a stable, if inefficient, system. Democracy worked in the sense that elections were held and people in power yielded peacefully if defeated. But almost everyone who ran for higher office came from the same elite. Differentiating between parties was nearly impossible; candidates jumped from one party to the other solely to enhance opportunity, and Liberals and Nacionalistas were ideologically indistinguishable. The oligarchy was shrewd enough to recognize that it had to allow upwardly mobile and acceptable newcomers to enter the establishment, provided they accepted the existing value system and played by the rules. Relative newcomers like Ramon Magsaysay could reach the top quickly if they had momentum. Rapidly coopted, welcomed to Baguio or the Polo Club in Makati, these newcomers infused energy without challenging the hegemony of the oligarchy.

The system was stable. If it was unjust and too preoccupied with wealth, it did apparently handle the problems of reconstruction, increasing population, and economic development. The society was not torn asunder by social revolution, despite its glaring contradictions. The Hukbalahap, a radical agrarian movement in central Luzon, did threaten the new nation in the early 1950s, but Magsaysay solved the threat by creating a program of resettlement in Mindanao for landless peasants, by revitalizing the army and the civil government, and by capturing the Huk politburo. The CIA and Colonel Lansdale played an important part, but ultimately it was Magsaysay's appeal as a leader that made his program work.

The Huk threat, recurring peasant movements such as the Rizalistas, and the obvious gap between rich and poor revealed a nation that had stability but not social justice. The continuity of power meant that the rich got richer and the poor got children. Land reform never succeeded because the landlords sat in Congress. The urban poor, the ethnic minorities, the landless peasants, and the small cultivators producing crops like copra have all been victims, often ruthlessly abused. Many were powerless if not disenfranchised. And yet, the central question is why the society had such stability. Observers, including this author, constantly prophesied that the social pressure would lead to an explosion that did not come.

Why not? Middle-class status was expanding, education seemed a valid ticket upward, training at home or abroad offered children vistas that perhaps had been denied to their parents, emigration to America and elsewhere was a safety valve, and the economy was growing, albeit unevenly. There was also a remarkable press (so free it often knew no restraint) that titillated, informed, and helped to curb abuses of power. The army was professional, small, and committed to remaining that way. If it lacked great combat skill or high visibility, it also had few political ambitions and played a passive role in the life of the nation. The judiciary was a real legacy of the United States. It was independent, powerful, and respected. It maintained the inherited system of checks and balances, preserving the constitution as the paramount political institution. Although the courts, the press, and the army were far from perfect, they all contributed to the new state's stability.

Moreover, the optimism and ebullience of the Filipino people invigorated the system. Politics was—and is—one of the archipelago's great national pastimes. Many Filipinos sustain a belief in the possibilities of progress. Even during what was called the "old order" by Ferdinand Marcos after he instituted martial law in 1972, the tendency toward venality was tempered by public opinion. The constitutional convention convened in the early 1970s expressed this optimism. At this convention, which Marcos both disdained and attempted to manipulate, the delegates debated both seriously and frivolously the liabilities and opportunities of various alternate systems. What was emerging, when martial law stopped the process, was a reinterpretation of Philippine democracy. There were plenty of flaws, and there was a lot of bargaining, but that convention was also a vote of confidence in the possibilities of an indigenous, domesticated democracy.

There are two possible interpretations about the old order, the period from 1946 to 1972. The first suggests that the oligarchy put group interest ahead of national need. Ferdinand Marcos, celebrating the third anniversary of martial law, said in 1975 that the Philippines was "a nation divided between urban and rural, rich and poor, majorities and minorities, privileged and underprivileged."[11] Revealingly, he further noted that martial law may "have liquidated an oligarchy only to set up a new oligarchy . . . , [establishing] massive opportunities for graft, corruption and misuse of influence—opportunities which are now being exploited within the government service."

The second interpretation of the old order is more benign. It notes the virtues of stability, of development, of new and enlarged opportunities for many through education and upward mobility. It highlights the vitality of the courts, the passivity of the army, and the role of the press. It sees in the domestic process a chance for popular opinion to decide leadership. If there was a frontier violence to politics, there was also a real symbiosis between the masses and the leadership, especially during the periods before elections when pork-barrel legislation and vote-buying recycled some of the wealth. Few would argue that the system was one to cherish, but many might argue that

[11] As cited in Robert Shaplen, *A Turning Wheel* (New York: Random House, 1979), p. 221.

the constitutional convention offered a genuine way to reform the abuses while preserving the core.

Philippine society has usually opted for evolution over revolution. It has usually chosen to preserve continuities and retain the baggage of the past. Even in the era of the Marcos administration, in which the army became a new and seemingly powerful threat to traditional structures, the fundamental priorities seem to have survived quite well. The same quest for upward mobility and economic gain that plagued the old order before martial law was the dominant characteristic of the Marcos era landscape. The players changed, new groups were allowed to feed at the trough, but the new groups acted just as the old ones did, and the momentum, at least superficially, seemed to be consistent.

In 1965 in his first inaugural address, Ferdinand Marcos warned: "The Filipino, it seems, has lost his soul, his dignity, and his courage. Our people have come to a point of despair. We have ceased to value order." Marcos claimed that the "government is gripping the iron hand of venality, its treasury is barren, its resources are wasted, its civil service is slothful and indifferent, its armed forces demoralized and its councils sterile."[12] His negative judgment eventually led to martial law and "constitutional authoritarianism." Whether his administration addressed the litany of social ills he identified, whether twenty years later the Philippines was a healthier, stronger society, was far more problematic.

[12] Ferdinand Marcos, Inaugural Address, December 30, 1965.

CHAPTER III

THE SOCIAL SITUATION

WILFREDO F. ARCE AND RICARDO G. ABAD

We often have occasion to travel in the provinces of the Philippines. And when we do we see the national society in ways that are very different from what one sees from the political heights of the capital. Here are two cases, paralleling many that we have encountered, that will give the reader a concrete sense of what we mean:

1. The government has a program to buy rice at prices that are designed to assure the rice farmer that he can sell his produce at a profit, or at least without a loss. However, the poor tenant farmer finds it difficult to take advantage of the program. First, he usually sells in small lots, that is, a sack of 52 kgs. Because he sells in small lots, his profit margin is limited. Also, for the same reason, the cost of transportation to the purchasing center is significant. When he gets there he may find that the queue is long, with some sellers like himself and others who haul rice by the truckload all taking their place in the same line. Once he gets to the head of the line, he finds that his rice has to conform to certain quality standards, such as moisture content. Finally, he is paid by check, and cashing this may be delayed overnight or over a weekend. The situation calls to mind the doleful comment of one official in the government purchasing agency: the efficiency and benefits of the price support program could be improved, he said, if only the small farmers could organize themselves into larger groups of sellers. Apparently this has not come about on any large scale. Instead, many small farmer-sellers continue to turn to the ubiquitous and traditional middlemen who may pay less, but who pay in cash, sometimes in advance of delivery, and usually with a minimum of other demands.

2. The government has delineated "water districts" in more urbanized areas of the country. These districts are to be pro-

vided with potable water for household and commercial or industrial use through the establishment of modern systems of
water treatment and delivery. However, some *barangays* (the
smallest official political units) are not served by the water district system in their locality because not enough households
can afford the price of individual connections. Now, the water
district system could set up relatively inexpensive outlets at
just a few locations that could serve as distribution points in
these *barangays*; and the local people could carry the water
from there to their houses. But the water district officials have
to worry about recovering the investment involved in providing the service. Some person or organization has to be billed
for it. Sometimes a *barangay* official will agree to list himself
as the subscriber with the understanding that he will collect
contributions from the other residents. Invariably, however,
after a few months, the contributions cease, the water connection is cut, and the residents go back to their traditional
sources of water.

Two Sectors

These examples are not chosen for their dramatic character.
They are simply part of the larger picture of Philippine society's attempt to cope with the present-day problem of achieving national development. In bolder strokes, the larger picture
that emerges looks somewhat like this:

On the one hand, there is a relatively small but significant
and powerful sector that derives its livelihood by controlling
much of the nation's resources and heading the country's public and private bureaucracies. The population in this sector includes government and business leaders, and other "influentials."[1] These people, and their families, are affluent. And in
accumulating and controlling their surplus resources they are

[1] Perla Q. Makil, *PAASCU/IPC Study of Schools and Influentials 1969-70*,
Final Report, Part 1 (Quezon City: Ateneo de Manila Institute of Philippine
Culture, 1970); and idem, *Mobility by Decree: The Rise and Fall of Philippine
Influentials Since Martial Law*, Final Report, Volume 1 (Quezon City: Ateneo
de Manila Institute of Philippine Culture, 1975).

assisted by a host of functionaries—the purchasing agency and water district staffs in our examples, and, among others, the white collar workers in various public and private institutions. They live largely in the country's urban areas. And the lifestyle they follow is modeled largely after that of people living in the developed Western nations.

On the other hand, the rest of the population is relatively disadvantaged. Most members of this disadvantaged social sector are rural people. They earn their living as upland farmers, lowland tenant farmers, loggers, fishermen, and workers in similar occupations that demand physical toil. In the urban centers, where their number is increasing, they may be squatters or slum dwellers who earn their living as peddlers or scavengers, or are otherwise engaged in activities for which the returns are marginal. Some are among the fully employed workers in the lowest rung of the income scale, such as domestics and factory workers. Some white-collar workers (such as the poorest paid teachers) are of similarly constricted means and might be included in this category. One important characteristic shared by members of this disadvantaged sector is their poverty. They are poor because they are unemployed or because the material rewards they command do not allow more than a mere subsistence level of living. They do not have the power or the resources to accumulate more resources and thus become less poor. Another equally important characteristic is their adherence to a traditional style of life.

This picture of a society divided into two distinguishable sectors—advantaged and disadvantaged—conjures up the concept of the "dual society" first described for the Netherlands East Indies by the Dutch economist, J. H. Boeke; it is also referred to by others who trace the concept to him as "sociological dualism." The broad notion behind these terms is that of a society consisting of two distinguishable parts that clash with each other.

Many important historical factors that help account for this dualism are treated in other chapters of this volume. Dualism in this society may also be linked with inequalities among nations, with the richer countries contributing to the perpetuation of dualism in the Philippines as a developing country. But our focus here will be on internal dualism in the Philippines.

Statistical Profile

Aggregate statistics testify to the gap between rich and poor Filipinos. Surveys conducted by the National Census and Statistics Office (NCSO) suggest that the income distribution in the country might even have worsened between 1971 and 1979. In 1971, the poorest 60 percent of the total households received a mere 25 percent of the total income; in 1979, the same group's share of the total income dropped to 22.5 percent. In contrast, the richest 10 percent of households increased their share of total income from 37 percent in 1971 to 42 percent in 1979. Workers also suffered declines in income. Central Bank figures show that although monthly nominal incomes for salaried workers and wage earners were higher in 1980 than in 1972, the monthly real incomes actually declined during the same period. Unfavorable wage trends could have been offset by increasing time at work. However, the NCSO estimated that between 1978 and 1983 the annual unemployment rate rose from 5.2 percent to 5.9 percent, underemployment increased from 10.2 percent to 29.0 percent, and the labor supply grew at an annual rate of 4 percent.

The rural population has carried the brunt of the economic malaise. The 1980 census reveals that 63 percent of the Philippine population resides in rural areas; other statistical sources indicate that the majority of these rural people are poor. Whereas only 15 percent of all households in Metropolitan Manila were classified as low-income, between 59 to 90 percent of households in the rural provinces fell in this category. At the end of 1983, the poverty threshold for food and other needs was set at 23,268.00 pesos per annum; in the National Capital Region, 43 percent of households had incomes below this poverty line; in other regions (predominantly rural) the percentage rises to 73. Indeed, at February 1984 prices, even the lowest poverty threshold estimate of 1,082.43 pesos per month was not reached by the highest-earning nonagricultural legal minimum wage worker who was the sole breadwin-

ner in a six-member household. The unemployment picture is
no better. Scrutinizing more closely NCSO data in the 1970s,
one study suggests that half of the working-age population in
the Philippines is not in the labor force; and two-thirds of this
unemployment is found in the rural areas.

The bleak statistical picture continues in the agricultural
sector. The number of farms increased from 2.4 to 3.4 million
between 1971 and 1980, but the average size declined from
3.6 to 2.6 hectares. The increase in the numbers of small farms
relative to larger farms has widened income gaps in agriculture. In addition, a comparison of NCSO labor force surveys
for the first quarters of 1971 and 1983 showed a 75 percent
increase in the number of agricultural wage workers, the lowest income earners in the Philippine economy. But agriculture's
share of total annual employment declined between the years
1978 and 1983; there is still a tremendous amount of surplus
labor found in Philippine farm families.

Lower income and unemployment tend to go together, and
are, in turn, related to other manifestations of rural poverty.
The literacy rate in urban areas, for example, stands at 93 percent; in rural areas it is 79 percent. Physician-population ratios
and the number of hospital beds per thousand population are
more favorable in urban than in rural areas. Statistics are not
available, but parallel differences in morbidity rates and the in-
cidence of malnutrition are likely. In 1970, the crude death
rate in the city of Manila was 8.4 for males and 6.1 for females; most other provinces registered higher rates. The infant
mortality rate has been declining on a nationwide basis, but
the contrast between rural and urban rates is dramatic. In
1970 the infant mortality rate for Manila was 67.9 for males
and 55.7 for females. Almost all other provinces registered
higher rates; in rural Surigao del Sur, the figures were 202.6 for
males and 176.1 for females.

Development Programs and the Dualism Block

Macro-societal statistics are heady stuff. Let us now take the
analysis back to the examples we started with, the widely

known government development programs, and the involvement of the two sectors in them.

At present, the relationship between the advantaged and the
disadvantaged sectors continues to be one of unequal partnership in the development enterprise; furthermore, in the unequal relationship, the disadvantaged sector continues to be
systematically deprived in many ways. In our example of the
potable water program, members of the advantaged sector can
pay the subscription fee which, in turn, can be used to maintain the system, compensate the staff for its services, and liq-
uidate the loan to the international lending agencies. Members
of the disadvantaged sector living in impoverished *barangays*
do not have the same capacity to pay; in monetary terms, they
do not deserve treated water for drinking.

Nor does it take much imagination to deduce from the an-
ecdote of the rice farmer that he, and many others like him,
with only one sack of rice to sell at a time, play a small part in
determining the price of rice. The Minister of Agriculture once
spoke of these farmers as being "caught in a squeeze" between
the price of fertilizers and what they receive for the *palay*
(husked rice). This unpleasant squeeze has been described by
one scholar for a village in Cental Luzon.[2] He says that the
benefits of the Green Revolution have accrued not to the farmers or even the landlords but to a newly emerging commercial
elite whose ranks are being joined by many landlords. Umehara contends that another important sharer in the profits is
the agribusiness sector, which is dominated by foreign capital;
about 70 percent of the country's fertilizer is currently imported, and paid for by foreign loans.

The limited effectiveness of Operation Land Transfer—the
latest in a series of generally emasculated agrarian reform programs—is the most recent demonstration of the weakness of
the disadvantaged sector in the rural areas. To be fair, credit

---

[2] Hiromitsu Umehara, "Green Revolution for Whom?" (an inquiry into its
beneficiaries in a Central Luzon village, Philippines) in *Second View from the
Paddy*, edited by Antonio J. Ledesma, Perla Q. Makil, and Virginia A. Miralao
(Quezon City: Ateneo de Manila Institute of Philippine Culture, 1983), pp.
24-40.

should be given to the Ministry of Agrarian Reform; by August 1982 certificates of land transfer had been issued to 430,273 farmer-beneficiaries, a total that exceeds the target set by the ministry for the whole program. But the same ministry report cites an even higher number of farmers (609,042) as being eligible only for leasehold arrangements, not for eventual ownership of the land that they till. Further, these two groups of tenant farmers are still only a portion of those who derive their living from the land but do not own a piece of it. The number of these in 1975 was estimated at 3.5 million. Indeed, as Gelia Castillo has pointed out,

> Land transfer, although regarded as a major instrument for achieving greater income equality, is not likely to drastically shake up the prevailing patterns of landownership because about three-quarters of the farm area is operated by full or part-owners whose holdings are not part of the redistribution plan. Furthermore, their farms are larger (3.9 and 3.5 hectares average for full and part-owners) than the tenanted farms (2.6 hectares average).[3]

The urban poor are better off than their rural counterparts, but this is probably the best that can be said about their situation. The fact is that they are poor, and most studies so far suggest that the growth of slum communities came about as a result of unplanned development, government apathy, and economic development plans that favor selected sectors of urban society. Left to their own devices, the poor have developed their own means of coping with poverty in an otherwise affluent urban environment, at least so long as they are not evicted to unacceptable resettlement sites.

We prefer not to comment on the various government programs that are supposedly intended to help redress the imbalances between the two sectors of society. And we will only mention in passing the abuses and corruption of power and authority by members of the advantaged sector, even though

[3] Gelia T. Castillo, *Beyond Manila: Philippine Rural Problems in Perspective* (Ottawa: International Development Research Center, 1979), p. 40.

we believe that these have seriously weakened the moral fiber and societal will of the nation. On the other hand, we do not impugn the motivations of all participants in this sector because, thankfully, there are still men and women of good will there. What we would like to stress is that the structural imbalance is perpetuated as much by members of the advantaged sector as by those in the disadvantaged sector themselves. Behind the water district official's complaint that poor *barangay* residents cannot get themselves organized to pay the cost of water, and behind the rice official's lament that greater efficiency benefiting all would be achieved in the price support program if only small-scale producers could pool their produce, is a common vision of what this society is like—its goodness, its limitations—and what needs to be done to achieve prosperity for all.

The members of the disadvantaged sector who are seemingly resistant to the most rational plans and efforts at development are following a different vision, or at least responding to different pressures. At the heart of their conception of the world is the individual's reliance on, and his or her expectation of support from, the extended family and a small group of personal allies. Castillo calls the large family "the mirror of society rather than vice versa" and continues,

> The Filipino family, large and functionally extended as it is, provides social security, old age pensions, jobs, scholarships, unemployment benefits, nursery services, credit, land, labor, capital, income redistribution, work sharing, companionship to the unmarried, care for the sick, home for the aged, counsel for the troubled, and most of all, love, affection, emotional maintenance, and social stability without which the Filipino's life is meaningless. On the debit side, the Filipino family has often been accused of harbouring nepotism, encouraging dependency, supporting social parasitism, promoting prolific childbearing, which are all inhibitory to the Filipino's integration into the community and larger society, and hence dysfunctional to national development efforts.[4]

[4] Ibid., 103.

There are qualifications and additions to this summary description that are worth noting. For instance, it is likely that many family-centered groups would include nonrelatives because of their propinquity, emotional closeness, and proven dependability to a given individual in the group. Frank Lynch has argued that the Filipino relies for most of his needs on a personal "alliance group" composed largely of kinsmen but also including selected nonkinsmen who have proved to be reliable in fulfilling expectations of mutual aid.[5] Thomas McHale has observed that the reliance on the small family-centered group means that the Filipino's "area of trust" in his social world tends to be limited.[6] But Castillo does provide a useful description of the perception that the individual has of the persons he can depend on and the persons who, in turn, depend on him. The solidarity of this group—nurtured through the centuries by the mutual benefits and security that individual members provide for one another and the mutual demands that they make on each other—has effectively blunted the formation and growth of other kinds of organizations, sincerely and competently conceived or otherwise, that the advantaged sector may have wanted for the disadvantaged sector. The *barangay* organization that the water district official would like to see, and the pool of small rice sellers that the purchasing agency official would prefer to deal with, have very strong competition indeed.

Confronted with the problems of poverty, the rural family resorts to a number of ways of coping. Members diversify their activities to include marketable crafts that can be done at home; call on wealthier relatives to help provide credit or a little land to grow vegetable crops on; rely on kinship ties and reciprocal arrangements to obtain resources from similarly poor groups that may have a momentary surplus; and simply cut down on the consumption of food and other basic neces-

[5] Frank Lynch, *Social Class in a Bikol Town* (Chicago: University of Chicago Philippine Studies Program, 1959), pp. 49-55; and idem, "Perspectives on Filipino Clannishness," *Philippine Sociological Review* 21:1 (1973), 73-77.

[6] Thomas McHale, "Econological Analysis and Differential Economic Growth Rate," *Human Organization* 21:1 (1962), 31.

sities. When all these mechanisms prove inadequate, the option of migration is available.[7] If a family migrates to another rural area, this cycle of coping is repeated. For those who migrate to urban areas, new pressures are faced, and new strategies have to be adopted. The family takes up low-income service occupations; there is greater need for women and children to contribute to family income; there is a critical need to locate one's home near one's place of work, even if this means occupying a piece of land illegally; and there is the ever-present danger of being evicted to another site where the level of living is surely to erode further. Those who have family connections, or who can amass the necessary resources, may opt to migrate abroad, to the United States or the Middle East, for example. Emigration provides short-term benefits for households and individuals, but it is doubtful that it contributes to the country's economic and political self-sufficiency.

The notion of disadvantaged individuals or family-centered groups turning to the agencies of the advantaged sector for assistance is accepted and even welcome, but only if they pose no threat to established coping mechanisms. The performance of many of these institutions is too unreliable, their red tape too costly, and the probability of success too low for people to risk significant changes in their already precarious lifestyle. Significant trade-offs—such as yielding some of the autonomy of the reliable family-centered group in favor of a government-initiated community organization that promises greater benefits in the long run—are to be scrutinized very carefully and tested through time. The more immediate dole is usually preferred.

Thus, the sociological dualism that we see seems to have produced a situation in which the advantaged sector is saying to the disadvantaged sector, "We want to help you, but you will have to take this help on our terms." And the disadvantaged sector in reply, "We will take your assistance, but only on *our* terms." The result is that gains continue to be made by

[7] George Carner, "Interdependence and Competition among the Philippine Rural Poor," in *People Centered Development*, edited by David C. Korten and Rudi Klauss (West Hartford, Connecticut: Kumarian Press, 1984), p. 135.

those who are already gainers and losses continue to be incurred by those who are already losers.

Alternatives

We believe that the maintenance of dualism in Philippine society perpetuates injustice and social stagnation, and will eventually lead to serious violence and bloodshed. It is evident, therefore, that the solution lies in breaking down the barriers that support this dualism, and enhancing interaction between the two sectors. Our recommendations for breaking down these barriers take each of the two sectors in turn, and then the society as a whole.

We advance three interrelated general policies for the *advantaged sector*. We will not be able to specify with any precision what these policies entail, but we can begin with the notion that what is being done in each of these policy areas at present is not achieving what we advocate.

First, acting basically through the government and cognizant of its self-interest in the long run, the advantaged sector should set up a system by which the acquisition and holding of wealth is controlled so that it narrows the gap between the rich and the poor. It is known, for instance, that the taxation of earned and inherited wealth, and the redistribution of resources to those in the population who need them and can use them to help themselves, is one way of flattening out differences. But the income gap continues to widen; hence the mechanisms for both taxation and redistribution need to be reexamined, and more effective mechanisms firmly pursued.

Second, the advantaged sector should set up equity goals and the mechanisms for achieving them. Besides redistributing income, this means providing greater access to basic needs and services in the areas of food, nutrition, health, clean water, sanitary facilities, shelter, and education; more widespread generation of employment opportunities; and a more widespread land redistribution system with the necessary support facilities and resources to make the whole program work.

Third, the advantaged sector should set up a long-range program to make the Philippines less dependent on dominant foreign economies. This may seem not to be the time to advocate this course of action, considering that the Philippine government has borrowed over $25 billion, is still negotiating for the loan of additional sums, and the economy is in its worst postwar crisis as a result. At the same time, some economists claim that projects funded by foreign capital might well be justified because of the controls imposed by international agencies. In the long run, these controls simply perpetuate the country's dependency status: they legitimize the need for an international watchdog to oversee the government's use of loan funds and its management of the economy. In the short run, however, these controls could help channel resources from abroad for projects that truly benefit the disadvantaged sector. We are not, in other words, necessarily arguing against foreign capital. Rather we see this resource as a doubled-edged sword, and think we should use the edge that benefits the majority of Filipinos.

The *disadvantaged sector*, for its part, should claim for itself what rightfully belongs to it. This is such a fundamental requirement that there is simply no way that the structural imbalances in this society can be righted unless the disadvantaged groups want rectification. In this regard, we see a need for the people to develop a capability for seeking solutions to problems beyond the family-centered unit; for organizing and mobilizing at the community level; for participating more actively in community affairs; and for assuming greater accountability and responsibility at the level of their own neighborhoods and communities.

Historically, efforts to mobilize the poor have occurred with the assistance of people from the advantaged sector. At least since the 1950s there have been regular efforts by the government to undertake community organization and to cultivate people's participation. But the successes have been severely limited. The benefits of participatory development, in Castillo's words, "have yet to substantially accrue to the rural poor."[8] Po's earlier comment, after an extensive review of the government's organizing efforts, still holds:

> It tends to be a process in which farmers come to meetings called by extension personnel, listen to the latest instructions, and respond in terms of the prescribed framework. Initiatives which may arise on the part of small farmers but do not fit the preordained format of rural organizations find little encouragement.[9]

Given the government's dismal record in this area and the need to mobilize the poor toward greater participation, it is not surprising that alternative movements have gained momentum. Witness, for example, the well-known efforts of the Communist Party of the Philippines, and its military arm, the New People's Army. Witness, also, the increasing efforts by individuals, mostly associated with the Church, to organize the poor into "basic Christian communities." Ideologically grounded in the "theology of liberation," this movement claims a membership of 600,000 people.

Less publicized but just as effective are efforts of other, small, private nongovernmental organizations that engage in community organizing work in poor urban and rural areas. Among some of the documented cases of success might be included the determined efforts of Kagawasan residents in Bukidnon to claim legal rights to their land, and the mobilization of San Jose residents in Leyte to set up their own credit cooperative. But behind every successful case is a trail of substantial opposition from vested interests in the advantaged sector, from government use of police power, and from tireless bureaucratic red tape.

In sum, the disadvantaged sector is powerless and needs

[8] Gelia Castillo, *How Participatory is Participatory Development? A Review of the Philippine Experience* (Makati: Philippine Institute for Development Studies, 1983), p. 597.

[9] Blondie Po, "Rural Organizations and Rural Development in the Philippines: A Documentary Study," in *Rural Organizations in the Philippines*, edited by Marie S. Fernandez (Quezon City: Ateneo de Manila Institute of Philipine Culture, 1980), p. 89.

help, not in terms of being presented with the option to accept or reject standardized development schemes, but in terms of being helped to help themselves. Unless the government is willing to alter its schemes drastically, much of the success in mobilizing the poor will come from nongovernmental sectors, or worse, from groups whose ideologies are inconsistent with the general aspirations of this society. But although the legitimate work of the nongovernmental organizations shows great promise, these groups are constantly vulnerable to harassment from parties with contrary interests in the advantaged sector, on the one hand, and to infiltration from groups with different designs, on the other.

John J. Carroll's recent prescription for one type of social change is very relevant to our recommendation. He argues for an "organized poor" that would apply pressure at the same time that the middle class, the media, and the churches ("the 'official' custodian of society's values") apply moral suasion to promote a type of social change that leads to "common values rather than to polarization and ultimately violence." Carroll continues,

> The strategy is a demanding one. It asks of the elite a creative response which will inevitably entail a loss of some of its power and wealth; and of the middle classes that they take a definitive stand with the poor for genuine structural change, change that will be costly to them as well. It asks of media and the churches that they speak out clearly on the basic moral issues facing the nation: on human dignity and the need to safeguard it in the process of both socio-political change and economic development; on human rights, including the right to organize, to participate in decision-making, to express dissent; on the need not only for a return to the rule of law and to integrity in personal and public life, but also for a more equitable distribution of power and wealth in Philippine society and for the structural changes which will bring this about; on national autonomy in relationships with foreign powers. Of the poor the strategy asks that they con-

tinue to organize in defense of their rights, and that they vigorously resist all of those forces—whether of the right or the left—which would take it on themselves to define the common interest and then impose their definition on the nation.[10]

Beyond all this is the more immediate task: the dismantling in an effective and orderly manner of the constitutional authoritarianism of the state. This step would at least help to avoid the egregious errors of policy and implementation that have brought the country to its present crisis. It also would remove the oppressive mechanisms of repression that constitute the most serious obstacle to public examination and participation in the shaping of the character of this society. Whether this dismantling will come about or not, at least in the near future, remains to be seen. This much is clear: the sociological dualism must be cut if this society is to survive and flourish as a free community.

Unfortunately, there is no easy way to bring this about. Already it is conceded that there is little to look forward to in the economy of the near future. Many Filipinos have already been forced to make hard economic choices. There may be hard political choices ahead as well for these same Filipinos.

[10] John J. Carroll, "Social Theory and Social Change in the Philippines," *Pulso* 1:1 (1984), 45-46.

CHAPTER IV
POLITICS IN THE MARCOS ERA

LELA GARNER NOBLE

In June 1983, Congressman Stephen Solarz, as chairman of the Subcommittee on Asian and Pacific Affairs of the Foreign Affairs Committee of the U.S. House of Representatives, held a series of hearings on U.S.-Philippine relations. Among those testifying was former Philippine Senator and Governor Benigno Aquino, who used the occasion to explain why he had decided it was time to return to the Philippines, at the risk of imprisonment or death.

Senator Aquino's essential points were these: The Philippines was facing an ever-deepening economic and political crisis. Repression, rampant military abuses, runaway corruption in the highest places and the gross mismanagement of the economy had pushed millions of Filipinos into opposing the regime, some violently. Yet there was no way to dislodge Marcos, who had the support of the "U.S.-backed military" and who controlled the bureaucracy, the legal system, the media, and much of the wealth of the country. Marcos, however, was old (sixty-six) and in poor health, and the collective leadership (his wife, the technocrats, the military, and his cronies) he hoped would succeed him were already feuding among themselves. After his death the military was likely to emerge victorious; their tactics and the disastrous economic situation could only result in a further slide into violence.[1]

The alternative, as Aquino perceived it, was the "formula for national reconciliation" outlined by leaders of the nonvi-

---

[1] "United States-Philippines Relations and the New Base and Aid Agreement," Hearings before the Subcommittee on Asian and Pacific Affairs of the Committee on Foreign Affairs, House of Representatives, Ninety-Eighth Congress, First Session, June 17, 23, and 28, 1983 (Washington, D.C.: U.S. Government Printing Office, 1983), pp. 74-76.

olent opposition on June 12, 1983. "They appealed to the armed opposition in the hills, to give democratic processes a last chance by joining in the forthcoming elections and to demand that they be free, orderly, and honest. To bring about peaceful reconciliation, the leaders urged Marcos to grant general amnesty to all political offenders, repeal the anti-subversion law, abolish the infamous Presidential commitment order, and discontinue the practice of military interference in purely civilian affairs." Aquino said that he shared their premise that without such actions revolution was imminent, and was convinced that revolutions exacted the highest price in human lives and values, producing only victims, not victors. Hence he was returning home to work for reconciliation.

Senator Aquino's testimony is significant not only because it announced intentions that led ultimately to his death, but also because it reflects the opinions of most foreign observers at the time. While not necessarily sharing Aquino's definition of what his personal role could or should be, they—perhaps I should say we, since I was among them—were convinced that economic deterioration was so marked that it was adding to the numbers and intensity of those opposed to the regime's policies and practices; that the regime seemed unable or unwilling to devise creative solutions for dealing with its problems, and instead continued to rely on manipulation and repression; and that the only hope for avoiding widespread violence was for Marcos to negotiate a transition to a new, more broadly based regime while he was well enough to do so.

The reasons for this consensus are found in the history of the Marcos period, which this chapter is intended to describe. It does so by examining two periods, 1966-1972, when Marcos was elected, then reelected president of the Philippines, and 1972-1983, when Marcos imposed and subsequently lifted martial law, but continued to dominate the government under new constitutional provisions. Events during the first period provided the justification for martial law and some of the means by which it could be established and maintained: a proto-ideology defining enemies and articulating the need for strong, populist leadership; a prominent role for technocrats and costly development programs; centralization of the police and appointment of Ilocanos to key positions in the armed forces; and quid pro quo arrangements with the United States. During the second period, Marcos' declared intent to achieve fundamental reform—as represented by the creation of both New Society and New Republic—failed; the base of the regime narrowed and socioeconomic conditions further deteriorated.

1966-1972

Marcos' election in 1965 was generally regarded with relief by both Filipinos and foreign observers. Although President Macapagal's election in 1961 had inspired similar enthusiasm, his promised New Era had not emerged. It was to have been characterized by an emphasis on the improvement of the "Common Man," with pledges of strong leadership, elimination of graft, and a massive socioeconomic program. Macapagal managed to push an agrarian reform bill through the Philippine Congress, and removed the controls from foreign exchange and devalued the peso, thus eliminating a major source of corruption and facilitating exports. Moreover, he branded as illegal the import of American tobacco that had been authorized by his predecessor, and impounded the tobacco, arguing that the importation was in direct contravention of laws designed to protect the Philippine tobacco industry. This act was perceived as symbolic not simply because it was aimed at vigorous enforcement of laws but also because, after Congressman Harold Cooley of North Carolina threatened to cut the Philippine sugar quota in retaliation, it demonstrated a willingness to stand up to U.S. pressure.

But the agrarian reform law proved too expensive to implement, and decontrol and devaluation hurt businessess protected by the earlier emphasis on import substitution; the result was inflation. There were few efforts to increase rice production, so the growth of population resulted in a widening gap between supply and demand, which was filled by imports. Even with imports (particularly high in 1965, since it was an election year), rice prices increased by a third between 1961 and 1965; prices of fish, pork, and poultry also increased. The graft associated with foreign exchange controls was replaced by widespread smuggling, aimed at avoiding the tariffs that substituted for exchange rationing as the main instrument for protecting local industry. Impounding American tobacco lost its symbolic significance when Harry Stonehill, the American accused of illegal importation, was suddenly deported, allegedly to prevent him from implicating too many Filipinos in high places, perhaps even President Macapagal himself.

Macapagal's foreign policies, moreover, produced no successes to counterbalance the problems with domestic policies. His inconsistent conduct of relations with the United States pleased neither Filipino nationalists nor Americans. His major regional initiatives, the announcement of a claim to North Borneo in 1962 and the subsequent effort to mediate between Indonesia and Malaya over the formation of Malaysia, resulted in the severance of relations with Malaysia and the dissolution of the association the Philippines had earlier formed with Malaya and Thailand.

Marcos' election, then, promised another new beginning. The son of a lawyer and politician from the Ilocos region, in northern Luzon, Marcos had first attracted public attention in 1939 when he earned the highest score on the national bar exam while appealing successfully his conviction of a charge of murdering his father's opponent in an election. Marcos' reputation was subsequently enhanced by accounts of his exploits as a guerrilla leader in World War II (he allegedly was protected by an amulet given him by the leader of the Philippine Independent Church, which had been formed during the rebellion against Spain); and his political base was established by his role in organizing a postwar government in northern Luzon and in securing back pay and other benefits for Filipino veterans from the United States. He was first elected to the House of Representatives in 1949, and reelected in 1953 and 1957. In 1959 he ran for the Senate and emerged as the front-runner, despite being a Liberal in a period of Nacionalista party dominance. He expected to win the Liberal party's nomination for the presidency in 1961 but was outmaneuvered by Macapagal,

who, though a Liberal, had been elected to serve as vice president to the Nacionalista President Garcia. Marcos then allegedly agreed to support Macapagal after Macapagal promised
that he would not seek a second term in office. When Macapagal reneged on that pledge Marcos switched parties and secured the Nacionalista party's nomination for the presidency.

For Every Tear a Victory, the Marcos biography published
in 1964,[2] asserted a record based on support for commerce
and industry; agricultural development and reform (he was responsible for the introduction of the cash crops of tobacco, on-
ions, and garlic in the Ilocos region, and authored the 1952
land reform code, the book said); protection and extension of
civil rights (he and Senator Claro Recto successfully challenged President Quirino's suspension of the writ of habeas
corpus in 1950); fairness to military veterans and their families; and a higher standard of professional ethics in politics and
the civil service. What mattered in the election, however, was
not whatever reputation Marcos might have had as a re-
former—Senators Raul Manglapus and Manuel Manahan
were clearly the reform candidates in the election, and their
third-party attempt lost decisively—but Macpagal's vulnerable record and Marcos' ability to link his northern Luzon political base with that of his wife's family and of his vice presidential candidate in the Visayas. Vice presidential candidate
Lopez' wealth also helped in the campaign. Marcos' own
wealth was a source of controversy—he claimed it came from
investing in real estate the earnings from his law practice; his
opponents attributed it to his having used his official positions
to personal advantage.

Like Macapagal before him, Marcos began his administration with speeches defining the current nature of the crisis in
the Philippines and outlining a program designed to cure the
country's ills. Most foreign observers of the next four years described his record of achievement as mixed, with the striking
exception of his adulatory American biographer, Hartzell
Spence, who produced a new edition of his book before the

[2] By Hartzell Spence (New York: McGraw-Hill).

next presidential election. More typical were David Wurfel and Jean Grossholtz, who wrote the yearly reviews of the Philippines for *Asian Survey* for 1966, 1967, and 1968. David Wurfel's account of 1966, for example, described a number of initiatives taken by Marcos. One of the earliest—and most surprising, given his opposition to a similar proposal by Macapagal—was a request to the Philippine Congress for an appropriation to support the sending of two thousand noncombatant troops to Vietnam. Marcos justified the request by citing the necessity of supporting an Asian neighbor in a fight against communism, but the effort was clearly part of a larger effort to consolidate relations with the United States and hence to get additional aid, trade, and investments. A second foreign policy initiative was the restoration of relations with Malaysia and the revival of the old Association of Southeast Asia, which was later to be the basis for an expanded five-nation ASEAN. The new Asian Development Bank was located in Manila, and relations with Japan were cultivated.

Meanwhile Marcos had assembled a team of technocrats who devised what appeared to be a realistic four-year development plan. To raise revenues he focused on curbing smuggling and improving tax collections. By appointing a vigorous and honest customs commissioner he immediately increased revenues, then moved to discipline corrupt Constabulary and Navy officers who were in collusion with smugglers. He justified a plan to centralize administration of the police, who heretofore had come under the authority of elected mayors, by reference both to their dishonesty and to their frequent involvement in vendettas. He moved to implement the 1963 Land Reform Act in the province of Pampanga, where a resurgence of the Huks was evident. The four-year budget for land distribution was matched by a military budget for 1967 that was twice the defense budget for 1962.

At the end of 1966 Wurfel was cautiously optimistic: the problems of the Philippines were enormous, but Marcos was "devoting more intelligent attention to major policy decisions" and showing "greater determination and impatience" then several of his predecessors.[3] Over the next two years, however, the annual reviews grew increasingly pessimistic. Initiatives continued—programs to increase rice production and to build roads, schoolhouses, and airports, for example—and progress occurred. Most notably, the Philippines temporarily achieved rice self-sufficiency in 1968. But other initiatives fizzled or were countered by subsequent actions. The efficient, honest customs collector was removed in late 1966. Diplomatic relations with Malaysia, carefully cultivated in 1966, and the anti-smuggling agreement, negotiated with Kuala Lumpur in 1967, ceased in 1968 in the wake of the Corregidor incident, when a Muslim special forces unit allegedly being trained to invade Sabah (North Borneo) mutinied and about twenty-eight were killed. Marcos protested that the incident was a purely internal matter, a characterization the Malaysians understandably rejected, particularly after the Filipinos used the occasion to revive Macapagal's old claim to North Borneo. Attempted negotiations only exacerbated the situation between the two countries, and threatened ASEAN as well. Finally, in late 1968 Marcos replaced his secretary of foreign affairs with elder statesman Carlos Romulo, and tensions subsided while both countries concentrated on election campaigns.

The economic situation remained precarious. The balance of payments was stabilized not by an increase in exports or investments but by U.S. aid and purchases related to the war in Vietnam. Indeed it was reported (and later confirmed) that Marcos' proposal to send troops to Vietnam, finally approved by the Philippine Congress in August 1966, followed a secret agreement that Washington would provide funds for engineering battalions to be used for road building and other community development projects in the Philippines and would subsidize the Philippine contingent in Vietnam. Meanwhile the national budget was affected by the Philippine Congress' refusal to approve thirty-seven of the forty tax measures Marcos

[3] David Wurfel, "The Philippines: Intensified Dialogue," *Asian Survey* 7 (January 1967), 52.

proposed, while supporting his request for a 100 million peso fund designed to give each barrio 2,000 pesos to use as it saw fit.

Violence appeared to escalate, some of it attributed to Huks (remnants of the Communist-led anti-Japanese guerrilla forces) or to government squads created to assassinate Huks. By 1969 violence was also clearly related to the election campaign, in which Visayan Senator Sergio Osmeña, Jr., led the Liberals in opposition to Marcos and the Nacionalistas. There was an increase in demonstrations and strikes, and organizations proliferated outside the formal bipartisan structure.

Nevertheless, despite all the indicators that caused concern to outside observers, the Filipino electorate voted solidly for Marcos, thus making him the first Philippine president to be reelected to office. Vice President Lopez was also reelected; Nacionalistas won all but one of the Senate races and 90 of 110 House districts. The reasons for the landslide were complex. Osmeña was not an attractive candidate, lacking Marcos' oratorical skills and his wife Imelda's charm and savvy. Nor was he able to build the organization or amass the funds available to Marcos. Marcos could point to visible accomplishments—highways, farm-to-market roads, schoolhouses, airports, electrification projects—that he supplemented by personally distributing government checks to every barrio captain and other funds (presumably from private sources) to friendly candidates. Moreover, by espousing a more independent policy toward Washington, closer ties with Asian countries, and the gradual establishment of relations with communist states, Marcos attracted the nationalist vote antagonized by Osmeña's pro-American, anti-communist rhetoric.

The triumph, however, was short-lived. Marcos' inaugural address on December 30 and his state-of-the-nation speech on January 26 lacked the resounding promises of costless reform characteristic of the post-election stage of the Philippine political cycle (the next stage was the abandonment of reform—which inevitably had costs—for more focused political payoffs, sometime before the mid-term elections). Yet Marcos' speeches were as idealistic as ever: emphasizing the need for discipline and dedication, he pledged that the country's leadership would exemplify these virtues (along with integrity and simplicity) and would lay the foundation for a revolutionary transformation of international and domestic policies. "I will not demand more of you than I demand of myself and the government—neither wealth nor power shall purchase privilege," he declared.[4]

More noteworthy was that, when the president and the first lady left Congress after the state-of-the-nation address, they were pelted with stones, bottles, and placards. Thereafter students and police battled for three hours. Five days later, on January 30, two protest rallies preceded an assault on Malacañang, the Philippine presidential mansion (students commandeered a fire truck and rammed through the gate), which in turn led to a night of fighting between police and the military on one side and students on the other. Six students died, and hundreds were injured.

Subsequent demonstrations, strikes, sermons, and articles suggested that the students' causes were shared even by those who did not support their tactics. Quite clearly Marcos had fallen from grace, but why, and why so quickly? Analysts cited student claims that the pre-poll campus elections (which had been overwhelmingly pro-Marcos) had been rigged, and the claims of others that the election itself had been the most dishonest in Philippine history; hence, they concluded, there was less support for Marcos than the election results indicated, and his fall therefore was less precipitous than it appeared. Alternatively it was argued that Marcos was simply the victim of excessive success: the electoral sweep was so great that the opposition, and hence legislative checks on Marcos' power, had been all but eliminated, thus frightening "intensely democratic Filipinos" and encouraging students and the press to take more assertive roles.

Both explanations are at least partially credible. There *was* widespread fraud and consequently outrage, and the outrage

[4] Claude Buss, *The United States and the Philippines* (Washington, D.C.: American Enterprise Institute for Public Policy Research, 1977), p. 57.

was not diminished by Marcos' announcement that he would use his wealth to set up a Ferdinand Marcos Foundation to help the people. The electoral sweep and Marcos' driving ambition *were* disturbing to many Filipinos, though Philippine political parties had never been sufficiently cohesive for the electoral sweep to constitute any real threat to democracy; indeed it was their lack of cohesion that was usually regarded with concern.

More plausible were explanations that focused on economic factors. Descriptions of political cycles in the Philippines, referred to earlier, assumed limited resources. The shifts from program to pork barrel occurred not simply because Filipinos were culturally predisposed toward more personalistic methods of distributing benefits, but also because in the short run the pork barrel appeared to be a more economically efficient way of getting votes. However, because both funds and positions were limited, the distribution of patronage was likely to alienate as many as it attracted. Those who lost, or believed they benefited insufficiently, switched to the other party; those rewarded remained or shifted, depending on their current affiliation.

Marcos, however, apparently ignored the limits even more than his predecessors had. If many of his programmatic initiatives fizzled, some of the projects—schoolhouses and roads, for example—continued. Even when subsidized heavily by U.S. aid, they were expensive and produced few immediate economic returns. But they were useful politically, functioning essentially as a more sophisticated pork-barrel without the disadvantages of reform programs: virtually all villagers would perceive themselves as benefiting immediately from a road or a school, for example, whereas land reform would produce both winners and losers, certainly in the short-term. Moreover, these projects (the label "infrastrasture" was an indicator of increased sophistication) were accompanied by old-style gifts from the public treasury directly to local officials. These, too, were economically unproductive, except as they increased the buying power of recipients. Hence Marcos kept his old supporters, gained new ones, and pushed the country closer to bankruptcy.

The costs of this process become obvious immediately after the 1969 election, when the government cut expenditures (there were simply no funds left to spend), curtailed some services, laid off employees, tightened credit and exchange restrictions, and dispatched official missions to renegotiate old loans and get new ones. The peso was under pressure, the stock market began a steady decline, and prices—particularly of fuel and spare parts and therefore of transportation fares—soared. In this context Marcos' emphasis on discipline, dedication, integrity, and simplicity appeared hypocritical, and produced explosive protests.

As the protests continued during the following months, Marcos seemed to be losing control of the political process. Students secured enactment of restrictions on campaign spending and on participation of elected or appointed officials in elections for delegates to the Constitutional Convention, which was scheduled to begin review of the 1935 constitution in June 1971. Although Marcos released $16,500 in pork-barrel funds to each Nacionalista Congressman before the election, the election was comparatively inexpensive and peaceful. Many of those elected were young professionals, not politicians; several politicians elected were perceived as anti-Marcos reformers. Students meanwhile had pushed Marcos into public announcements that he would not seek a third term, which would have been legally possible only if he secured an amendment to the constitution.

Violence escalated markedly during the mid-term election campaign, as political warlords used "guns, gold, and goons" to secure electoral victories. Because of or despite this, Marcos-supported Nacionalista candidates lost heavily. Vice President Lopez had already split with Marcos and shifted his political affiliation to the Liberal party. (Accounts of the reasons for the Lopez-Marcos split vary. Marcos apparently blocked an attempt by the Lopez family to increase its already extensive holdings, and also accused Lopez of funding left-wing student activists.) Meanwhile the new pro-Chinese Communist

Party of the Philippines had linked with one faction of the Huks (the others had been arrested, killed, and/or become brigands) to constitute the New People's Army, which was active in areas of central Luzon where problems of tenancy and abuse were particularly acute, and by 1972 the NPA was spreading north and south.

More generally, radical ideologies had growing appeal among intellectuals and labor and peasant leaders, though the left included a wide spectrum of opinion and was highly factionalized. "Nationalist" was a more inclusive rubric, and included many who found the source of their ideology in neither Marx nor Mao but rather in resentment of American influence and involvement in Philippine economic life. Few of these people were placated by Marcos' moves to expand trade and diplomatic relations with socialist states, or reassured by Japan's growing challenge to U.S. domination of the Philippine market. Instead they focused on the postwar agreements that had given Americans special privileges (parity with Filipinos) in owning and exploiting national resources and in participating in trade. Many also opposed either U.S. bases (seeing them as endangering rather than enhancing Philippine security by drawing the islands into American wars) or the terms on which the bases existed (as violations of Philippine sovereignty).

National disasters and a general deterioration of law and order added to the political ferment. Volcanic eruptions, a devastating earthquake, and severe droughts had occurred during Marcos' first term; in 1970 there were more earthquakes and terrible typhoons. The typhoons were less intense in 1971, but still caused considerable damage; then 1972 brought the worst floods in Philippine history, causing over 400 deaths (from drowning or cholera) and widespread destruction. An increase in kidnappings, robberies, and murders was perhaps due in part to the desperation caused by these events and to other economic problems. Bombings presumably had political causes.

Marcos' reaction to these developments varied. His initial reaction to the student protests of December 1969 and January 1970 was to retreat into Malacañang for several weeks. When he finally emerged he made some compromises—agreeing to a nonpartisan Constitutional Convention, for example, an agreement he then underminded by releasing funds to Nacionalistas for the obvious purpose of supporting sympathetic candidates. Alternatively, he used force against the protesters, negotiating permission to use the Philippine Constabulary against them in Manila and sending both police and regular army units into the University of the Philippines campus the following year.

Increasingly, he was prone to draw a firm distinction between supporters and enemies. Although the latter category was elastic and included at various times not only students but also union leaders, journalists, politicians, Muslim secessionists, oligarchs, church people, and foreign governments with a range of ideological orientations, "enemies" most frequently meant "communists," against whom extreme measures were justified. Hence the Yuyitang brothers, respected journalists and publishers of a Chinese language newspaper in Manila, were identified as procommunist and deported without full due process (they had published articles carried by a French news agency and some stories by Han Suyin, who was regarded as sympathetic to the Maoist government). "Communists" were responsible for grenades thrown during a Liberal party rally at Plaza Miranda at which nine were killed and ninety injured, including eight senatorial candidates; Marcos thereupon suspended the writ of habeas corpus. When Senator Aquino and Diokno protested (as Marcos had earlier, when President Quirino had taken the same action in 1950), Marcos called them communists and said he would do everything possible to prevent Aquino's becoming president, including asking his wife Imelda to run in opposition. Apparently "everything possible" also included bribing delegates to the Constitutional Convention to support a change to a parliamentary system that would allow Marcos himself to remain in office—or so a respected member of the Convention claimed. On July 7, 1972, a majority of delegates supported such a change, and the resolution to disallow Marcos from becoming prime minister failed, though by a small margin.

As for the armed communists in the field—the NPA—their reputed numbers rose and fell, depending on whether the need was to justify greater military expenditures and operations or to demonstrate the government forces' effectiveness. The need for combat effectiveness similarly justified the replacement of older officers on whose loyalty Marcos could not rely with younger ones, frequently Ilocanos like Marcos.

There was also a new book, not a biography this time but a manifesto bearing Marcos' name as author, *Today's Revolution: Democracy*.[5] Rejecting both the old system, in which "the aim of free and popular elections had been frustrated through the control, corruption, and manipulation of the political process," and the alternatives of a replacement from below (the masses) or above ("the ruling classes giving up their privileges, rather than their heads"), it argued for a revolution from the center, initiated by the government. Such a revolution would be dependent on a leader who would educate the people to the realization that government is an instrument of achieving collective well-being and not personal interests alone. It would be democratic because it would be characterized both by authoritarian rule and submission to the people, not by the former alone because then it would not merit the name democracy, not by the latter alone because it would not face the need of "controlling the rising level of expectations, which if allowed full play may very well threaten stability."

Marcos' moves in turn produced reactions. It was widely suspected that the government (Marcos and/or the military) itself was responsible for the Plaza Miranda bombing, since the NPA had nothing to gain from the act unless it was pursuing a policy of random terrorism, in which case it would claim to have done so. Nor was it plausible that Senator Aquino was involved, as the government later charged, since he was the Liberal party's leading candidate for the presidential nomination in 1973, and needed those injured to run on the slate with him. As unsolved kidnappings continued, and bombs ex-

[5] Manila, n.p., 1971.

ploded late at night in empty buildings, both Senator Diokno
and Aquino charged that Marcos was using if not creating incidents as a justification for perpetuating his power.

Finally, Senator Aquino charged in the Senate on September
15 that sources in the Philippine Armed Forces had revealed to
him plans for "Oplan Sagittarius," which would impose martial law on the country. Marcos denied the existence of such
plans, told the National Security Council there was no need for
martial law, and assured the Senate he would consult before
taking any such drastic action. But on the night of September
22, 1972, Defense Secretary Enrile's car was ambushed (again
there were no injuries and Enrile has recently admitted the incident was staged); early on September 23 martial law was announced.

In the following weeks Marcos' reasons, goals, and methods
became increasingly clear. In the statement with which he announced his proclamation of martial law, Marcos cited provisions in the 1935 constitution authorizing such action "in case
of invasion, insurrection, or rebellion or imminent danger
thereof," then proceeded to give evidence that a state of rebellion did exist, and affirmed his intention both to remove anarchy and maintain peace and order and to reform the country's institutions. The proclamation itself charged that lawless
elements motivated by "Marxist-Leninist-Maoist techniques
and beliefs" and supported by a foreign power were attempt-
ing to destroy the existing government through violence and
propaganda. Their intentions and activities, plus "the equally
serious disorder in Mindanao and Sulu resulting from the unsettled conflict between certain elements of the Christian and
Muslim population of Mindanao and Sulu, between the Christian 'Ilagas' and the Muslim 'Barracudas,' and between our
government troops, and certain lawless organizations such as
the Mindanao Independence Movement," necessitated his
placing the entire country under martial law.

The statement accompanying the martial law declaration
also identified the agenda for the regime:

We will eliminate the threat of a violent overthrow of our Republic. But at the same time we must now reform the social, economic and political institutions in our country . . . to remove the inequities of that society, the cleanup of government of its corrupt and sterile elements, the liquidation of the criminal syndicates, [and to encourage] the systematic development of our economy.[6]

The goal, then, was the creation of a New Society; constitutional authoritarianism was to be the method; the anarchists on the left and the oligarchs on the right were the chief targets. The link between the left and right, elaborated by Marcos in subsequent speeches, was both general and specific. Generally, he claimed, the left exploited the popular disaffection resulting from an oligarch-controlled society characterized by inequities and corruption: thus left and right were jointly responsible for violence. Specifically, there was a conspiracy between some members of the left and right to secure his assassination. Marcos argued that he, in contrast to either group, represented a way to achieve fundamental change without violating the law: he was the elected president; he had authority under the constitution to do whatever was necessary to save the country.

The first step was the "removal of anarchy and the maintenance of peace and order," a goal that in practice meant the demobilization of any individuals or groups willing and able to take autonomous action. Thousands were arrested: members of the oligarchy accused of conspiracy; politicians associated with private armies or outspoken opposition to Marcos; journalists; members of labor, student, or peasant organizations; petty criminals. Equally important in terms of effect were restrictions on labor organization and action, and on travel outside the country. Congress was suspended. Approximately 500,000 guns were collected. A curfew was imposed.

The demobilization program was primarily the responsibility of aides directly associated with Marcos and of the military, who were charged with its implementation. The reform pro-

[6] Statement published by the Office of the President of the Philippines, September 22, 1972.

gram—aimed at restructuring Philippine society—reflected the development and philosophy of the technocrats and the specific interests of the Marcos family and their associates. To encourage rationality and efficiency, decision making was centralized in a number of executive agencies whose recommendations were issued by Marcos as decrees. Both communication and popular participation were controlled, the media through transfers of ownership from unreliable oligarchs to reliable associates of the Marcos family, popular participation through new consultative structures and procedures.

Land reform was identified as the "cornerstone of the New Society"—an essential first step of a program of agrarian reform legitimized as revolutionizing socioeconomic relations in the countryside and hence guaranteeing stability and justice. Industralization was to emphasize export as well as import substitution. External financing was regarded as essential to success and was deliberately encouraged by cooperation with international lending agencies, concessions to foreign investors and traders, and inducements to tourists. The government's role in the economy was to remain primarily directive and facilitative: it was to provide the legal and economic infrastructure within which Filipinos, now imbued with discipline and social consciousness, could "develop."

In summary, the analysis shared by Marcos and his advisers was that the institutions of the Old Society had reflected and perpetuated inequality; they had encouraged conflict and discouraged development. By centralizing decision making, effective programs could be designed. Popular participation, although critical, was to be channeled toward the ratification, elaboration, and implementation of the planners' programs. Only thus could comparative prosperity be achieved.

Not surprisingly, the reactions of both Filipinos and outsiders to Marcos' analyses and actions varied. Those convinced that the the existing system had failed and that the country was falling into chaos or communism supported martial law and the reform efforts they believed it portended. Regarding Marcos as a messianic figure, they placed their loyalty and faith accordingly. Others, at the opposite extreme, believed neither his statement of reasons nor his commitment to reform. Some, like Diokno and Aquino earlier, charged that Marcos had created the conditions he now deplored, and had acted only because he could not retain power under the old constitution and could not assume that he would get a favorable vote to support a new constitution, without drastically changing the political environment. Marcos had declared martial law, then, not because the system had failed but because he had planned for it to so appear, and/or had simply panicked (the versions differed); in either case he was held to be motivated by ambition and greed, not by patriotism or revolutionary fervor.

There were also commentators who focused not on personal factors (Marcos' character and motivations) but on what they identified as structural factors. They, too, differed among themselves in their identification of relevant structures and the conclusions they drew from their analyses—whether the system was evolving in ways conducive to broadened participation and hence to greater justice, equality, and prosperity for the masses, or was so overloaded by demographic factors that it could no longer function effectively for anyone. In the first instance, the conclusion was that evolution threatened patterns of development to which Filipino elites and outside (primarily American) investors and donors were committed. Authoritarianism was required to stop nationalism. The second line of analysis exemplified a commitment to those patterns of development criticized in the first; accepting authoritarianism as at least temporarily preferable to the chaos it perceived as the alternative, it dismissed Marcos himself as either cause of chaos or source of hope.

Most Filipinos, however, apparently withheld judgment. The more sophisticated reasoned that they were willing to accept Marcos' ruthlessness against politicians and the press, and his suspension of civil liberties, "if he [could] actually create a new national consensus and carry out his technological and developmental revolution."[7] Others, wary of costs, scep-

[7] Robert Shaplen, "Letter from Manila," New Yorker (April 14, 1973), p. 119.

tical but needful of benefits, simply said they would wait and
and see.

Over the next decade Marcos' constitutional authoritarianism continued to evolve through statements and actions, and
popular reaction to it shifted accordingly. It seems possible to
identify three stages in this evolution, distinguished primarily
by the nature of political initiatives taken by Marcos and by
the scope and intensity of the opposition to them. By describ-
ing these initiatives, the power balances within the regime they
reflected, their economic consequences, and the nature of the
opposition they produced and to which they in turn responded, the transition from the hopeful scepticism greeting
the regime in 1973 to the despair more characteristic of 1983
can be traced.

Briefly, the first stage was the period from 1973 to 1975,
when Marcos' New Society seemed characterized by initiatives
framed by technocrats to create both a political base in the
countryside and an agricultural surplus, the one to destroy the
power of the oligarchs and the appeal of the Maoists, the other
to provide food and foreign exchange to support industrial development. Economic indicators, while mixed, seemed predominantly positive. With the significant exception of the
Muslim rebellion in the south, opposition was generally expressed in the form of protest against specific government actions, like price increases or raids on churches.

During the second stage, from 1976 to 1980, initiatives
shifted away from the countryside toward the formation of national representative structures and modern, capital-intensive
economic projects, with a corresponding increase in power of
the Marcos and Romualdez families and of friends referred to
as cronies; the military also increased its power as economic
conditions deteriorated and armed rebellion in the countryside
spread apace, with at least rudimentary organization in the cities. The Church began to challenge the values and practices
characteristic of the regime, articulating alternative values and
developing and defending its own programs of social action.

At the beginning of the third period, 1981-1983, moves toward further political normalization—the formal ending of

martial law and the inauguration of the New Republic—coincided with the near collapse of several of the conglomerates identified with crony capitalism, declining returns from exports, and a burgeoning debt burden. Both political and economic policies narrowed further the base of the regime, pushing many former supporters (or at least tacit acceptors) of the regime into opposition; pushing earlier critics into opposition; and the desperate and the idealistic into armed resistance. Thus isolated, the regime was increasingly reliant on coercion, and hence on the military, and on the outside aid negotiated by those technocrats remaining. The system was precarious, and critically dependent on Ferdinand Marcos.

1973-1975

Both the imposition of martial law, with its accompanying restrictions on speech, press, and assembly, and the completion of constitutional revision by the Constitutional Convention in late 1972 gave evidence that the structures and procedures associated with Philippine democracy in the past were to be changed. Initiatives during the next three years defined a new base for democracy, the *barangay*, and new channels of communication between people and government. Historically, *barangays* were pre-Hispanic communities; in the New Society they were clusters of 100-500 families organized as citizens' assemblies "designed to broaden the base of citizenship participation in the democratic process to afford ample opportunities for the citizens to express their views on important issues." As indigenous forms (in contrast to the Western institutions Marcos believed ill-suited to Filipino character), they were to be used, as Belinda Aquino has summarized, to:

> ratify the new Constitution in a national referendum in January 1973; vote on national issues such as the continuance of martial law and the necessity of elections; handle the sale and distribution of government-controlled rice and other commodities in local communities; maintain peace and order; monitor "subversive" activities like the

clandestine distribution of anti-martial law literature; implement development projects like the "Green Revolution"; promote tourism; organize cooperatives; and act as the basic units of local government in lieu of the old system of elective barrio councils.[8]

By 1975 the community organization had been linked through indirect elections and appointments to provincial and regional councils, and supplemented by parallel structures aimed specifically at young Filipinos. Referenda had allowed Marcos to suspend the implementation of transitional provisions in the new constitution, and hence to postpone the assembling of a national body with an alternative political base, and had authorized him to appoint officials to formerly elected positions at local and provincial levels.

Whereas the activities of the *barangays* were directed and controlled by the Commission on Elections and the Department of Local Government and Community Development, other government agencies were involved with development programs at local as well as provincial and regional levels. Since the regime described agrarian reform as the cornerstone of its development efforts, and was equally committed to increasing agricultural productivity—particularly in rice and corn—the countryside was the focus of much activity. Essentially, the land reform program was directed at all rice and corn holdings above seven hectares in size, and was intended to provide tenants on these holdings family-sized farms (three hectares if the land was irrigated, five if it was not). Tenants were to be distributed land transfer certificates, land prices were to be fixed at 2.5 times the value of the average gross harvest, and payments were to be amortized over a fifteen-year period. At the end of that period farmers would own the land and the landowners would have been compensated at approximately 92 percent of the calculated value of their holdings. Meanwhile the former tenants would be assisted through bank

[8] Belinda A. Aquino, "Politics in the New Society: Barangay 'Democracy,' " paper delivered at the annual meeting of the Association of Asian Studies, New York, March 1977.

loans (commercial banks were required to make a fixed percentage of their loans for rural purposes); through their membership in barrio associations called Samahang Nayons, which they were required to join before being given land transfer certificates; and through direct government programs of providing roads, electrical power, and other services.

The food production drive was carried out primarily through a program called Masagana 99, which was intended to triple rice yields per acre. The program provided cheap credit for a seed/fertilizer/pesticide input mix specified by the government. The government also required large employers to provide rice for their workers, either through importation or through their own production.

Other measures were directed toward producers of crops other than rice and corn. Agencies were created to centralize marketing of both sugar and coconut, and the secretary of agriculture was directed to reserve public lands for large scale commercialized farming in joint ventures with foreign corporations.

Infrastructure programs were designed to support both agricultural and industrial development. The first plan allocated roughly 35 percent of the funds available for transportation (roads, harbors, airports), 35 percent for power and electricity, 20 percent for water resources, 10 percent for social development (such as schools and hospitals), and 2 percent for telecommunications, with a foreign exchange component comprising 42 percent of the total. Beyond these programs, a range of investment incentives was devised to encourage the inflow of foreign funds: constraints on labor organizing and strikes, relaxed rules on investment limits and repatriation of profits, and tax advantages.

Both political and economic initiatives appeared to reflect a predominant influence of those identified as technocrats, as part of a new coalition being built by Marcos. Writing in late 1975, Jeffrey Race identified the coalition as being composed of the "common man," the military, the technocrats and the bureaucracy, part of the business community, and certain for-

eign groups.[9] Certainly these groups seemed to be the beneficiaries of at least some of the accomplishments reflected in statistics during the period. According to the *Far Eastern
Economic Review*'s *1976 Yearbook*, of the 450,000 rice and
corn tenants falling under the stipulated requirements (half of
all rice and corn tenants), 183,647 had been issued land transfer certificates by October of 1975, and 15,000 had become
amortizing owners. The government claimed that productivity
in areas covered by the Masagana program had increased by
44 percent. Construction projects created jobs for the landless.
Both the budget and benefits of the military increased, resulting in a reported tripling of spending for the armed forces during the first three years of martial law. Growth of the gross national product was marked in 1973 (10 percent) and remained
respectable in 1974 and 1975 (5 to 6 percent), despite oil price
increases of 350 percent in 1974 alone, increases of 50 percent
in prices of other imported goods, and plummeting export
prices. Foreign investment rose in both 1973 and 1974.

There were, however, negative indicators as well, which
called into question the existence and/or stability of the coalition Race described. At best, the agrarian reform program did
not cover landless agricultural laborers, tenants on farms less
than seven hectares in size, and either tenants or workers on
land producing anything other than rice or corn. Rice- and
corn-producing farms less than seven hectares in size covered
an estimated 46.7 percent of the land area, with 57 percent of
the tenants and 90 percent of the landowners; the average size
of tenant holdings on these lands was 1.3 hectares. But even
within its defined scope, the program quickly bogged down.
The predominance of small landlords, many of whom were
teachers and government employees, meant that implementation of the program threatened Marcos' supporters; in many
instances those involved in administering the programs were
those whose families would suffer from their efficient implementation. Efforts at systematizing rules and procedures were

[9] Jeffrey Race, "Whither the Philippines?" paper given at the Institute of
Current World Affairs, November 30, 1975, p. 6.

subjected to innumerable bureaucratic delays. A series of schemes for fixing land prices was tried; each proved liable to landlord obstructionism. Participation in barrio associations apparently dropped (membership figures are unreliable), and defaults on bank loans reached such proportions that the Philippine armed forces were ordered to help in their collection. Meanwhile the policies favoring commercialized farming and requiring large farmers to provide rice for their workers, but allowing them to do so through their own production, worked at cross purposes with land distribution policies.

Policy in regard to sugar was also problematic. Planners decided to promote the expansion of the sugar industry and to withhold large portions of the crop from the market in 1974, on the assumption that prices would continue to rise. Instead, price increases reduced demand and prices plummeted, leaving the Philippine government with stockpiles exceeding its storage capacities. Aggressive salesmanship eventually succeeded in reducing the surplus, but at price levels at or below the cost of production. The government raised the domestic price on sugar, refused loans to marginal producers (in effect, those with the smallest and least capitalized farms), and exempted land transferred from sugar into rice or corn production from the application of land reform decrees. These measures generally meant that the losses of large plantation owners and millers were buffered, while wage laborers, small farmers, and consumers suffered. Since workers on sugar lands were already among the worst paid in the Philippines and were restrained from organizing to protest their situation by both landlords and government officials, their plight was particularly desperate. They were hired and paid as the owner's finances dictated. For marginal producers there was at least the possibility of a successful transition to other crops, if capital was available. Consumers had the choice of paying higher prices or buying less sugar.

In a broader sense, as William Overholt commented, "Philippine [agrarian] reform programs [were] tied neither to any integrated view of the national economy and its principal trends (e.g., industrialization, urbanization, rising popula-

tion), nor to any explicit vision of the national political future."[10] Major infrastructure and industrial projects planned
for areas outside Manila seemed likely to have (and in some
cases already had had) a negative impact on both the natural
and human environment, destroying traditional and comparatively productive sources of livelihood and displacing people.
Similarly, programs for modernizing Manila resulted in the
demolition of squatters' housing and the deportation of the
squatters themselves to places outside Manila where neither
jobs nor adequate relief aid were available.

Some statistics were also troubling. Inflation reached 40 percent in 1974, causing real wages to decline by about 20 percent. By 1975 inflation had been reduced to 10 percent, but increases in imports, decreases in the value of exports, and
declining investments had produced a deficit in the balance of
payments. Real wages continued to decline, though more
slowly, but the government refused to raise the daily minimum
wage "for fear of raising the cost of exports and scaring away
foreign investors."[11] Instead, it subsidized certain commodities
such as rice. Despite these subsidies and the programs for expanding food production, government studies showed a decline in food consumption in both urban and rural areas.

Finally, in 1975 there were signs of shifts in the regime's internal balance of power. Imelda Marcos, who earlier had been
associated with a number of infrastructure projects not included in the technocrats' plans or reflected through their ac-
counting systems (the Folk Arts Theatre and the Heart Center,
for example), and with extravaganzas like the Miss Universe
Contest and the Ali-Frazier championship fight, was named
Mayor of Metro-Manila. Defense Secretary Enrile left the
country in late September, after a massive purge of government bureaucrats, including his under-secretary, and after his
teenage son was charged with killing another youth. But Enrile
returned in October, after his son was cleared of the charges,

[10] William Overholt, "Land Reform in the Philippines," *Asian Survey* 16
(May 1976), 428.
[11] *Asia 1976 Yearbook* (Hong Kong: Far Eastern Economic Review Ltd.,
1976), p. 264.

and in December Executive Secretary Alejandro Melchor, whose staff had allegedly been responsible for the purge, was fired. Since Melchor had been identified as the regime's chief technocrat, and was reported to have clashed with Mrs. Marcos as well as Enrile, his ouster was significant.

Not surprisingly, these developments produced both protest and pessimism. The protest was primarily of two kinds: that of lawyers and church leaders who challenged the legality or ethics of the existence and policies of the martial law regime; and that of ethnic groups, agricultural laborers, urban workers, squatters, and their sympathizers, who opposed the regime through armed rebellion (in the case of the Muslims in the south), resistance (as by tribal Filipinos whose lands were to be flooded by hydroelectric projects in Luzon), and demonstrations (in Manila and other cities). The Muslim separatist movement, fueled by centuries of alienation, specific grievances resulting from recent Christian migration, and outside support from Muslim states and organizations, was successful in mobilizing about thirty thousand armed combatants and dominating much of central and southwestern Mindanao and the Sulu archipelago. In so doing it justified, at least from the regime's perspective, the military build-up and the continuation of martial law, but it also resulted in programs and bounties from which at least some Muslims benefited.

Other forms of protest had less success. The Supreme Court consistently ruled in favor of Marcos, though sometimes with mixed votes and ambiguous rulings. Although many of those detained were subsequently released, Aquino and two members of the Lopez and Osmeña families remained in jail. Reports of torture of prisoners persisted, raids of church premises continued, and the press remained controlled, though the means of keeping it so shifted from direct censorship to self-monitoring by selected owners. Resistance slowed some development projects, but most were pushed through with whatever degree of force was required.

The pessimism resulted from growing evidence that it had been easier to change governmental structures and personnel than to create a New Society. Many of the problems of the old society had simply taken on new manifestations. Corruption, patronage, extravagance, and abuse of authority continued, sometimes with different beneficiaries and victims. Party-switching was replaced by defections; policy making, once subject to executive-legislative stalemate, was now hampered by bureaucratic rivalries. Shoot-outs occurred not between political factions but between military ones. A political cycle that had once depended on elections now depended on executive initiatives. If in the short run the regime was now more centralized and secure, in the long run it was not necessarily more just or stable.

1976-1980

After early martial law initiatives disassembled old political structures and disrupted old political patterns in late 1972, the regime had set about building a new mass base in the *barangay*, relying on bureaucrats to provide leadership and linkages and the military and police to maintain control. Between 1976 and 1980, Marcos both topped off this structure and modified it. On the top he created a national legislative council that advised him to proceed with the constitutional amendments he proposed, secured approval of the amendments in a referendum, and called elections to select members of the new kind of interim assembly the amendments provided for. Meanwhile he created a political party, the Kilusang Bagong Lipunan (New Society Movement), or KBL, to identify candidates and conduct the campaign, and reorganized military and police structures so as to parallel more closely the hierarchy of political ones. These moves made possible a new succession formula, if Marcos were to become incapacitated or to die, and also allowed the election, rather than the appointment, of local officials.

More generally, the moves demonstrated the regime's desire to institutionalize itself in ways that could henceforth define "normality." Judged by this criterion alone, the election returns for both the April 1978 interim Assembly elections and the January 1980 local elections indicated success. In both in-

stances restrictions on speech, press, and assembly were relaxed during the campaign (in 1978 Benigno Aquino, the opposition's chief symbol, was allowed a TV appearance from
prison), voting was encouraged, and KBL candidates
triumphed—amidst widespread charges of fraud and corruption. Imelda Marcos led the KBL slate to a full sweep of all 21
seats in Manila despite intense campaigning by, and incon-
trovertible evidence of support for, the opposition. In the assembly as a whole—composed of 165 members popularly
elected from regions, 14 selected to represent "sectoral" organizations, and 20 appointed by the prime minister—there
were only 13 non-KBL members from the central Visayas, one
from northern Mindanao, an outcome also regarded as im-
plausible. Marcos, moreover, served as president and prime
minister, and maintained his extraordinary powers, including
the rights to approve (through Cabinet members) any bills introduced and to veto any he disliked, and to dissolve the Assembly if he thought it was not doing its job properly or if he
decided there was a national emergency.

In August, after the Assembly was inaugurated on June 12,
1978, Marcos announced the contents of a succession decree,
one of many signed on June 11. It specified that the Assembly's
speaker would become president if Marcos died or became incapacitated, and that the more powerful post of prime minister
would be filled by the deputy prime minister. Marcos did not,
however, respond to KBL pressure to name his wife (by then
also minister of human settlements) to the post of deputy
prime minister, and it remained empty.

The 1980 campaign for local offices differed from the 1978
one in its brevity (the January elections were not announced
until December); the regime also defined new rules that cir-
cumscribed the opposition's activities, and distributed funds
to *barangay* officials for infrastructure and development during the month before the elections. But whatever the regime's
fears, it again managed to sweep the polls. KBL won 69 of 73
governorships, and 1,550 of 1,560 mayoral elections. President Marcos' sister was reelected Governor in Ilocos Norte;
Ferdinand Marcos, Jr., was elected vice governor at age 21.

Accompanying these efforts at institutionalization were announcements of other moves toward normalization. On September 21, 1977, for example, Marcos marked the fifth anniversary of martial law with a speech to the World Law Conference in Manila, in which he announced not only his intent to hold local elections by the end of 1978 (which he did not do) but also the easing of restictions on international travel and the lifting of the nationwide nighttime curfew. In response to persistent reports of torture from Filipino and international sources, and complaints from various U.S. officials and groups, he defended his country's human rights record and affirmed his commitment to the maintenance of human dignity. Periodically he denied the existence of political prisoners, ordered the release of anyone held without charges, or proclaimed the arrest of military men accused of abuses. By 1980, the U.S. Department of State's review of human rights reported improvement in the Philippine record, though this conclusion was not universally shared by observers.

The Muslim south was usually not included in normalization efforts, but did receive considerable attention from the regime. Although neither the tentative settlement nor the ceasefire negotiated in late 1976 with the Moro National Liberation Front, representatives from the Islamic Conference, and Colonel Qaddafi of Libya produced lasting peace, the regime's initiatives did contribute to a reduction in both the scale and scope of the fighting. (Libya had provided diplomatic support, funds, and weapons for the MNLF.) By 1979 two KBL-dominated "autonomous" governments had been constituted in the two regions with substantial Muslim populations, and a Commission on Islamic Affairs, headed by Admiral Romulo Espaldon, was established in Manila to oversee government programs toward Muslims. Apart from these efforts, funds were provided to support the reentry into civilian life of those rebels who decided to return to "the folds of the law."

The subsiding of conflict in Muslim areas was fortunate, because the NPA and other groups opposed to the government increasingly claimed the government's attention. Although military and economic policies had destroyed much of the

NPA's old base in the early years of martial law, and the army managed to arrest its top leadership (Bernabe Buscayno, Victor Corpuz, Jose Maria Sison) in 1976 and 1977, the organization continued to spread. Consequently army units moved to occupy new areas, particularly in Samar and eastern Mindanao.

The regime's economic initiatives between 1976 and 1980 seemed more diffuse than its political ones. Efforts at increasing agricultural productivity continued, with primary attention given to achieving self-sufficiency in rice and encouraging plantation agriculture. Self-sufficiency in rice was achieved by 1976, though at a high cost to government banks, which were forced to write off substantial defaults on loans. Plantation agriculture also expanded, despite opposition from those who had earlier farmed the lands and their supporters.

Equally controversial was a program designed to make Manila more attractive to tourists, and specifically to conventions. Initiated in 1974, following a presidential decree easing government loans for new hotel construction, the program included the building of fourteen new hotels and a huge convention center. The total cost was never made public, and estimates varied. Government press releases, for example, cited a cost of $20 million for the convention center; President Marcos gave it as $106 million; observers guessed $130 million. According to the *Far Eastern Economic Review*,

> The cost of the 14 new hotels (representing 11,000 new rooms) was also never revealed, though a realistic estimate was $300 million. All the hotels had promised the Central Bank that they would be open for business by October 1976, in time for the IMF/World Bank annual meeting which was held in the new conference centre from October 4-8. Many were not, and most opened only partially. Following the IMF meeting, construction on the incompleted hotels slowed considerably as the government lending agencies tightened up on loans already committed and had second thoughts about financing building cost increases.

... Analysts calculate that 1 million hotel guests ... will be required yearly to keep the hotels at 75% of occupancy, assuming each tourist stays six days. Total tourist arrivals ... are expected to total 600,000 in 1976.[12]

Other infrastructure projects stressed road building and the development of alternative sources for energy, both receiving a large share of the country's budget and the bulk of its foreign borrowing. Late in 1979, however, the government decided to shift its emphasis (and consequently its allocation of earned and borrowed funds) from roads toward basic industries. The shift was in part recognition of the success of the road building programs, beginning with Marcos' first term in 1966, in part a reflection of the conviction that "it was time to provide a bigger outlay for improving production capacity."[13] Hence the government identified eleven projects involving the establishment of nine new industries ranging from integrated steel making to integrated pulp-paper making. It also sought the rationalization and expansion of the cement and coconut industries.

Meanwhile, the energy program was accelerated toward a goal of fully tapping indigenous energy sources in five rather than ten years, with an overall objective of reducing dependence on oil from 88 percent to 55 percent of total energy requirements. An earlier decision had left oil and coal to the private sector, but had provided for direct government involvement in the development of geothermal steam, hydro-electricity, diesel power plants, and the nuclear power plant in Bataan. Since Philippine oil exploration had not proven promising and since the intent was to reduce dependence on all oil, the effect of the government's accelerated program was to supplement the shift from basic infrastructure to industries. The increased availability would be for industrial plants and commercial establishments, not cars, jeepneys, and buses.

Amid these developments, the regime's political base seemed to be changing. The effort to include the common man, exemplified by the agrarian reform program and by "*barangay*

[12] *Asia 1977 Yearbook*, p. 279.
[13] *Asia 1981 Yearbook*, p. 232.

democracy" in the early years of martial law, showed few signs of existence, let alone success. Medium and small landowners, however, seemed solidly supportive, particularly in central Luzon, where government programs had been concentrated and comparatively effective. The bureaucrats outside Manila, who in the earlier period had provided links between *barangays* and the capital, had been joined by appointed and elected officials, and were now part of party as well as administrative networks. From them, patronage apparently produced loyalty. The military also appeared loyal, though undisciplined at lower levels and fraught with factional rivalries at the top. In many areas the military constituted a governing structure paralleling and dominating the civilian, and retired generals filled posts in government agencies.

In Manila, meanwhile, the technocrats seemed increasingly isolated. The bureaucracies they nominally headed seemed to have shifted in focus and function from the days they were identified as responsible for the regime's development programs, and were correspondingly less accountable to standards of competence or honesty. Instead, the bureaucrats increasingly shared the values and styles of the old politicians with whom they were now allied in KBL, receiving and distributing benefits designed to deliver votes.

As for the development programs, their nature and benefits seemed increasingly dependent on the Marcos-Romualdez families and those associates identified as cronies. Quite clearly, Mrs. Marcos was influential in Manila's redevelopment, and she and family friends were directly involved in the hotel construction that the regime's top planners had unsuccessfully opposed. Other projects she sponsored (and for which she secured public and private funds) both technocrats and others identified as unnecessary and undesirable extravagances. But the focus of criticism after 1978 was less Mrs. Marcos than those like Herminio Disini, Marcos' relative (by marriage) and allegedly the recipient of a "commission" of at least $4 million from Westinghouse for the Bataan nuclear plant contract. The Westinghouse scandal, first made public by the *Asian Wall Street Journal*, not only called into question the nuclear project (which was to be built in an earthquake zone, had been bid by Westinghouse at a price considerably above General Electric's offer, and had subsequently been characterized by massive cost overruns), but also the Herdis conglomerate that Disini had built since 1972 with help from the government. By 1979, similar conglomerates, also benefiting from direct or indirect participation by the Marcos family, had been documented in "Some Are Smarter Than Others," the title taken from Mrs. Marcos' response to a question by a *Fortune* magazine writer about why relatives and friends had enriched themselves during martial law.[14] The study, hurried into typescript for circulation on the seventh anniversary of martial law, identified the holdings of members of such families as Benedicto, Cojuangco, Cuenca, Elizalde, Enrile, Espino, Floirendo, Silverio, Velasco, and Villafuerte, as well as those of the Marcos and Romualdez clans.

Thus the technocrats seemed limited to developing plans, which were not necessarily implemented, and to negotiating the outside funding required to subsidize an increasingly expensive system. This role, ironically, alienated them from those businessmen who were also opposed to the malversations they attributed to the Marcos family and their friends, but who believed that the terms imposed by the World Bank and other lenders were in neither the national interest nor their own.

Under these circumstances, economic indicators were not simply mixed but apparently contradictory. Thus the *Far Eastern Economic Review's Yearbook* reported of 1978,

> as the year progressed, certain economic indicators seemed to contradict each other. The trade balance was running a bigger deficit, yet the peso performed strongly against the U.S. dollar. The country's external debt was at

---

[14] A revised version, written by John F. Doherty, S. J., and titled "Who Controls the Philippine Economy: Some Need Not Try as Hard as Others," was published in Belinda A. Aquino, ed., *Cronies and Enemies: The Current Philippine Scene*, Philippine Studies Occasional Paper No. 5 (Honolulu: Philippine Studies Program, University of Hawaii, 1982).

an all time high, yet overseas lenders were not only granting local borrowers new loans, but also extending debt re-
financing and restructuring facilities. Inflation was within
control, yet the budgetary deficit widened and expansion
of money and credit aggregates went through the ceiling.
There was a slowdown in growth, and big projects were
unable to get off the ground. Yet unemployment remained
low. Notwithstanding the welcome sign to foreign investors, few were coming and some of those already in the
Philippines were even leaving. Either the official facts and
figures reflecting all this were less than accurate, or there
were offsetting factors at work.[15]

But for the period as a whole, from 1976 to 1980, the indicators were even more complex and puzzling. In 1976, for example, the recession seemed to be easing, growth accelerated
slightly, unemployment fell, and international reserves were
up. Yet the consumer price index rose even more than growth
rates, unemployment rose in critical sectors (agriculture, for
example) and underemployment remained high, and the external debt increased by almost 29 percent in the first nine months
of the year. In 1977 the same trends continued.

Another "oil shock" took its toll in 1979, and by 1980 negative statistics appeared to be predominant. Inflation soared to
over 20 percent in January-June before dropping to 14 percent
in August; price increases eroded purchasing power, cut demand for all but the most essential goods and services, reduced
profits, and caused layoffs—according to government statistics over 64,000 in Metro-Manila alone in January-June. Declining prices for coconut products and bananas made life particularly difficult in agricultural areas. Foreign borrowing
continued, but concerned lenders were imposing more strin-
gent limits. The continuation of a heavy reliance on foreign
trade and borrowing had obviously left the country highly dependent on international economic conditions and decisions;
and the lack of any direct, consistent mechanisms resulting in
income redistribution meant that the share of the rich grew,

[15] *Asian 1979 Yearbook*, p. 284.

that of the poorest shrank. The Food and Nutrition Research Institute of the Philippines estimated that 70 percent of the population were malnourished.

Both political and economic developments shaped the nature of opposition to the regime. The regime's announced moves toward normalization failed to placate a moderate elite composed of former top government officials and politicians, who branded announcements of relaxation false and elections fraudulent. Their allegations were substantiated by other observers, both within and outside the Philippines, who documented continued abuses of basic rights (detention, torture, and, increasingly, "salvaging"—the killing of those seized and tortured), and who agreed that massive fraud characterized the elections, particularly the 1978 elections in Manila. Protests achieved some successes—Mrs. Trinidad Herrera, a leader of a Manila slum-based organization challenging government relocation efforts, was released after the World Bank held up funds pending her release from prison, where she had been tortured; and U.S. intervention apparently secured the release from prison of Senator Aquino so that he could leave the country for a heart bypass operation.

Broader efforts at organization among the opposition were frustrated by disagreements over leadership, issues (the "correct" position on U.S. bases, for example), and tactics (to boycott or contest elections). But in August 1980 about seventy people representing eight opposition groups, most regionally based and formed to contest the 1978 and/or 1980 elections, issued a National Covenant of Freedom. The Covenant "denounced the Marcos government, demanded an end to martial law, called for free elections to establish a democratic system of government, and proposed the 'liberation of the Philippines' from all forms of foreign domination in all aspects of our national life."[16] Later the leaders announced the formation of a United Democratic Opposition (UNIDO).

[16] Larry A. Niksch and Marjorie Niehaus, *The Internal Situation in the Philippines: Current Trends and Future Prospects*, report No. 81-21 F (Washington, D.C.: Congressional Research Service, Library of Congress, 1981), pp. 64-70.

Some of these moderates had at least ideological ties to the "Third Force," a movement of Manila-based, affluent, college-educated professionals who began to consider the use of violence to overthrow the regime after the 1978 elections. The Third Force was apparently subdivided into the Light a Fire group, which was uncovered by the government in late 1979; the United Party of Democratic Socialists (the "soc dems"), which was responsible for a wave of bombings in Manila in August and September 1980; and the Christian Social Revolutionary Forces, which was identified with the U.S.-based Movement for a Free Philippines. The strategy, as described in a Congressional Research Service report, was "to weaken the Manila citizenry's confidence in the government and, through the bombings and perhaps more severe acts of violence, to scare off tourism and foreign investment, two vital parts of Manila's economy."[17] It was hoped that success in these endeavors would encourage political protests that would shut down the city's economy.

Meanwhile the New People's Army was offering support to those suffering from the forceful implementation of development projects (the World Bank-financed Chico Hydroelectric Dam Complex in Northern Luzon, or banana plantations in Mindanao) and, more generally, from deteriorating economic conditions (coconut farmers in Bicol, Samar, and Mindanao). Although its strategy remained one of the "strategic defensive," it was building both alliances and an infrastructure. In the cities its affiliates in the National Democratic Front were directing their attention to urban problems like inflation, the ban on strikes, and low wages.

The church had members (priests, pastors, nuns, and laypeople) in all three groups, but also increasingly articulated an independent stance. Most marked during this period was the sharpness and comprehensiveness of the critique of martial law leveled by the Catholic Bishops' Conference of the Philippines under the leadership of Jaime Cardinal Sin. Earlier balanced between progressives (primarily from the country's pe-

[17] Ibid., pp. 73-74.

riphery) and conservatives, with Sin leading a moderate group espousing "critical collaboration," by 1978 the CBCP responded to a series of developments: a wave of arrests of priests, nuns, and laypeople involved in Church-sponsored social action programs; an increased government tendency to discredit the Christian left as subversive; military abuses against civilians; fraud, deceit, and connivance in the 1978 elections; and the government's ineffectiveness in bettering socioeconomic conditions for the masses. Pastoral letters and statements, whether issued individually or collectively, moved from the identification and condemnation of specific acts and policies to a call for the end of martial law. Meanwhile the Task Force on Detainees of the Association of Major Religious Superiors continued to monitor human rights violations, Catholic media provided an alternative to government-controlled sources, and church workers helped to organize and defend the poor or persecuted.

Within or among groups of students, workers, and urban squatters, however, there was little evidence of sustained political organization and action. Particular government actions occasionally sparked protests, which even more rarely resulted in change—an increase in the minimum wage, for example, or modifications in a proposed education code intended to give the regime more direct control over universities.

1981-1983

Despite its shrinking coalition, deteriorating economic indicators, and the increased scope and organization of the opposition, the regime was sufficiently confident of its strength to take further moves toward "normalization." On January 17, 1981, President Marcos announced the ending of eight years of martial law. The right of habeas corpus was restored, except in two regions of Mindanao; military trials and military detention of civilian offenders were phased out; some prisoners were released; and legislative powers were formally transferred to the Interim National Assembly. Marcos retained, however, the right to issue decrees, and all decrees issued under martial law remained in effect. Twelve days later Marcos made another announcement: because of popular dissatisfaction with the parliamentary system adopted in the 1973 constitution he would ask the Assembly to consider constitutional amendments that would establish a French-style presidential-parliamentary system.

As submitted to the Assembly, the amendments provided for a president (at least fifty years old, thus excluding Senator Aquino from candidacy) elected for a six-year, renewable term and empowered to appoint and remove a prime minister and a fourteen-member Executive Committee. The committee was to be authorized not only to assist in supervising the government but also to run the government in case of the president's death, incapacity, or resignation. Presidents and those acting on presidential orders were granted immunity for their official acts during or after their terms of office. There were also provisions establishing procedures for accrediting political parties, determining party membership, and defining representation of various electoral boards.

The Assembly approved the amendments, which were submitted to a plebiscite in April. The presidential election followed on June 16, 1981. The regime campaigned hard and not entirely fairly for both. Before the plebiscite, for example, thousands of forged tally sheets were discovered in a raid on a Zamboanga City hotel room occupied by government officials (Zamboanga had an oppositionist mayor, Cesar Climaco, who has since been murdered). Before the presidential election, in which the opposition candidates were exemplified by someone from a faction of the old Nacionalista party whom Marcos had allegedly persuaded to run, and someone else who urged that the Philippines join the United States as the fifty-first state, the regime first issued summonses to those who had boycotted the plebiscite, then offered amnesty for those who voted in the election. Marcos also issued land titles in Tondo (a slum area in Manila), released funds in oppositionist areas, and gave $750 to *barangay* chairmen.

Marcos was, of course, reelected, and proceeded to appoint Cesar Virata (a respected technocrat) prime minister, reorganize the Cabinet and Cabinet-level offices, constitute an Executive Committee, and name new leadership for government-controlled financial institutions and the military. Doubtless as intended, these moves gained the approval of the new U.S. administration. Secretary of State Haig, in Manila for an ASEAN meeting, congratulated Marcos for a "wonderful victory," and Vice-President Bush, who attended the inauguration of the New Republic, praised his "adherence to democratic principles and to the democratic process." Marcos and Reagan reportedly had a cordial meeting in October at the Cancun North-South conference, during which Reagan invited the Marcoses for a state visit eventually scheduled for September 1982. The visit produced any number of occasions fully covered by the Philippine media and a few agreements, including $204.5 million from the U.S. Export-Import Bank for the Bataan nuclear power plant project and a commitment to renegotiate the terms for U.S. bases in the Philippines no later than December 1983.

Meanwhile, in May 1982, elections had been held for *barangay* officials (a captain and six councilors in each of approximately 42,000 *barangays*). Although unpaid and officially nonpartisan, the officials were expected to play an important role in the Assembly elections scheduled for 1984, the mayoralty and gubernatorial elections scheduled for 1986, and the presidential election set for 1987. By early 1983 Marcos was considering revamping the electoral code for the Assembly election to allow UNIDO (then a coalition of twelve opposition parties) to field candidates, to shift from large regional voting areas to the smaller provincial level, and to abolish block voting for an entire party slate.

But if between 1981 and 1983 Marcos appeared to have total control of political initiatives, he had considerably less success with economic factors that in both the short and the long term decisively affected the regime's political base and stability. In January 1981 news coverage of the Philippines focused not simply on the lifting of martial law but also on a major financial scandal caused by the disappearance of business tycoon Dewey Dee, who left behind approximately $70 million in debts, and on one of several critical reports on the Philippine economy issued by international agencies.

Although the Dee scandal revealed the fragility of the Philippine economic system and brought about immediate reforms in banking and investment regulation, it was equally significant in pointing up the extent of the crony problem and in escalating a debate over the proper use of government funds. Three major firms especially hard hit were the Construction and Development Company, headed by Rodolfo Cuenca; the Silverio Group, a conglomerate owned by Ricardo Silverio; and Disini's Herdis Group. The government responded to their problems (and those of others) by buying time with central-bank emergency loans and eventually transferring equity to other public-sector institutions.

Also in January 1981 the *Asian Wall Street Journal* published a summary of a World Bank study of poverty in the Philippines. It and other Bank reports subsequently leaked to the press revealed the Bank's concern about the regime's economic strategies and their results, and about its administrative capabilities and political stability.

Economic figures for 1981 and 1982 did not alleviate the Bank's concerns or those of other lenders. Growth rates were estimated at 3.8 percent for 1981 (by the Philippine government; the International Monetary Fund said 2.5 percent), and 2.6 percent for 1982. The current account deficit grew from $2.29 billion in 1981 to $3.33 billion in 1982, as exports declined in value, imports increased, and debt servicing costs escalated. Whereas the coconut, banana, sugar, and copper industries were all affected by marked declines in prices or demand, the coconut industry (on which one-third of the population, and two-thirds of those in certain areas of Mindanao, were dependent) was particularly hard hit. And whereas electronics and garments exports grew, the business sector generally was plagued by reduced sales (down as much as 30 percent in some areas of the country), mounting debt, and declining new investment. Unemployment rates for urban workers reached 25 percent or more in Manila and other cities, even with an estimated 500,000 Filipinos working overseas.

The immediate consequence of these circumstances was an apparent increase in the authority of the technocrats, as exemplified by Cesar Virata's appointment as prime minister and by their predominance in the new Cabinet. But their charge—to restore domestic economic stability and maintain foreign economic support—was not conducive to their popularity. By early 1983, the combination of the bail-out program dictated by the regime's internal structures and the austerity program mandated by the IMF and World Bank had left the technocrats even more isolated than in earlier years. Businessmen, including many not usually known as nationalistic, were opposed to what they perceived as the regime's continued subsidies to the incompetence and profligacy of the cronies, and to the insistence of the IMF and World Bank on opening the country further to foreign trade and capital.

Within the regime the cuts in government expenditures and other efforts to free or rationalize the economy affected those whose own political base depended on particular structures providing access to funds. If the technocrats dominated the Cabinet, their critics were well represented in noncabinet posts and in the executive committee, and they controlled the KBL. Hence they won some early skirmishes (as, for example, over Virata's desire to eliminate coconut levies—successfully opposed by Defense Secretary Enrile and "crony" Eduardo Cojuangco), and mounted a full-scale attack in April 1983. The result was Virata's resignation, which Marcos refused to accept.

A less obvious beneficiary of the economic crisis was the military, whose power grew as additional force was required to cope with dissent. General Ver, particularly, was given increased status. Marcos gave him secret instructions regarding the succession as he left for Saudi Arabia in March 1982, and Cojuangco reportedly shifted from his linkage with Enrile to support Ver and Imelda Marcos after a deal involving the San Miguel Corporation in March 1983. Outside the Manila area, where Ver directly controlled all troops, transfers of units from the Muslim areas to areas where armed dissidence was increasing made the military an even more visible and powerful presence. But the military appeared to remain split at the top, undisciplined at the bottom.

Amid these developments, popular support for the regime declined markedly. Observers noted three trends. Perhaps the majority of Filipinos—cynical and alienated but passive—simply withdrew their support. Others continued to work through political parties and, while indulging in endless factionalism, seemed increasingly able to rally support. An estimated 34 percent of the population boycotted the constitutional plebiscite in 1981, and a majority "no" vote was registered in nine provinces and eleven cities. UNIDO announced four conditions for participating in the June presidential contest (revamping the Commission on Elections, purging the voters' lists of names of dead and unqualified people, extending the campaign period to 120 days, and accrediting UNIDO as the minority party). When the regime refused to respond, UNIDO refused to run candidates and joined others in another boycott.

Within or outside party contexts, the trend among moderates was to continue their public criticism of particular policies authorized or tolerated by the regime (such as "salvaging" or "strategic hamleting"), or simply of its ineptitude (as with drought relief in Mindanao). Their charges were documented and publicized by international agencies such as Amnesty International, which issued a strongly critical report during Marcos' triumphant Washington visit. The subsequent arrest of some of the Filipino critics (Mayor Aquilino Pimentel of Cagayan de Oro, and staff members of the newspaper *We Forum*, for example) also received international attention. By early 1983 moderates were focusing on demands for a broadening of participation and hence of the regime; thus they proposed the "formula for national reconciliation" that Aquino referred to in his testimony, with the intent of preparing for the 1984 parliamentary elections.

But the most significant trend was apparently radicalization, as the regime's corruption and lack of openness, the evident failure of its economic policies, its repressiveness and military abuses, and its support from the United States convinced more and more Filipinos that there was no alternative to violence.

The NPA's ranks were swelled by those who did not necessarily share its original Maoist ideology but who agreed with its choice of tactics to defeat the "enemy"; NPA fronts expanded to virtually all of the country's provinces, with students and professionals joining peasants in organizing and fighting. Labor groups, also radicalized, staged rallies and organized strikes.

As for the Catholic Church, if there was a conservative trend after Pope John Paul's visit in 1981, as some observers believed, actions of the regime quickly provoked a return to the earlier level of criticism. Cardinal Sin remained particularly outspoken, urging Marcos to resign because he had lost the respect of the people and criticizing the role of U.S. military aid (given as "rent' for the bases) in supporting the regime. And in January 1983 the CBCP declared the Church-Military Liaison Committee useless and withdrew. This action was followed in February by a pastoral letter that was a sweeping denunciation of the regime's abuses of human rights (among which it cited torture and murder) and its substitution of lavish projects and empty propaganda for genuine economic development.

The Reagan administration also seemed less enthusiastic about the regime, an opinion that brought it more in line with the U.S. Congress and particularly with the House of Representatives. Although it negotiated base agreements increasing U.S. aid from the $500 million over a five-year period arranged by the Carter administration in 1979 to $900 million for the following five years, and significantly liberalized the terms for military sales credits, its intelligence agencies apparently shared the World Bank's view that the situation was "precarious," and had little hope that the regime had sufficient insight or will to recover. In June 1983 an aide to Secretary of State Schultz told a *New York Times* reporter that "The Marcos regime is entering its twilight zone and we don't want to find ourselves in the same position as we did in Iran when the Shah was overthrown."[18] The analogies also included Nicaragua and, for economic reasons, Mexico.

[18] Sheilah Ocampo-Kalfors, "No More Irans," *Far Eastern Economic Review* (July 21, 1983), p. 16.

But even though his public statements indicated both testiness and defensiveness, Marcos himself showed no signs of yielding to pressures for more fundamental change in the regime, either to make its structures and policies more responsive and less repressive or to guarantee a clear and orderly succession. Yet his health was reportedly deteriorating. Rumors varied as to the cause—lupus was usually mentioned—but the fact seemed confirmed by an announcement in early August that he was going into seclusion for three weeks to write books.

These, then, were the circumstances in which Aquino decided to return, hoping for enough time before the 1984 elections to persuade Marcos to allow a transition to a regime that included the opposition, and the opposition to unify to take advantage of whatever opportunities were offered. The alternative, he and others were convinced, was a cycle of repression and revolution from which no Filipino would benefit.

CHAPTER V

THE POLITICAL CRISIS

CARL H. LANDE

A political crisis erupted visibly after the assassination of former Philippine Senator Benigno Aquino, Jr., on August 21, 1983. That event triggered widespread public demands for President Marcos' resignation. It set off a rapid decline in business confidence, leading to a massive flight of capital and to the inability of the Philippine government to service its foreign debt. It stimulated an outburst of organizational activity by the democratic opposition and an expansion of the scale of military and political action by the revolutionary opposition. For President Marcos, it brought a precipitous decline in legitimacy and authority and in his ability to shape the course of events. It led also to efforts on the part of important friends, both domestic and foreign, to distance themselves from the Marcos regime.

Yet the crisis did not have its beginning in September 1983, but had been some years in the making. It was made possible, and perhaps inevitable, by gradual changes in the roles and attitudes of various groups that were affected by the institutional and policy results of martial law. The later behavior of these groups cannot be appreciated without an understanding of their recent past.

The Aquino Assassination and Its Aftermath

The son of a prewar senator from Tarlac Province, Benigno Aquino, Jr., had been successively the youngest elected mayor and senator in Philippine history as well as a provincial governor. Quick of mind, brash, and endowed with a winning personality, he had become, before the imposition of martial law, the most likely opposition Liberal party nominee for the pres-

idential elections scheduled for 1973. Martial law and the new
constitution devised by a Marcos-dominated Constitutional
Convention prevented that election from taking place. Instead,
Aquino found himself under arrest and accused of a variety of
crimes, including responsibility for a political killing.

Thereafter Aquino's political history was that of a David
challenging Marcos' Goliath—though with a less happy ending. At the first elections for a new Interim Legislative Assembly in 1978, while still under military detention, Aquino led a
slate of opposition Laban party candidates in Greater Manila,
after besting the secretary of national defense, Juan Ponce Enrile, who had attacked him, in a brilliant televised rebuttal.
Had the elections been conducted fairly, Aquino undoubtedly
would have outpolled all other Manila candidates. Instead,
that honor went to Mrs. Marcos, and Aquino was denied a
seat.

Later, released from jail through the intervention of the
Carter administration to undergo heart surgery in the United
States, Aquino quickly displaced less charismatic figures to become the principal leader of the exile opposition. In 1981,
while Aquino was still abroad, Marcos held presidential elections, but not before amending the Constitution to raise the
minimum presidential age to fifty, thereby excluding the forty-
eight-year-old Aquino. By 1983, taunted by Marcos' spokesmen for his failure to return home to jail as he had promised,
impatient with the new American administration's Philippine
policy, and worried by reports of Marcos' uncertain health,
Aquino decided to return to the Philippines in the hope of per-
suading the president to arrange for a peaceful transfer of
power to the opposition, or failing that, to assume leadership
of that opposition himself. He had been previously warned by
Mrs. Marcos and others that his life might be endangered by
such a return.

The fatal ending of Aquino's homeward flight is too well
known to need recounting here. Its consequences were pro-
found, because of the widespread belief, later supported by the
Agrava Commission's reports and by the testimony in the subsequent trial, that members of the armed forces, and not a lone

communist assailant, were the killers. Local and provincial political rivalries had often led to the killing of minor political
leaders or their retainers. But the murder of the most prominent leader of the opposition convinced the upper and middle
classes that no opponent of the present regime was safe, no
matter how high his social position.

Aquino's return to his country in the face of dire warnings
of his probable fate also reminded many Filipinos of their past
timidity in opposing the regime. Aquino's courage was infec-
tious. The result was a wave of anti-government demonstrations, and a belief that the president could be forced thereby to
yield to at least some of the demands of his critics. A side effect
of these demonstrations was the indefinite postponement of
President Reagan's scheduled 1983 visit to the Philippines, and
the beginning of the American administration's efforts to
lessen what was widely believed to be its close identification
with the Marcos government.

The New Political Activism of
the Middle and Upper Classes

The imposition of martial law in 1972 and the resulting
changes in government policies had divided both the upper
and the middle classes. Those directly affected—opposition
political leaders, parents whose children were incarcerated for
their political activity, members of once wealthy and powerful
families whose properties were taken over under near-confis-
catory terms, as well as nationalistic businessmen who were
placed at a disadvantage by the government's increased efforts
to attract foreign capital—condemned the imposition of martial law from the outset. But what was probably a majority of
the upper and middle classes and perhaps of the lower class as
well had welcomed the prospects of a period of centrally imposed order. They had watched the growth of radical political
activism in the schools and the labor movement, and the wave
of urban political demonstrations, with growing unease. To
them the old political system, and in particular the Philippine
Congress, appeared discredited. The prospects of a change in

the country's political institutions through the promised introduction of parliamentary government on British lines, after
what was supposed to be a brief period of martial law, held out
the hope for a new beginning. Most of all, the revival of the
Philippine economy during the early 1970s, which appeared to
be a consequence of the imposition of law and order and the
resulting inflow of foreign capital, provided for a few years
broadly based support for President Marcos and martial law.

By the middle of the 1970s however, approval for martial
law and for its author began to decline. One reason for this
was the downturn in the economy, which could be blamed
only in part on the worldwide increase in the price of petroleum and on the fall in prices for some Philippine export commodities. Marcos' mismanagement of the economy also appeared to be to blame. Another reason for the decline in
support for the administration was the widespread realization
that authoritarian government was not likely to come to an
end as soon as had been promised, and a growing awareness of
the violations of civil rights and the other abuses of power that
were made possible by the abolition of the pre-1972 system of
checks and balances.

Disenchantment with martial law expressed itself in growing sympathy for the student demonstrations that, after a period of relative quiet, resumed in 1977. Until the following
year, however, such sympathy was expressed mainly in private. It became more open and widespread at the Interim National Assembly Elections of 1978. In Manila these were preceded on election eve by a "noise rally" in support of the
opposition, which brought a large number of the city's lower-
and middle-income inhabitants into the streets.

The demonstrations that followed the Aquino assassination
in 1983 were much larger and were sustained longer than any
that had preceded them. For the first time, prominent businessmen took a major part in the organization of such demonstrations, which now took place not only in the university
belt but also in the financial and upper-class residential district
of Makati.

The growth of political activism of the business community

could be attributed to a combination of factors. Even before the Aquino assassination, it was clear to businessmen that the country was fast approaching a financial crisis brought on by excessive government borrowing in support of what were too often unproductive projects, and by the collapse of the business empires of several favored crony capitalists which had to be rescued by the government. A flight of capital reminiscent of that of the premartial-law years had begun some time before Aquino's death. The periodic illnesses of the president brought fears of a post-Marcos succession that seemed likely to bring to power Mrs. Marcos and her ally, Chief of Staff General Fabian Ver. Neither of these two individuals enjoyed the confidence of the business community.

Demonstrations could, of course, be suppressed if they became violent or allowed to run their course if they did not. But there was little that the government could do to prevent capital flight or to force Filipino businessmen to invest. Nor could it prevent businessmen from communicating to foreign lenders their doubts about the competence or viability of the regime. These weapons were used with considerable effect to pressure the government into a new sensitivity to the views of the financial community.

Finally, the business and professional elites began to create a variety of organizations which, although distinguished from political parties—the instrument of professional politicians— became an important part of the political opposition.

The Role of the Catholic Church

In a predominantly Catholic country undergoing a political and social crisis of extraordinary proportions, it was to be expected that the Catholic Church would play some political role. Yet it took up this role gradually and reluctantly.

During the Spanish colonial period, the Church had been an active partner with the state in fulfilling the dual mission of carrying Spanish rule and the Catholic faith across the seas. As in other Spanish colonies, several religious orders were granted land for their support. At the same time, they were entrusted with broad responsibilities for the welfare of their native parishioners, including the provision of their education and the oversight of their elected municipal governments.

American colonial rule brought major changes in the position of the Church. It introduced both the principle of separation of Church and state and that of religious toleration. Parish priests no longer supervised municipal governments. The religious orders lost their landed estates, though not without compensation. A predominantly Protestant colonial administration welcomed Protestant missionaries, and for a time placed mainly under the control of their native converts an extensive new system of free, secular public education.

To a large degree these innovations survived the passing of American rule. Both the separation of Church and state and religious toleration were accepted by the clergy and laity of what remains a predominantly Catholic country. Except where the Church found itself under legislative attack, as in the case of measures that conflicted with its doctrines (such as divorce), attacked its reputation, or threatened its economic interests, the Church as an institution sought to avoid involvement in politics. Thus it was only slowly, and with some hesitation, that the hierarchy of the Church, the Council of Bishops and Manila's Jaime Cardinal Sin, became at first cautious, and then increasingly outspoken, critics of the Marcos government. Such hesitation was not, however, found in all sectors of a very broad Church.

Both among the religious orders and among individual parish priests, opposition to martial law developed soon after its imposition in 1972. Early during the martial-law period, the Association of Major Religious Superiors, that is, the superiors of the religious orders, created a Task Force on Detainees, which took for its special mission the investigation of the mistreatment of political prisoners. Its findings were published in a succession of mimeographed news sheets. At about the same time, there was formed a Church-Military Committee to provide a regular means for bringing complaints of military abuses directly to the attention of the armed forces.

In addition, particular religious orders found themselves

drawn into the roles of critics and opponents of the Marcos government through their involvement with politically active students and graduates of the Church-related universities and colleges, as well as through their ministry among the poor. Long before martial law, graduates of the Jesuit-run Ateneo de Manila University had taken a leading part in the formation of both a labor and a peasant federation. As ordinary members of these organizations found themselves under arrest, their clerical friends came to their defense. In the tribal highlands of northern Luzon and of Mindanao, as well as in the Muslim areas of the south, members of other religious orders became articulate champions of the victims of military abuse. In the slums of Manila, parish priests as well as members of the religious orders helped to organize or to defend squatters' associations that championed the interests of the urban poor.

A small number of priests and nuns joined the communist New People's Army as active combatants, or came to support it through the Christians for National Liberation, a member of the communist-led National Democratic Front. Some were killed in action or were captured by the armed forces. Others remained in the hills. Most prominent among them was Fr. Conrado Balweg, S.V.D., an NPA guerrilla leader in the Northern Cordillera, and himself a member of the Tingguian tribal minority. His account of his conversion to revolution was published in the Church-sponsored newspaper VERITAS, and helped to legitimize the NPA, its doctrines, and its guerrilla war among a predominantly Catholic population. In criticizing or actively opposing the Marcos government, the Catholic clergy were joined by Protestant ministers in a display of ecumenical cooperation.

The hierarchy of the Catholic Church, divided among bishops of conservative, moderate, and liberal views, moved more slowly toward a politically active stance. When it took a position, it placed itself firmly on the side of the moderate rather than the radical opposition. Its voice was heard through pronouncements of the Catholic Bishops Conference of the Philippines, through the statements of such individual conference members as Bishop Francisco Claver of Bukidnon (like Fr. Bal-

weg a cleric of highland tribal origins), and through the country's most prominent churchman, Manila's Jaime Cardinal
Sin.

During the first years of martial law, the cardinal confined
himself to protesting specific infringements of the rights of the
Church and the clergy. From there he moved gradually toward
broader criticism of the actions and policies of the regime, notably its inattention to the poor and its misuses of economic
and military power. By 1982, the cardinal was calling for the
restoration of democracy and urging Marcos to make way for
a new leadership. In March 1983, he asked the United States
to halt military aid to the government in view of its probable
use for the killing of Filipinos by Filipinos.

After the Aquino assassination, the cardinal became outspoken, sometimes in coordination with political and business
leaders, in urging President Marcos to give up power and,
more discretely, in offering to help make such a transfer of
power a relatively painless one for the president. Unsuccessful
in that endeavor, he continued to press for a restoration of
Philippine democracy.

In short, the Church, against its wishes and tradition, was
propelled into an active though changing political role. During
the eleven years between September 1972 and August 1983,
while fear of criticizing the Marcos government hung heavily
over most of Philippine society, the Church was almost alone
in upbraiding the president and his associates for the excesses
of their rule. It did so publicly and with increasing bluntness
through its premier cardinal and through lower members of
the clergy, thereby providing a shelter for the small number of
laymen who added their voices to that of the Church.

After the Aquino assassination broke the dam of previous
inhibitions and let loose a torrent of attacks on the government
by leaders of all social classes, the Church no longer found it
necessary to serve as the principal open critic of the regime. Its
now equally important function, as Cardinal Sin appeared to
see it, was to provide a brake against an escalation of violence
from either the government or the opposition. As the crisis
deepened, the cardinal offered himself to President Marcos as

a moderator for a peaceful transition. In the meantime, more radical members of the clergy offered to Christians who wished to be revolutionaries both role models and moral support.

The Opposition Political Parties

Before martial law, political competition in the Philippines expressed itself through the biennial electoral rivalry of two nationwide political parties. So similar were these parties in their policies and their broad, societywide sources of support that many politicians, as well as ordinary voters, found it both possible and advantageous to shift their allegiance from one party to the other, depending on their calculations as to which party would win the next elections. Indeed, two presidents, Ramon Magsaysay in 1953 and Ferdinand Marcos in 1965, changed parties shortly before being nominated and elected to their country's highest office. Because of the instability of support for both parties, control of the presidency and the Congress changed from one party to the other on the average of once every eight years between 1946 and 1972.

The imposition of martial law brought an end to the cyclical alternation of power between two political parties. The Congress was disbanded and its building turned into a storehouse for government documents. Some members of Congress, among them Senator Aquino, were placed under arrest. Still the two political parties were not abolished, perhaps because Ferdinand Marcos remained the nominal head of the Nacionalista party. The leaders of the Liberal party, as well as some anti-Marcos Nacionalistas, maintained their now inactive parties in skeletal form, if not in the expectation of an early restoration of elections then as symbols of their nonrecognition of the legality of the new political order.

When President Marcos announced that a newly created Interim National Assembly would be elected in 1978, both Liberals and anti-Marcos Nacionalistas disagreed among themselves as to whether to take part. Some wanted their parties to boycott what they expected would be unfree and unfair elections for a weak and constitutionally dubious new legislative body. Others, including the still imprisoned Benigno Aquino, felt that the opposition should not miss an opportunity to put its case before the electorate. Thus it was agreed that Liberals and Nacionalistas who wished to become candidates could do so, but that they should not use their old party names. They ran instead under the names of several newly formed parties to contest seats in particular regions. In Manila, the new regional party called itself Laban (fight). In the Visayas there was the Visayan Fusion. In Mindanao candidates ran under the name of the Mindanao Alliance.

Although Laban was not allowed to win a single seat from Manila despite its obvious popularity there, some thirteen candidates of other regional opposition parties did manage to win places in the new Interim Assembly. This modest success, and a growing belief that the Marcos regime was in decline, kept both old and new opposition parties in being and led to the subsequent formation of several additional opposition parties.

After the Aquino assassination, there appeared a welter of new political organizations. Some of them, led by veteran politicians of the premartial-law period or by younger aspirants for elective offices, called themselves political parties. Among these were the remnants of the old Liberals and Nacionalistas and of the parties that were created in 1978. Several of them, notably the United Nationalist Democratic Organization (UN-IDO), were represented in the Assembly elected in 1984. Other organizations, led by individuals who disclaimed personal political ambitions—businessmen, professionals, labor leaders, and heads of neighborhood associations—also were formed. Those of leftist orientation described themselves as "cause-oriented groups." These devoted their efforts to organizing mass demonstrations, and made up what has been called the "parliament of the streets." They included the August Twenty-One Movement (ATOM), a businessman's group; the Alliance of Multi Sectoral Organizations (AMA); and GABRIELLA, an alliance of women's organizations. New ones sprang up continually.

There were, in addition, several umbrella groups led by well-known political figures, which brought together a wide variety of organizations that shared a common point of view. Before the 1986 presidential elections the most prominent of these were UNIDO, PDP-Laban—a composite group, as its name suggests—chaired by UNIDO leader Salvador Laurel, and the Coalition of Organizations for the Restoration of Democracy (CORD), a rival umbrella group that included among its leaders Agapito Aquino, brother of the late senator, ex-president Diosdado Macapagal, and former senators Jose Diokno, Lorenzo Tañada, and Raul Manglapus. Several of these leaders had smaller umbrella groups of their own. There was, in addition, the August Twenty-One Coordinating Council (ATOCC), designed to coordinate demonstrations by other umbrella groups, a sort of umbrella over other umbrellas. It remained to be seen whether and how these organizations would regroup themselves in the wake of the 1986 election.

Behind this confusing and changing collection of names lies a quite clear and stable tripartite division, reflecting differences in policy and ideology. Fr. Jose Dizon has described the three ideological types as conservative reformist, liberal democrats, and militant progressives. As Dizon put it, they differ "in their perception of the root cause of the present crisis, the manner in which they address the political question, their alternative to dictatorship, and their methods of changing society or liberating the people from the present situation." Thus:

> Conservative reformists and the liberal democrats see the Marcos dictatorship as the root cause of the crisis whereas the militant and progressive groups blame the "US Marcos dictatorship." The conservative reformists address the central political question through peaceful and clean elections, the liberal democrats through active non-violence and the militant progressive groups through militant mass struggle.
>
> The alternative to the dictatorship, according to the conservative reformists, is a return to the 1935 Constitution with the changes in society effected through clean elections. For the liberal democrats, the alternative is a re-

turn to the liberal democratic society and the means is through mass actions as pressure tactics on the dictatorship. For the militant progressives, on the other hand, the alternative to dictatorship is the dismantling of the regime through mass struggles and the establishment of a coalition government through mass undertakings where the people chart their own history.[1]

The main vehicle of the conservative reformists is UNIDO, PDP-Laban. It took part first in the May 1984 elections, and won most of the opposition seats. Its leaders, Corazon Aquino and Salvador Laurel, won the election of February 1986, and now head the new government. The Liberal Democrats are represented mainly by CORD, the successor to the JAJA Movement ("Justice for Aquino, Justice for All"), which boycotted the elections. Many of its sympathizers, however, appear to have gone to the polls at both the 1984 and 1986 elections, and probably voted for UNIDO, PDP-Laban candidates, as a way of registering their opposition to the Marcos government.

The militant progressives, also known as the national democrats, are led by the Communist Party of the Philippines and include its guerrilla force, the New People's Army, and its political front, the National Democratic Front. A new political party, BAYAN, a coalition of mass organizations, also appears to be an instrument of the communists. Initially it included a group led by Agapito Aquino. But that group withdrew when BAYAN's dominance by the Communists became clear. The NDF and Bayan boycotted both the 1984 and 1986 elections, while the NPA attempted to disrupt them by force in some localities. The communist-led groups will be discussed in greater detail below.

As the middle group, the liberal democrats will have to de-

---

[1] Jesselynn Garcia Dela Cruz, "Uneasy Alliance in 'Parliament of the Streets,' " *Philippine News*, October 12-23, 1984, pp. 6-7. From An American policy maker's point of view, the three groups might be designated simply though not inaccurately as the pro-Americans, the noncommunist anti-Americans, and the communist-led group.

cide in the future whether to ally themselves either with the conservative reformers or with the militant progressives, or whether to reject cooperation with both of the other groups. Their decision will have important consequences for the post-Marcos Philippines.

The Student Movement and Philippine Nationalism

A foreign visitor to a Philippine university campus in the early 1950s might have been struck by the seeming lack of student interest in national politics and public affairs. At a time when a communist-led peasant army was at the gates of Manila, students at the University of the Philippines, the country's pace-setting institution of higher learning, were preoccupied with social competition between American-style Greek-letter fraternities and sororities and, secondarily, with the rivalry between the "Greeks" and U.P. Student Catholic Action.

Twenty years later however, in the late 1960s and early 1970s, Manila was in turmoil as radicalized anti-government student demonstrators battled the police. By the close of the Marcos years, a communist-led guerrilla force, created and led by former university instructors and their students, and inspired by the slogans and strategy of Mao Zedong, was gaining ground on the armed forces of the Philippines. Clearly the change in student attitudes has been dramatic. How did it happen?

The politicization and radicalization of university students, and in their wake of students at secondary schools as well, was the result of several intellectual currents, summed up in the 1960s slogan of "opposition to imperialism, feudalism, and fascism." The most important of these three evils, which was seen by the radical spokesmen as the cause of the other two, was imperialism, the enemy of Philippine nationalism.

In an island country marked by strong local and linguistic-regional loyalties and subjected to long periods of foreign colonial rule, nationalism as a call to sacrifice in the name of a higher loyalty has served repeatedly as a powerful spur to collective political action. It inspired the revolution against Spain and then the protracted resistance against America. It was the rallying cry of the country's most effective political party when the electoral arena replaced the battlefield early in the century. It was used to justify both cooperation with and resistance against the Japanese occupation. It continues to be a powerful, indeed an irresistible, force today.

Post-independence nationalism, spearheaded first by the student movement before martial law and then by the militant progressive wing of the opposition, was nourished during the early post-independence years by several grievances against the United States. In the economic sphere, the protest was against the imposition in 1946, as a precondition for the provision of badly needed reconstruction aid to a newly independent but physically devastated country, of the Philippine-U.S. Trade Agreement, which gave parity rights in the exploitation of Philippine natural resources to American citizens and corporations. That imposition and its continuance under the Laurel-Langley Agreement of 1955 left a lasting legacy of nationalistic resentment against the United States among the business community. With the ending of parity in 1974, economic nationalists found a new grievance in the Marcos government's trade liberalization policies which, together with an aggressive effort to attract foreign investors, seemed to threaten the position of the new Filipino manufacturing community.

At the universities, meanwhile, nationalism took the form of a reexamination of Philippine history. Historians, led by Teodoro Agoncillo, directed attention to the part played by nonelite, working class leaders in the revolution against Spain. At the same time, they sought to revise the conventional benign portrayal of the American colonial period by rediscovering atrocities committed by American troops during the early years of the American occupation.

In the cultural sphere, other nationalists, most prominent among them a long-time senator, Claro Recto, and the writer Renato Constantino, described with great eloquence, in their writings in English, the stultifying effect upon the emergence of a genuine Filipino identity of the uncritical acceptance of an alien language, alien ideas, and alien values—an acceptance that, in their view, separated Filipino intellectuals from their own traditions and people.

The capstone of the increasingly strident nationalism that guided the student movement of the 1960s, and that continues to inspire it today, was Marxism. This was not a new ingredient in Philippine thought. But prior to the 1960s its influence among university faculty members and students had been quite limited. During the decade before martial law, however, Marxist thought and membership in communist-led organizations spread rapidly through the universities and colleges. Its most influential instrument for recruitment was the Kabataan Makabayan, or Nationalist Youth, founded in 1964 by Jose Maria Sison, a University of the Philippines instructor who later would emerge, under the pseudonym of Amado Guerrero, as the leader of the Maoist Communist Party of the Philippines. Joined soon by other newly formed student organizations, some founded at Church-related institutions but all strongly nationalistic, the KM became the principal organizer of numerous anti-government and anti-American demonstrations culminating in the "Battle of Mendiola Bridge," an attempt to storm the presidential palace grounds, and in the short-lived Diliman Commune on the campus of the University of the Philippines.

The increasing violence of demonstrations by students, joined by newly radicalized labor unions, was cited by President Marcos as one of his reasons for imposing martial law. That imposition put a temporary end to open student demonstrations, and led to the arrest of many student leaders. Others escaped to the hills, however, where they joined the recently formed New People's Army. As an alternative to the suppressed organizations, the government created its own youth organization, the Kabataan Barangay, which was placed under the leadership of the president's elder daughter, Imee. Modeled upon the Soviet Komsomol and subsidized by the government, it drew its membership mainly from among the children of the poor. Most upper- and middle-class youth, the mainstay of the college population, reacted to martial law by withdrawing from active participation in politics. A small minority, however, maintained the KM as an underground organization.

Student activism began to revive in the mid 1970s with the reemergence of the Kabataan Makabayan. At first the KM limited its public protests to such school-related issues as the rise in college tuition. But a radical activist phalanx was visible at the mass rallies that were held during the 1978 Assembly election campaign. The Aquino assassination fanned the smouldering embers of the movement into a brushfire that came to involve a large number of students. Again there were many different student organizations, but again the radical elements formed the militant core of anti-Marcos student demonstrations.

The history of the radical wing of the student movement merges with that of Philippine communism, a major actor in the current Philippine drama.

The Communist Opposition

Differing from both the conservative reformist and liberal democratic elements of the former moderate opposition are the communist-led militant progressives. After the capture and imprisonment of Communist party chairman Jose Maria Sison some time after the imposition of martial law, and until his release from jail by President Aquino, the Communist party's leadership was almost unknown, which placed it in sharp contrast to its democratic rivals, as well as to the Marcos government. The general public knows of the communist movement mainly by its organizational designations: the New People's Army (NPA), its noncombatant political counterpart, the National Democratic Front (NDF), and the more secretive body which appears to control them both: the Communist Party of the Philippines (CCP).

This revolutionary opposition had no representative in the National Assembly. Its influence was felt not through the pronouncements of well-known public figures but through the military operations of its guerrilla units and through its presence as a disciplined core of the demonstrations that rocked Manila after the Aquino assassination.

Communist-led revolution is not new to the Philippines. The NPA's war against the government was preceded by a similar war, four decades ago. That earlier struggle, the Hukbalahap rebellion of the late 1940s and early 1950s, was confined mainly to the high-tenancy rice-growing plains of central and southern Luzon, and relied almost wholly upon fighters of peasant origin. It began, during the early 1940s, under the leadership of the merged Communist and Socialist parties, as a movement of resistance against the Japanese occupation and, simultaneously, against collaborators among the landowning class. Denied postwar recognition of their contribution to the resistance and deprived of several congressional seats that had been won by their leaders and sympathizers at the 1946 elections, the Huks resumed their military campaign, this time against the new Philippine Republic. By the early 1950s they had become a serious threat to the state.

The tide was turned against the Huks by Ramon Magsaysay, a young member of Congress who had been appointed secretary of national defense, and then in 1953 was elected to the presidency. Magsaysay's strategy of "all out force and all out friendship" combined the use of concentrated military power against Hukbalahap strongholds in central Luzon with positive inducements in the form of offers of frontier homesteads for surrendered Huks, a program of rural improvements, and promises of land reform. A not insignificant contributor to the collapse of the Hukbalahap rebellion was the charismatic populist president's immense personal appeal to the common man. By the early 1950s, even before the Philippine Congress had emasculated Magsaysay's land reform proposals, many of the party's leaders had been captured, had surrendered, or were weakened by internal division. Most Hukbalahap units had been disbanded, some had degenerated into bands of armed rural racketeers, and only a few continued to fight against the government. By 1954 the old pro-Moscow leadership of the Partido Komunista ng Philipinas (PKP) had abandoned revolution for parliamentary struggle. In 1974, some of the remaining older leaders formally surrendered to President Marcos. A few of them served in his government.

The New People's Army rebellion was begun by a younger group of communist intellectuals, most of them products of the University of the Philippines. These broke with the PKP's older leadership, and in December 1968 founded a new Communist Party of the Philippines (CPP). Looking to Peking instead of to Moscow for doctrinal guidance, they returned to a strategy of armed struggle, but with major modifications. Their New People's Army, organized early in 1969, three years before Marcos imposed martial law, had guerrilla units in a large majority of the country's provinces, usually based in their more isolated, forested and mountainous regions, by mid-1985. In addition, the CCP, through the National Democratic Front that it organized in 1973, created a complex structure of supporting organizations operating openly and underground in the archipelago's major towns and cities. Their long-term strategy follows that devised by Mao Zedong: to build up military strength in the countryside in preparation for an assault on the cities, where the NDF stands ready to join in the final battle to take power. The method to be used for taking control of the cities was developed in Davao City in Mindanao, where "armed city partisans," that is, assassination squads of the NPA, took control of many squatter areas away from the police. In 1985, the organization of similar units in Manila was reported to be under way.

With their slogan, an end to the "U.S.-Marcos dictatorship," the CCP, NPA, and NDF built a much broader constituency than did the mainly peasant Hukbalahap. Their appeal was directed to all who opposed the Marcos government and who despaired of ousting it by peaceful electoral means. It was directed also to those who attributed Marcos' survival to the support of the American government and who blamed their country's many other problems on the continuing American military and economic presence. Their willingness to risk their lives against the forces of an unpopular ruler and their strident nationalism struck a deep chord among a people who admire bravery and patriotism. Their leaders appear, however, to be committed to dogmatic Marxism-Leninism-Maoism. Their guerrilla units, according to a reporter who has spent some time with them, have probably killed more civilians over the last five years than have the government's armed forces.[2]

Essential to understanding the rapid growth of the post-1960s communist movement is the fact that it has been led at all levels by members of the educated class, that is, by university-trained instructors and their students. This gives the new movement a great advantage over its Hukbalahap predecessor, and makes it a more threatening opponent for the government. Whereas support for the Huks was confined mainly to central Luzon, the present movement's Manila-educated, middle-class core enabled it to form a nationwide organization with surprising speed. During the mid-1960s, Kabataan Makabayan members from many parts of the country were spending their school vacations away from Manila, indoctrinating peasants in their respective home provinces. The formation in the same provinces of NPA units after 1969 was a relatively easy further step.

In a country where in the past all types of nationwide coordinated action were plagued by the divisiveness of regional loyalties and interests, a sophisticated, Manila-educated leadership, commanding separate units in widely scattered islands, has been able to adapt itself to the need for tactical and operational decentralization without sacrificing unity in its strategy for the long-term struggle. To assure coordinated action, non-combatant middle-class sympathizers, traveling between the islands, provide communication links for the NPA. Finally, an articulate phalanx of intellectuals serve as propagandists for the revolution both in the Philippines and abroad.

The heavy involvement in the communist movement of members of the educated middle and upper classes also has given that movement invaluable connections with the Philippine elite. Many upper-class families still have younger members fighting in the hills. Others have seen their children im-

[2] Ross H. Munro, "Dateline Manila: Moscos's Next Win?" *Foreign Policy*, No. 56 (Fall 1984), p. 184.

prisoned, tortured, or killed by the armed forces. In such families political loyalties, if not leaning toward to the NPA, at least are divided. From such families and their friends have come material aid and protection, as well as the increasingly widespread view among the upper classes that the NPA are not subversives but patriots who deserve the nation's gratitude for having been the only effective opponents of the Marcos government. In this respect too, the communist movement during the Marcos years had advantages not possessed by its Hukbalahap predecessors.

No Marxist-inspired revolution can justify itself, however, if it does not rely heavily on the peasant and working classes whose interests it professes to serve. The middle-class leadership of the party has been effective in organizing peasants, trade unionists, and the urban poor, and in coopting self-made leaders of such groups who achieved prominence before joining the movement. It may continue to do so unless the new Aquino government can improve the living conditions of these groups.

To win support among the lower income strata, the communist movement appealed to a wide variety of grievances, many of them of a specifically regional character. The old Hukbalahap movement, originating in a region distinguished by its high rate of agricultural tenancy, relied heavily on promises of land distribution. The Marcos administration's land reform measures and its programs of rural development in the rice- and corn-growing regions defused land reform as an overriding issue in these regions. There instead, the NPA has appealed with particular success to the increasing number of rural unemployed youth who, because of the growing population, had no access to agricultural land, either as owners or even as tenants.

In the highlands of the interior and in the frontier regions of the outlying islands, the NPA has offered arms, training, and leadership to tribal peoples or settlers who have lost their land to logging concessionaires, agri-business developers, or to the government's hydroelectric projects. In the cities the movement has appealed to the many squatters who lost their homes to make way for the government's urban redevelopment projects. Among labor, the movement's organizational efforts benefited from the no-strike, low-wage policies adopted by the Marcos government as a part of its effort to achieve greater export competitiveness. In addition, the NPA found considerable support among those who were alienated by the abuses of governmental power that were made possible by Marcos' removal of checks that predated martial law and a then omnipotent civil and military governmental establishment.

The advantages that the communist movement derived from its modern, middle-class leadership were made all the greater by certain premodern traits of the Marcos regime. After 1972, that regime relied increasingly upon what, by contrast with the Marxists, were quite traditional values, incentives, and methods of rule. Though effective in keeping Marcos in power, these characteristics of his regime tended to undermine its ability to achieve a precondition for effective government: the sympathy of the general public. The problem was especially serious for the military.

The Armed Forces as Political Actors

It has been said of the Indian army that it is "the only institution in the country to have transcended corruption, political meddling, and feudal disputes." This has made it "a bulwark of Indian democracy." Thus it could "be called upon to settle or oversee the resolution of civilian political crises."[3]

That, unfortunately, could not be said of the Philippine military under Marcos. Yet until he assumed the presidency, and to some degree until the imposition of martial law, the Philippine military played an essentially nonpolitical role. Modeled upon the American armed forces, with many of its older officers trained at American service academies, it was accustomed to being the nonpartisan subordinate of successive civilian

[3] Mary Anne Weaver, "Rajiv Gandhi Faces Daunting Task," *The Christian Science Monitor*, November 2, 1984, p. 36.

governments under the alternate control of one political party and one elected president or another.

True, before martial law the military were not totally isolated from politics. Officers who hoped for advancement to the rank of full colonel and above were obliged to curry favor with the congressional Commission on Appointments, an offense to their pride and sense of professionalism that is still remembered with bitterness by older officers. And officers of the Philippine Constabulary, a separate branch of the armed forces created in American colonial times as a national rural police force, usually found it necessary to develop close ties with town mayors and provincial governors. To limit their involvement in local electoral politics, the then nonpartisan Commission on Elections, which was empowered to take control of the Constabulary at election time, could transfer such officers temporarily to other provinces. Finally, most Philippine presidents, even before Marcos, gave certain key posts, notably the position of Chief of Staff, to officers in whom they could place special trust, which usually meant officers from their home region or province. On the whole, however, before martial law the officer corps saw itself as the nonpolitical servant of the nation and not as the partisan of any president or political party. It had little respect for those of its members who allowed themselves to become involved in local politics. This helps to explain the low esteem in which the Constabulary was held by other branches of the service.

The role of the military changed fundamentally under President Marcos, who was himself once an ROTC officer and an anti-Japanese guerrilla. During his first two terms as elected chief of state, some critics began to express alarm at Marcos' tendency to give undue preference in promotions to officers from his home Ilocos region and at his unprecedented generosity to the armed forces. The decision to impose martial law, taken some time before the events that served as its pretext, was made with the agreement and participation of a group of the president's senior officers. Only one officer, General Rafael Ileto, opposed that move. He was soon exiled to a diplomatic post abroad. He has now returned as deputy minister of defense in the Aquino government.

After 1972, the military became an active, privileged, and essential bulwark of the Marcos government. They increased from a force of 54,000 to almost three times that number. With their growth came rapid promotions, pay increases, generous opportunities for outside and post-retirement incomes—both legal and extra-legal—and the assumption by the military of numerous previously civilian functions. In the provinces, military commanders replaced mayors and governors as the principal holders of power.

The post-1972 years led to a continuing "Ilocanization" of the officer corps, especially at its high levels, as well as to a special reliance on Ilocano enlisted men. Most heavily infused with Ilocanos were the security and intelligence forces based in or near Manila. These were composed of the Presidential Security Command (PSC) of some 15,000 men, including the Presidential Guard Battalion, of the National Intelligence and Security Authority (NISA), the Metropolitan command of the Philippine Constabulary (METROCOM), the Manila unit of the Integrated National Police, and the 2nd Army Division.[4] This massive concentration of forces in or near the national capital was designed to provide absolute security for the presidential family and for other members of the regime. It was created by and remained under the direct control of General Fabian Ver, who after 1981 was also the armed forces chief of staff. The officers of the Presidential Security Command swore personal loyalty to the president and then to General Ver. They formed a privileged elite within the armed forces. Some were assigned temporarily to other units, where they served as the eyes and ears of the president. It was one of the remarkable aspects of the February 1986 military revolt that this powerful force of presumed Marcos loyalists failed to save him.

The Marcos years brought changes not only in the size and

[4] Larry A. Niksch, "The Armed Forces of the Asia-Pacific Region, The Philippines: Uncertainties After the Aquino Assassination," *Pacific Defence Reporter*, February 1984, pp. 22-23.

structure of the armed forces but also in their values and behavior. These changes were apparent especially among the security forces. The rise to dominance of personnel from the
president's home region was but one example of a growing
tendency to make assignments and promotions not on the basis of competence or seniority but of favoritism, personal loyalty, and familial connections. Loyalty in turn was rewarded
by a growing tolerance of corruption, of the arbitrary use of
power, and of other abuses. There was, in short, an increased
reliance on primordial ties and traditional incentives rather
than on the rewards commonly associated with military
professionalism. Although this use of traditional incentives
undoubtedly cemented the loyalty of its beneficiaries to the regime, it also contributed mightily to the loss of public respect
for the military.

In the countryside away from greater Manila, the armed
forces face an increasingly serious problem of internal defense.
The growth of the NPA, the source of the most threatening insurgency, has been discussed. A serious threat during the early
martial-law years came from a quite different rebellion, one
from within the Muslim minority of the large southern island
of Mindanao and of the smaller Sulu island chain. The Muslim
rebellion was a probably inevitable reaction to the southward
migration of Christian Filipino settlers, which threatens to
turn Muslims into a minority in their own homeland. For a
time the "Moro" rebellion, which received outside assistance
from Libya by way of Eastern Malaysia, occupied most of the
attention of the anti-insurgency forces. The Moro rebellion
now appears to be on the wane, but the growing strength of the
NPA in Mindanao has more than replaced it as a challenge to
the armed forces of the Philippines.

Under Marcos, the government's prospects of halting the
growth of the NPA, let alone of defeating it decisively, did not
seem promising. Under President Aquino, these prospects have
improved to some degree, but the NPA remains a serious
threat. In contrast to the situation in the 1950s, the military
now face not a peasant army confined to a densely inhabited
plain where they could be overwhelmed by concentrated gov-

ernment forces, but numerous bands of highly mobile guerrilla units operating in difficult highland and forested terrain among a friendly—or intimidated—population. The NPA's opportunities for attack and retreat are limitless. Their communication system in the field appears to be equal, if not superior, to that of the armed forces.

The Philippine military under Marcos thus suffered from a schizophrenia induced by two very different missions: to support and defend the Marcos regime, and to protect the nation against external and domestic armed threats. This schizophrenia was reflected at the level of organization and on the ground, as well as in the social and prestige structures of the military establishment. Regime support was the task of various elite units concentrated in the environs of Manila. These units were composed largely of Ilocanos. They provided the most attractive career opportunities for their rank and file. For advancement to their highest levels, absolute personal loyalty to the president and to General Ver were the principal prerequisites.

National defense, on the other hand, remained the primary function of the forces outside Manila: the Navy, the Air Force, and the many small units assigned to the frustrating and life-threatening task of combating the communist and Muslim insurgencies. Assigned to these duties in Marcos' time were officers and soldiers deemed least suitable for the task of regime maintenance: that is, non-Ilocanos and officers of uncertain loyalty to the president, as well as junior officers who had yet to win their spurs. Their life was unpleasant and their rewards were meager, unless they were willing to live off the land. They saw themselves inadequately supplied because equipment purchased for them had been sold off to enrich their superior officers, and sometimes found their paychecks delayed. They took the brunt of civilian dislike of a government that in NPA-infested areas had lost much of its popularity to the military's guerrilla opponents.

Among the junior officers of these units, there grew up between 1981 and 1982 a Reform the Armed Forces Movement (RAM), also called "We Belong," which hoped to restore professionalism within, and public respect for, the armed forces by bringing nonprofessional behavior of their colleagues and their superiors to the attention of the president. RAM was to play a significant role in the downfall of the Marcos regime.

Elections under the Marcos Dictatorship

During the first few years of martial law, Marcos ruled alone, unimpeded by a legislature. From the outset, however, he had promised to recreate a legislative body in due time. That promise was made good to some degree in 1978, when the president called national elections for an "Interim National Assembly." Though endowed with less power to check the president than the pre-1972 Philippine Congress, the new Assembly did represent a cautious step towards a return to normalcy. But conducted at a time when martial law inhibited the campaign activity of opposition candidates and their followers, when the media and the Commission on Elections were wholly controlled and used in its own behalf by the Marcos administration, and while the economy remained relatively sound, the elections brought the opposition only thirteen Assembly seats.

Buoyed by his party's sweep of the Assembly elections, Marcos in 1981 sought a new mandate for his own rule by holding presidential elections, the first since 1969. But convinced that these elections would be no more free or fair than those of 1978 or than the several national referenda that had been held by Marcos in preceding years, all major opposition groups agreed among themselves to field no candidate against the president. As a result, Marcos was reelected virtually unopposed.

Had the Aquino assassination not intervened, the next Assembly elections, in May 1984, might have been a replay of the elections of 1978 or 1981. Most, if not all, opposition groups would have refused to run candidates. Aquino's murder, however, changed the political climate. Filipinos of all social classes were in the streets in a virtually continuous round of demonstrations. The 1984 Assembly elections seemed to offer an opportunity to register a desire for political change that actually could affect the process of government.

Since 1978, furthermore, there had been a substantial loosening of the administration's controls over the channels of mass communication. Several opposition newspapers now were sold openly, and their sales had cut significantly into the circulation of the pro-administration press. Radio Veritas, the station of the Catholic Church, now provided nonofficial and largely pro-opposition information. Finally, the American government, disturbed by the economic and political effects of the Aquino assassination and convinced of the need for a restoration of an open, that is, freely competitive, political system, was pressing Marcos, both publicly and privately, to make the 1984 elections "free, fair, and honest."

Opposition parties were divided over whether to take part in the new elections or to repeat their 1981 boycott. UNIDO, PDP-Laban (the conservative reformist coalition) decided to run a slate of candidates. The JAJA movement, then the main vehicle of the liberal democrats, chose to boycott. A boycott also was urged by the militant progressive National Democratic Front, while the New Peoples Army attempted to disrupt the elections in some localities.

Neither the call for a boycott nor forceful disruption achieved its announced goals. An estimated 80 percent of eligible voters cast ballots.[5] But the boycott helped the opposition in a perhaps unintended way: by not running candidates, the liberal democrats avoided creating an electoral rivalry between the two major democratic opposition groups, with the result that a single major opposition candidate usually confronted each candidate of the president's KBL party.

An essential part in making the 1984 elections cleaner than the preceding ones was that played by the National Movement for Free Elections (NAMFREL), a citizens' organization harking back to the time of President Magsaysay. NAMFREL's

---

[5] Marjorie Niehaus, "Philippines in Turmoil: Implications for U.S. Policy," Issue Brief No. IB84113, Library of Congress Congressional Research Service, August 20, 1984, p. 2.

chairman, businessman Jose Concepcion, supported by the opposition leadership and by quiet pressure on Marcos from the American Embassy, persuaded the government to introduce various changes in the election procedures designed to lessen the chances of "election anomalies."

These changes did not go as far as the opposition had hoped, but they made the elections cleaner than those of 1978. On and after election day, NAMFREL mobilized some 200,000 volunteer poll watchers to monitor the casting and counting of the votes as well as the reporting of the final results. Undoubtedly, NAMFREL's presence made a difference, though not as great a one as had been hoped. Early partial returns showed the opposition leading in more contests than did the final returns. This could be attributed to last-minute "cooking" of the results at COMELEC, or to the fact that the later returns came from outlying areas where NAMFREL was least likely to have an effective representation. According to its chairman, where NAMFREL was present, the opposition usually won. Where it was absent, the victory usually went to administration candidates.

Even so, the election results came as a surprise to many observers. The president had predicted that his opponents would win no more than 20 seats. For a time it appeared that the opposition might capture close to half the 181 elective Assembly seats. The final results, which in the opposition's opinion were alarmingly delayed, gave the opposition 59 elected seats to 122 for the president's supporters. An additional 17 seats in the Assembly were appointive ones, filled by persons selected by the president. After the elections, Marcos reportedly toyed briefly with the idea of adding some more appointive seats, but then thought better of it. In any case, the opposition's share of the seats fell short of the 33 percent needed to file an impeachment motion against the president—which had been one of its announced goals. Such a motion, duly filed in August 1985, failed to get out of committee. In a sense, both sides won the 1984 elections. The president still controlled the legislature. The opposition's showing, however, convinced most Filipinos as well as foreign observers that the opposition, rather than the administration, was the real choice of the electorate.

The End of the Marcos Era

In February 1986, momentous events changed the Philippine political landscape. The murdered Benigno Aquino achieved a victory denied him in life: his widow Corazon became president of the Philippines, while his rival, Ferdinand Marcos, took refuge in disgrace in the United States.

Continued decline in the Philippine economy, the unrelenting growth of the communist insurgency, and increased American pressure for reforms had led Marcos to call a "snap" presidential election for February 7, 1986. Cheered by partial success at the 1984 Assembly elections, and urged on by the fear that this was its last chance to unseat Marcos before the initiative passed to the communists, the democratic opposition decided to contest the elections with presidential and vice-presidential candidates of its own: PDP-Laban member Corazon Aquino and UNIDO leader Salvador Laurel.

Among Mrs. Aquino's effective supporters during her campaign were large numbers of men and women of the middle and upper classes who had been politicized by the Aquino assassination. Some contributed by participating in her campaign staff. Many more—some 400,000 on election day—were volunteer workers in the nominally nonpartisan but clearly pro-opposition NAMFREL. Although only partly successful in guarding the balloting process against massive pro-Marcos fraud, NAMFREL nonetheless won widespread domestic and foreign recognition for the accuracy of its count and for the detailed nature of its reports of fraud.

The Catholic Church, too, played a major role as an ill-disguised ally of the opposition candidates. It was Cardinal Sin himself who persuaded Corazon Aquino to join forces with Salvador Laurel, and who persuaded Laurel to accept second place on their joint ticket. It was Catholic laymen and women, and priests and nuns, who provided the bulk of NAMFREL's volunteers and leaders. It was the Church's radio station, and the Bishops' pastoral letters, read in all Philippine Catholic churches, that broke the government's monopoly of mass communication. Finally, it was Cardinal Sin who mobilized "people power"—the human barrier that protected the military insurgents from the superior firepower of the president's loyalist armed forces.

The military, so favored by Marcos, proved in the end to be undependable. The growing rift within the armed forces between defenders of the regime and protectors of the nation came to be the president's undoing. Marcos' post-election move to arrest members of the reform movement—including their patrons, Defense Minister Juan Ponce Enrile and General Fidel Ramos—provoked a preemptive and successful revolt. Marcos loyalists, faced with a choice between crushing the barrier of "people power" and defying the orders of their chief, chose not to move. Within four days, Marcos' military defenses had crumbled and he was on his way to Guam.

Although political parties may change their names and enter into new alliances, the tripartite division among the conservative reformists, the liberal democrats, and the national democrats will endure. Thus, Corazon Aquino and Salvador Laurel, as leaders of the conservative reformists, will need to contend with the more nationalistic and social reformist elements of the democratic opposition, who did not run candidates in the elections of 1984 and 1986, and thus were not represented among the elected members of either the executive or legislative branches of government in the immediate post-Marcos period. Still, a few were appointed to the Aquino cabinet. Some of these, or others of similar political persuasion, are likely in time to form a second major party that may challenge Mrs. Aquino's government. That would restore a two-party system, one with more distinctive parties than those of the pre-martial-law period, that is, one party of the moderate right and one of the moderate left.

While Catholic students were active in supporting the Aquino-Laurel candidacies and in working with NAMFREL, the more radical student members of the Kabataan Makabayan sat out the presidential elections. One may expect, however, that they will assert themselves as an active political force in attacking those policies of the new government that appear to violate the radical agenda of nationalist and social reform. Their presence, together with that of their allies in the labor movement, is likely to make itself felt in street demonstrations.

The Communist Party of the Philippines and its various front organizations also played no part in the Aquino-Laurel victory. Indeed, Mrs. Aquino declined their offers of help. Having won, she reached out to the communists with an offer of reconciliation, on condition that they lay down their arms and enter the electoral arena as a nonrevolutionary political party. The prospects for that seem unpromising. Having come within a few years of bringing the Philippine army to a stalemate in combat, the NPA is not likely to give up its military gains in return for the uncertain prospects of electoral competition against a popular new president. More likely, it will keep its guerrilla forces intact while lending electoral support to liberal democratic candidates.

Having offered reconciliation to the New People's Army, President Aquino will be better able than her predecessor to deal with its military challenge. Her chances of reducing the NPA threat will also depend on her ability to give the country not only renewed economic growth and restored civil rights, but also a sense of moving toward social justice.

CHAPTER VI

THE ECONOMIC CRISIS

BERNARDO VILLEGAS

The Philippine economy was one of the worst victims of the world recession that resulted from the second oil shock in 1979. Faced with increased costs of oil imports, declining world prices of its major export crops, and a steep rise in the interest on its foreign borrowings, the country experienced its worst balance of payments crisis at the end of 1982.

Before the Philippines could respond favorably to the economic recovery in 1983 of its major trading partner—the United States—the country suffered great political turbulence when former Senator Benigno Aquino was assassinated on August 21, 1983. The ensuing social turmoil caused a massive capital flight that drained the country's already meager international reserves. In October 1983, the government announced that it could not pay its foreign debts and asked for a moratorium from some 483 creditors. The debt crisis stopped the flow of trade credit of over $3 billion, causing a huge drop in imports. For all of 1984, the country had barely enough foreign exchange to import oil and food. The gross national product declined for the first time since the end of the Second World War.

Even the usually deodorized figures coming from the government described a grim picture at the end of 1984: the gross national product dropped by 5.3 percent; inflation averaged 50 percent for the year; and the underemployment rate rose to 36.5 percent of the labor force. The Center for Research and Communication reported a decline in industrial production of 20 percent and mass layoffs of more than 400,000 workers in 1984. The durable goods industries suffered the worst fate: volume declines of 50-70 percent were common in such industries as car assembly and appliances. Investment dropped by

more than 30 percent in 1984. The gravity of the crisis can be
better appreciated if one considers that in the 1970s, the Philippine economy posted an annual rate of growth in GNP of
about 6 percent; average inflation was about 14 percent per
annum; the rate of underemployment (more meaningful than
the unemployment rate in a Third World economy) was only a
little over 10 percent; industrial production grew at an average
of 8 percent per annum; and investment expenditures posted a
yearly increase of about 10 percent.

The Philippine economy went into a tailspin in 1984 as a result of a severe foreign exchange crisis that lasted through a series of debt moratoria from October 1983 to May 1985. It
took that long for the Philippines to come to terms with its 483
creditors on a debt rescheduling and credit package that involved $12 billion (out of a total of $26 billion of foreign
debt), even though the IMF had given the Philippines its much-
coveted "seal of good housekeeping" by late November 1984.
The final package called for a formal rescheduling over ten
years of $5.77 billion of foreign debt (including $1.1 billion
from bilateral public lenders), the reactivation of about $3 bil-
lion in trade credits from commercial banks that dried up in
October 1983, and the granting of $925 million in new com-
mercial bank credits.

Furthermore, new official development assistance (ODA) of
about US$2.5 billion would be required to help finance the ex-
pected resources gap during the program period. A January
1985 meeting of the Consultative Group for the Philippines
(the twenty-one "Paris Club" member countries plus the
World Bank, the Asian Development Bank, and other multilateral lenders) decided on this fresh ODA.

Missed Opportunities

Under more normal political circumstances, the debt rescheduling could have been completed as early as March 1984, as
some members of the twelve-bank Advisory Group for the
Philippines had anticipated early in 1984. The Philippines was
no tyro in dealing with the IMF, having signed seventeen

standby credit agreements since 1962. Besides, as an econometric model developed by Dr. Vaughn Montes of the Center for Research and Communication showed through a statistical simulation, the economic fundamentals were such that, without the acute political crisis, the IMF and the commercial creditors would readily have agreed to a debt rescheduling.[1] Just a month before the assassination of former Senator Benigno Aquino, the World Bank issued an annual report in which the Philippines was classified as a newly industrializing nation, along with South Korea and Thailand. The Bank attributed most of the difficulties encountered by the Philippines in the early 1980s to "the sharply deteriorating external environment." The Bank openly complimented the Philippines in the following words: "Despite the difficulties, the Philippines has embarked on a program of needed structural changes. The program includes measures of energy conservation and self-sufficiency, industrial restructuring, poverty alleviation and human resource development."[2]

Without the total collapse of investor confidence precipitated by the Aquino assassination and the ensuing political turmoil, the balance of payments problem would have been under control by the end of 1984. One need only reflect on the tremendous opportunities the Philippines missed by not being able to expand significantly its nontraditional exports to the booming U.S. economy—which registered in 1984 its highest rate of growth in GNP in thirty years. By the end of 1982, a full 60 percent of Philippine commodity exports was accounted for by semiconductor components, garments, finished wood products, houseware and giftware, leather goods and footwear, and a host of nontraditional fresh and processed food products, such as shrimp and mangoes. It would not have been impossible for Philippine exports to have grown by more than 20 percent in 1984—instead of the paltry 6 percent they registered because of the loss of business confidence and the ensuing pa-

[1] Center for Research and Communication, *1985: More of the Same?* (Manila, December 1984).
[2] World Bank, *Annual Report: 1983.*

ralysis in foreign trade. Keen interest was shown in the Philippines by investors in semiconductors, garments, and other export-oriented industries just before the Aquino assassination. The export growth of Taiwan, Hong Kong, South Korea, Malaysia, and even Indonesia ranged from 20 percent to 40 percent in 1984. And the Philippine economy used to be one of the most responsive in the region to a U.S. economic recovery.

The Causes of Delay

The negotiations with the IMF and the 483 creditor banks took more than a year to complete because of a serious credibility crisis suffered by the Marcos government. Almost from the very start of the debt moratorium, the IMF and the creditors had valid reasons to doubt the sincerity of the Philippine government in complying with the austerity measures that would be necessitated by the economic adjustment program.

In the last quarter of 1983, the international financial world was shocked by the revelation that Philippine government officials had overstated the country's national reserves by $600 million. To this insult was added the injury of a large jump in money supply during the same period. The amount of money in circulation and in demand deposits increased by an unprecedented rate of 38 percent. Although the explanation given was not totally unreasonable (that the government had to prevent a total collapse of the financial system by pouring massive doses of funds into distressed firms and financial institutions), it revealed to the outside world the very precarious state of an economy strewn with moribund industrial firms (such as the Marinduque Mining Corporation and the Construction Development Corporation of the Philippines), many of which are large dollar debtors.

To make matters worse, the government threw caution to the winds during the months preceding the National Assembly elections of May 1984. Fearing a strong anti-Marcos feeling among the population as a result of the protest moves that mounted after the Aquino assassination, the government pumped some P5 billion into the economy in the form of election-related spending activities. Too late were the words of caution of the governor of the Central Bank in his first quarter report, which indirectly acknowledged the undesirable increase in government borrowing: "An equally important policy objective should be the appropriate distribution of credit between the private and public sectors. The experience in the last quarter requires the establishment of appropriate controls over the disbursement mechanisms of the National Government if we are not to witness a continuance of the crowding out effect on the private sector in a rigidly enforced monetary program."[3]

The excess liquidity issue was a cause célèbre in June of 1984. Even the president himself admitted that there was an urgent need to "mop up excess liquidity" as a "prior action" requirement for the IMF stamp of approval. Also unpalatable to the IMF authorities was the continued overvaluation of the Philippine currency, which was fixed at P14 to $1 when the free market rate was closer to P20 to $1. It took several more months for a truly floating rate to prevail, even after another devaluation in early June 1984 brought the official "guiding" rate to P18 to $1. This partial devaluation move established a de facto multi-tier system: a black-market rate (at about P22 to $1); a P18 to $1 rate for government priority imports such as oil products, food, and fertilizer; and a P19.80 to $1 rate for service payments that were subject to 10 percent excise tax for all foreign exchange sold for reasons other than financing merchandise exports.

Another unfortunate incident occurred in July of 1984. The biggest savings bank in the country, Banco Filipino, faced serious liquidity problems. Instead of allowing the monetary authorities to institute disciplinary measures, President Marcos pressured Central Bank Governor Fernandez into bailing out the bank. Such a politically inspired move (the owners of the Bank had special connections with Malacañang) once again

---

[3] Governor of the Central Bank, *Report to the President: First Quarter 1984*. (Mimeo).

pumped excessive amounts into the money supply, causing yet another delay in IMF approval.

Toward the last quarter of 1984, Central Bank Governor "Jobo" Fernandez was generally free from political pressures and was able to put some order into the Philippine monetary system. Through the issuance of Central Bank notes (aptly termed "Jobo bills"), the monetary authorities succeeded in mopping up excess liquidity. The whole economy, however, had to pay a high price for monetary discipline: interest rates skyrocketed to levels exceeding 50 percent. Even relatively healthy industrial firms were on the brink of financial collapse because of the high cost of money.

As the economy continued to drop precipitously as a result of the delays in debt rescheduling, the politicians were forced to allow the government officials concerned more elbow room in complying with the IMF conditions related to monetary and fiscal discipline, as well as market-oriented reforms (such as the dismantling of the sugar, coconut, and grains monopolies). To use a graphic description by Governor Fernandez himself, the Philippine monetary authorities were preoccupied with preparing a launching pad, with the Philippine economy representing the vehicle to be launched, and the arrangements that had been made with domestic institutions and external organizations representing the closure of leaking valves that would otherwise endanger the launch. At least for the time being, the politicians refrained from producing more leaks.

During the last month of 1984, speculation about the deteriorating health of President Marcos and the lack of a credible system of succession threatened to derail once again the debt-rescheduling agreements. However, as the president's health bounced back, fears about a chaotic political environment started to subside during the first weeks of 1985. The debt rescheduling package was eventually finalized in May of 1985.

The Remote Causes

It is not hard to identify the immediate cause of the 1984 economic crisis experienced by the Philippines. The national trauma was obviously caused by the brutal slaying of Benigno Aquino. But as a group of economists from the University of the Philippines concluded in a widely read "white paper" on the economic crisis, the Aquino assassination "simply tore the already weakened fabric of the economy."[4] Although I believe that the fabric was not beyond repair in mid-1983 because of the booming market for nontraditional exports and the political reforms initiated during the first half of the year, it would be instructive to identify the more remote causes of the crisis.

The weakness of the fabric can be traced back to the 1950s, when government policy makers decided to focus on an import-substitution path to industrialization. Through a host of monetary, fiscal, and trade policies, the country's financial, technical, and managerial resources were concentrated on industries that merely processed or assembled raw materials and supplies imported from abroad. The import-substitution strategy accomplished its goal with great efficiency: the manufacturing sector grew at a rate of 12 percent per annum in the 1950s, transforming the Philippines into the most developed and industrialized economy in Southeast Asia by the early 1960s. Its GDP per capita grew at a robust rate of 3.6 percent per annum during the 1950s, compared to 1.3 percent of Singapore, 1.0 percent of Malaysia, 2.8 percent of Thailand, and 1.9 percent of Indonesia. Its per capita income growth was faster even than that of South Korea, which was just recovering from the Korean War.

The fundamental flaw in the development strategy of the fifties was the neglect of agricultural development. The emphasis on import substitution distracted national leaders from the urgent task of improving agricultural productivity, especially in such food crops as rice and corn. Even traditional export crops such as sugar and coconut suffered a continuous decline in farm productivity. Export volume was increased primarily through the expansion of acreage rather than through improvements in yield. Whereas the present-day strength of the

[4] University of the Philippines, School of Economics, *An Analysis of the Philippine Economic Crisis: A Workshop Report* (June 1984).

economies of Taiwan, Thailand, and Malaysia can be attributed largely to their having laid a solid foundation in rural and agricultural development early in the years following the Second World War, Philippine leaders waited for more than a quarter of a century after the war before taking serious measures to improve agricultural productivity.

The emphasis on import substitution at the beginning of Philippine efforts to industrialize was not an altogether unenlightened policy. It must be remembered that today's "tiger economies" (Hong Kong, Taiwan, South Korea, and Singapore) also started off in this way. However, in less than a decade these countries were able to dismantle their protective barriers and aggressively launch export-oriented industries. Almost overnight, the East Asian countries that succeeded in veering away from import substitution and toward an export orientation overtook the Philippines in per capita income growth during the sixties. By the end of the sixties, the Philippines had the slowest growing economy in the Asia Pacific region.

Understanding the Policy Errors

Why the Philippines lingered so long with an inwardly oriented industrialization program can be traced in part to its having been colonized first by Spain for close to four hundred years, and by the United States for over forty years before it became the first country in Asia to obtain independence in 1946. Because of rich agricultural and forest resources, the Philippine economy managed to finance its imports through the export of such products as sugar, abaca, coconut, timber, and other resource-based raw materials. Under the colonial rulers, the country introduced a relatively modern plantation sector side by side with primitive peasant agriculture, thus creating the base for the technological and economic dualism that has been the bane of the countryside since at least the 1930s.

It is especially instructive to examine the contrast presented by the colonial experiences of Korea and Formosa (now Taiwan) with Japan and those of the Philippines with its two colonial masters. As colonies of Japan, these two East Asian countries saw the introduction of small-scale intensive agriculture in the production of food crops in which the Japanese were highly interested for export to their home markets. As a result, the Japanese helped to improve the productivity of peasant agriculture in Korea and Taiwan during the years immediately preceding the Second World War. Except for a small Japanese presence (for espionage purposes) in some farms in Mindanao during the prewar days, the Philippines did not benefit from this early case of the transfer of appropriate technology.

However, the burden of an inefficient agricultural sector was hardly felt by the Philippine economy during the early years of the Republic. First, because of a free-trade relationship with the United States that lasted until 1974, the country had easy access to cheap food imports, particularly because the exchange rate was fixed at P2 to $1 until President Macapagal devalued the peso in 1962. Furthermore, with a relatively low population-to-land ratio in the fifties, there was ample room to expand coconut and sugar production for export without any improvement in farm productivity. There was also wanton destruction of forest resources through indiscriminate logging—which was a substantial source of foreign exchange earnings for at least thirty years after the war.

The lack of interest in improving peasant agriculture was aggravated by a pricing policy that was biased against the farmers in the short-sighted desire to provide urban consumers with cheap food and thus keep industrial wages down. This policy to control the prices of foodstuffs lasted almost until the 1980s. Although it may be cold comfort, this policy error has been a common trap into which many Third World countries have fallen.

Lack of Political Will

For a brief moment in 1962, there was some expectation that the Philippine economy was moving toward an export-oriented industrial strategy when the Philippine peso was devalued by almost 100 percent. After witnessing several years of

massive balance of payments deficits, President Diosdado Macapagal realized that the Philippine peso was significantly
overvalued. While the appetite of Philippine industries for imported raw materials was increasingly voracious, there was
less room for expansion of land devoted to the traditional export crops. Thus there lingered the hope that a sufficiently
massive devaluation would dampen imports and boost exports.

Unfortunately, the government leaders of the time did not
have the political will to dismantle the heavy tariff protection
that Philippine industries still enjoyed. The favorable effects of
a devaluation on the export sector were significantly counter-
acted by a tariff system that still highly favored the import-
substituting industries and discouraged manufactured exports. This ambivalent policy would last till the late 1970s.
Even the authoritarian regime that President Marcos introduced in 1972 took almost eight years to open the Philippine
economy to the international economy. As late as 1979, the
average protection rate of Philippine industry was 36 percent,
as compared to less than 10 percent in the East Asian region.
Manufacturing enjoyed an effective protection of 44 percent.

It also took almost two decades before the Philippine economy could remove the bias against labor-intensive industries
that was built into a low-interest regime. Interest rates were
kept at artificially low levels by government edict. Many of the
import-substituting industries benefited from the availability
of cheap capital, and, therefore, had the incentive to adopt
capital-intensive technologies. In sum, the foreign exchange,
tariff, and credit policies that prevailed for close to thirty years
encouraged the growth of capital-intensive industries that contributed very little to solving the underemployment problem,
while putting a great strain on the country's international reserves.

If one were to look for a political explanation for this flawed
economic policy, he could find it in the imperfections of a
fledgling democracy in which political power was still concentrated in the hands of the former landed gentry who turned
into manufacturing entrepreneurs during the fifties and sixties.

The Philippine legislature, through which tariff, fiscal, and monetary reforms had to pass, was dominated by groups that represented the very industrial sector that had been pampered by overprotection. Such vested interests fought hard against any attempt to open the economy to greater international competition. Under the martial-law years of the seventies, there were half-hearted attempts to reform the tariff structure. But these efforts were often negated by the granting of special privileges to favored businessmen who obtained undue advantage in domestic business. Instead of making Philippine industry more competitive, the practice of what was subsequently called crony capitalism encouraged the rise of some highly inefficient business conglomerates.

The Proximate Causes

This reference to crony capitalism leads us to an examination of what can be called the proximate causes of the present economic crisis, which causes are directly related to the authoritarian style of government that was ushered in by the Marcos administration in September of 1972.

The martial-law years (1972-1980) came after the initial period of massive government spending that characterized the first two terms of Marcos as president (1966-1972). Staking its reputation on a program of vast infrastructure projects, especially in the southern island of Mindanao, the government widened the gap between investment and savings from an excess supply of savings in 1961-1965 to an excess of investment over savings at a rate of P294 million yearly during the 1966-1970 period. This domestic savings deficiency was inevitably reflected in the current accounts deficits in the balance of payments, the levels of which increased almost tenfold. Generally, however, the infrastructure projects during this period were of a productive nature, significantly improving the road network in agriculturally rich Mindanao, and laying the foundation for rice self-sufficiency through the construction of irrigation systems throughout the archipelago.

The heavy spending continued during the second half of the

seventies, particularly in energy-related projects. Although the energy self-reliance program paid off handsomely in terms of a much-reduced dependence on imported oil (81 percent in 1974 to 58 percent in 1984), there were other capital expenditures financed by foreign borrowings that had very dubious utility because of poor planning or outright mismanagement by businessmen who received special favors from the Marcos government.

As heavy spending increased government deficits fourfold during the late seventies, foreign borrowings inevitably rose from $2.6 billion to $10.5 billion between 1975 and 1980. Especially responsible for this big jump in foreign borrowings was the government's practice of guaranteeing foreign loans made to certain favored groups in the private sector. With the very high interest rates that prevailed in the late seventies, the current account deficits increased nearly twelve times between 1971-1975 and 1976-1980.

Despite the huge current account deficits, the government decided to maintain the foreign exchange rate at virtually the same level. This was accomplished through a constant replenishment of the international reserves with fresh foreign loans that were relatively easy to obtain because foreign banks were aggressively recycling the burgeoning petro-dollars of Middle Eastern countries awash with oil revenue. The peso continued to be overvalued, thereby discouraging a faster growth of exports, especially the manufactured ones. During the 1972-1982 period, the foreign exchange rate was allowed to depreciate from an average of P6.67 to $1 in 1972 to P8.54 to $1 in 1982. In contrast, the equilibrium or open market rate (based on purchasing power parity which compares rates of inflation in the Philippines and the United States) should have been P11.00 in 1982.

The First Oil Shock

The first five years of martial law were generally characterized by sound economic policies. Chastened by the experiences of the late sixties in fiscal irresponsibility, the leaders in the initial martial-law years trimmed government deficits to lower levels primarily through increasing the efficiency of the tax collection machinery. The overall deficit of the central government dropped from an annual average of P889 million during the 1966-1970 period to P842 million during the 1971-1975 period. The government succeeded in finally running significant surpluses on current expenditures. During this period the capital outlays of the government were mostly in infrastructure projects, and not in corporate equity or "other capital outlays," which include construction by ministries not directly related to public works.

It cannot be denied that it would have been difficult for the Philippine economy to have survived the first oil shock of 1973 if the very volatile political environment of 1969-1971 had persisted. Most people in and out of government welcomed a stronger government, especially as they witnessed the very destabilizing effects of the quadrupling of oil prices in the world market. In 1974, Filipino consumers suffered the worst inflation (34 percent) since the end of the war. The government's ability to bring the inflation rate back to single-digit levels by 1975 was another evidence of a more responsive leadership.

Especially significant during this period was the decisive move of the government to launch an energy self-reliance program in order to combat frontally the "oil bill" problem. The oil bill of the economy jumped from $187 million in 1972 to $651 million in 1974 and $2.5 billion in 1980, although the physical volume had decreased. In the face of this serious threat to the country's balance of payments, the government acted in lightning fashion to set up the Philippine National Oil Company (PNOC), hardly a month after the quadrupling of oil prices in October 1973. The PNOC was assigned to provide and maintain an adequate supply of oil and petroleum products for domestic requirements; promote the exploration, exploitation, and development of local oil and petroleum sources; and foster oil or petroleum conditions that would be conducive to a balanced and sustainable growth of the economy.

Under the aegis of the PNOC and the Ministry of Energy,

the country reduced its dependence on imported oil by 20 percent during the ten-year period 1974-1983. By 1983 importation of oil (in million barrels of oil equivalent) dropped to 63.5 million barrels as domestic energy sources increased by 12.6 percent to 34.0 million barrels. This reduction was largely due to increased energy production from geothermal, hydro, coal, and nonconventional energy sources. By 1979, the Philippines became an oil producer when the Nido oil field in offshore Palawan started commercial production. By 1983, geothermal energy became a significant source, supplying about 7.03 million barrels of oil equivalent or 7.1 percent of total energy consumption.

Although there are critics of the energy program who argue that the foreign borrowings that were necessary to undertake the program greatly contributed to the present foreign debt crisis, an analysis performed by an economist at CRC demonstrated that the Philippine energy program was a net saver of foreign exchange, even after taking into account the amortization payments on the loans. Furthermore, the study pointed out, the program succeeded in lowering the country's dependence on the unstable energy source (in terms of supply and prices)—oil. Thus, it has substantially achieved the strategic objective of making the domestic economy resistant to oil shocks. Despite the shelving of several indigenous energy projects for lack of foreign exchange, the energy sector can still manage to cut Philippine dependence on imported energy to 50 percent by 1987.

Another noteworthy feature of the energy program initiated in 1973-1974 was the general reliance on market forces, despite the great temptation to an authoritarian leader of putting up the equivalent of a Pertamina or a Petromin, that is, a monopoly in the refining and distribution of petroleum products. Although PNOC took over the former ESSO Philippines (the Philippine subsidiary of EXXON), President Marcos was prudent enough to allow three other multinational firms (Shell, Caltex, and Mobil) to continue operating in the country. Thus, there was a regulated oligopoly instead of a government monopoly. The presence of the multinational corporations came in good stead during the most difficult period of the first oil shock; their contacts with the Middle Eastern suppliers provided the Philippines with much-needed oil supplies while the neophyte PNOC was just beginning to learn the ropes in direct government-to-government trade. It is a pity that this early model of how the government should intervene in a strategic industry was not replicated in the less fortunate sugar, coconut, and grains industries, where monopoly reared its ugly head in the late seventies.

Other Early Accomplishments

There were two other significant achievements of the early martial-law years. The earnest efforts to lay the foundation for an export-oriented industrialization began during this period. Through a series of incentives and programs designed by the Board of Investment and the Ministry of Trade (later merged in the Ministry of Trade and Industry), the Philippines was able to boost significantly its export of nontraditional products (defined as any item that accounted for less than US $5 million of exports in 1968). These nontraditional exports represented less than 10 percent of total exports in 1970. By 1975 their share rose to 23 percent, and by 1983 to 58 percent. The most important categories are electronic components, garments, finished wood products, leather goods and footwear, houseware and giftware, and fresh and processed food products such as tuna, shrimp, and mangoes.

The increasing importance of these products insulated the Philippines somewhat from the very volatile prices of such traditional export products as sugar, coconut oil, copper, logs, and lumber. The decision of more countries to obtain their supplies of these products from the Philippines reflected the confidence they had in the stability of the Philippine economy and the attractions of a more liberal trade policy. Moreover, there was industrial peace in the Philippines, and the wage policies adopted reinforced the advantages of locating labor-intensive industries in the Philippines.

Some critics miss the point when they denigrate these export-oriented industries because of their heavy dependence on imported materials. First, there are at least three major categories of nontraditional exports that have minimal import requirements: finished wood products, houseware and giftware, and fresh and processed food products. Each of these has a potential of $1 billion a year in exports before the 1980s are over. Second, even in the cases of the semiconductor and garment exports, in which net foreign exchange earnings may be as low as 10 percent of gross dollar receipts (although our own estimate is 25 percent in the semiconductor industry), the major contribution of these industries is the creation of jobs that are relatively well paid compared to those offered by local employers. This benefit cannot be underestimated in a country in which 700,000 new workers are added to the labor force annually. Any net foreign exchange earnings are to be considered a bonus. Furthermore, one cannot belittle 10 percent of $2 billion (which is what semiconductor exports could have been in 1984 if the Philippines had not been hit by a political crisis). Net earnings of $200 million still compare well with the less than $200 million earned in 1984 by the sugar industry, for example, after the costs of fertilizers and other imported inputs are deducted.

The other equally important achievement during this first phase of the martial law regime was the attainment of rice self-sufficiency, after decades of importing this staple food. Although the foundations of the Masagana 99 program were laid in the late sixties, when rice sufficiency was attained for a brief spell, the definitive victory came in 1977, after which the Philippines had enough rice to export some $153 million worth during the 1977-1983 period. The temporary reverses in 1984 and 1985, during which the country was forced to import rice once again, were results of abnormally poor weather and the credit squeeze that paralyzed the whole economy in 1983-1984.

During the period 1978-1983, the yield of *palay* (husked rice) recorded an increase of 19.5 percent (from 2.0 metric tons to 2.39 metric tons per hectare) or a 3.6 percent annual increase. Prior to the launching of the Masagana program, *pa-*

lay yield was only 1.71 metric tons per hectare. The program included a delivery system involving high-yielding rice varieties, credit facilities, fertilizer, and other production inputs. Extension services were provided to guide the effective implementation of the new technology. A credit scheme was initiated to provide off-season credit to farmers. Likewise, a price support program was instituted to ensure farmers of stable prices and reasonable profits. For the first time in the postwar economic history of the country, a total-systems approach was used in tackling the land reform problem. Up to this period, land redistribution programs had failed because they were not sufficiently backed up by the physical, financial, and social infrastructure the farmers needed in order to be productive. Despite the high rates of loan default in the Masagana program, it is our view that the land reform program of President Marcos was a success.

The Profligate Years

Unfortunately, the relatively good results of the early martial-law years were marred by unsound economic policies and blatant political interference in the workings of the economy during the late seventies and the early eighties. The first telltale signs appeared in the shift of government capital outlays away from infrastructure projects toward the "other capital outlays" category. Whereas public works accounted for more than 50 percent of capital outlays during 1970-1976, by 1981-1983 this share dropped to 36 percent. The "other capital outlays" component gained greater prominence, ballooning to 20 percent of total capital outlays in 1977-1980, whereas previously it had been insignificant. It may be recalled that the holding of the IMF meeting in Manila in 1976 marked the beginning of major construction expenditures whose value to the economy was highly questionable, such as the Manila Bay reclamation and building complex, the five-star hotels financed by government banks, the University of Life facilities, and the three highly sophisticated medical centers. Anyone who travels to various cities in East and Southeast Asia would observe

that the Philippines boasts the most showy and expensive government office buildings and other public edifices. It was this
propensity for ostentation in construction that prompted a
wag to comment that Imelda Marcos was suffering from an
"edifice complex."

Even more alarming was the trend discernible in the early
eighties. During the 1981-1983 period, corporate equity investments became the single most important capital outlay,
surpassing even infrastructure spending (46 percent as compared with 36 percent). This trend was mainly attributable to
the massive bail-out operation that became necessary when
large private firms—many of which were so-called crony conglomerates—had to be rescued from financial collapse. The
government was forced to make equity contributions, that is,
to pay out money in return for shares, to the Central Bank, the
Philippine National Bank, the Development Bank of the Philippines, the Land Bank, and the National Development Company—all government institutions that were charged with taking over the ownership and control of the distressed firms or
extending new loans to them. About 30 percent of equity cash
disbursements in 1981-1982 was allocated to these five government institutions, which in turn used these funds mostly for
bailing out or subsidizing the operations of ill-conceived companies.

All this rampant waste of capital—in nonproductive construction projects and ill-advised business enterprises—
showed clearly in the rapid rise of what is termed the incre-
mental capital-output ratio (ICOR) for the whole economy.
An ICOR of 2, for example, means that to produce an additional peso of income, P2 of investment is required. Its reciprocal, therefore, might be regarded as an index of the productivity of investment. If ICOR rises through time, there is an
indication that capital is getting less productive. ICOR in the
Philippines rose from 4.2 in the sixties to 5.0 in the seventies.
By the early eighties, ICOR was closer to 10. This is additional
hard evidence that a lot of investment spending was not increasing the country's productive capacity. What else could be
expected from half-empty hotels, nonoperating textile mills,
wastelands of reclaimed areas, and so on?

Crony Capitalism

The late seventies and early eighties saw the deleterious effects of what has been called crony capitalism in the Philippines. Such a practice is not original to Filipinos: in many developing countries, including the "tiger economies," financial power is concentrated in the hands of a few large conglomerates whose interests often encompass trading, mining, and manufacturing, with an "in-house" bank to boot.

By the mid-seventies, the almost absolute power given to President Marcos by the martial-law regime enabled him and a small group of relatives and friends to perfect the art of interlocking directorates. Two rationalizations have been offered by government apologists for the concentration of economic privilege in the hands of the "palace cronies." The first one has an ethnic undertone. It has been alleged that when Marcos came to power, he was shocked to realize that the economy was largely in the hands of the Chinese elements in Philippine society. In the name of nationalism, it is said, he proceeded to wrest control from the Chinese by encouraging the rise of native entrepreneurs (reminiscent of the Bumiputra policy of Malaysia). But the real thrust of the policy is found in the candid remarks of a high official in many a briefing: "Whom else could we possibly build up among the natives? Definitely not our enemies!" In fact, President Marcos used naked power to destroy the industrial empire of his political archenemy, Eugenio Lopez, and his family, who were forced to sell their interests in the Manila Electric Company to some of the palace cronies.

Another version of the defense of crony capitalism comes from a well-known ghost writer of the president. According to him, there was a deliberate policy to build the equivalent of "Japan, Inc.," that much-vaunted and much-imitated system through which the Japanese skillfully welded together the government and the private sectors in a common pursuit of what was good for Japan. Taiwan and South Korea had succeeded in emulating the land of the rising sun; why couldn't President Marcos appoint his relatives and friends to head the Philippine *zaibatsus*, which in turn could support the government in at-

taining the national objectives of growth, equity, and employment? Why couldn't Shogun Marcos have his economic samurais?

One does not have to be an anthropologist or an economic
historian to demolish these rationalizations. In the first place,
some of the favored groups were not non-Chinese. Second, if
the Chinese are predominant in economic activities, the main
reasons are business acumen and hard, persevering work. A
decision to shower economic privileges on palace friends can
easily lead—as it did—to serious investment failures. There is
no guarantee that one's cronies are competent, hard working,
or enlightened entrepreneurs. But even if, by sheer luck, the
majority of the cronies turned out to be truly entrepreneurial,
there was still the question of whether or not they would act as
economic samurais, that is, put the good of the nation above
their private interests. The "Japan, Inc." model works because
one can assume that the orientation toward the common good
is almost second nature to the Japanese businessman. When
the good of the whole country demands it, he is willing to sacrifice his private interests. That is authentic samurai culture.

Unfortunately, the palace was surrounded by robber bar-
ons, not samurai. Sad to say, Philippine capitalism took its
shape from the American version of capitalist growth in the
early decades of this century—in which the robber baron was
a dominant figure. With a few notable exceptions, the cronies
cared very little about what they were doing to the national
economy. It is very likely that they were more interested in en-
riching themselves in the short run than in building lasting industrial empires. It is no secret that a number of the cronies
whose businesses failed are now living well in the expensive
capitals of the world. That is prima facie evidence that they did
a great deal of "dollar salting" while they could.

The Agricultural Monopolies

What made the situation worse was the establishment of gov-
ernment-mandated monopolies in key agricultural sectors,
which adversely affected the lives of millions of farmers and

their dependents. These monopolies—in sugar, coconut, and grains—were in the hands of some of the closest associates of President Marcos.

Strictly speaking, there was nothing wrong with the creation of a single trading agency in the sugar industry. The example of the Australian Sugar Board is well known: it is the sole agency that exports Australian sugar. But it is democratically managed by all the participants in the sugar industry, who are represented in the Board. The managers are fully accountable for their decisions. In contrast, the decision makers of the Philippine Sugar Commission (the regulatory board) and the National Sugar Trading Company (NASUTRA)—the single trading agency—gave out grossly incomplete information about their operations to the planters, millers, and other industry participants. Because of this lack of accountability, the managers of the monopoly inflicted the following damages on the industry, almost with impunity, as reported in the University of the Philippines "white paper":

a. a loss to the producers of between P11 billion and P14 billion during the 1974-1983 period;
b. an increase in the marketing chain resulting in either more mark-up or a redistribution of income from actual traders to favored "paper" traders, or both;
c. no increase in trading efficiency, and consequently no increase in foreign exchange earnings (total export revenues were even slightly less than total revenues that would have accrued to producers in the free market);
d. a loss of foreign exchange as a result of the need to resort to foreign loans in order to finance operations;
e. a loss to the economy because of the operating losses of the agencies, despite estimated gross profits enjoyed from the differential between export revenues and purchase costs.

Furthermore, the managers of the monopoly used their influence to obtain government financing for additional sugar mills, despite an overcapacity that was already leading to ruinous competition for the short supply of sugar cane. Such intervention resulted in:

a. an increase in foreign debt by $508 million, represented by letters of credit issued by the Philippine National Bank for the mills' construction;
b. losses of the new mills because of insufficient cane supply, poor infrastructure, and insufficient equity investments of the owners;
c. liquidity problems of the PNB because of past due loans amounting to P1.5 billion.

Finally, one of the most bitter criticisms hurled against Philsucom and Nasutra concerns the loss of a substantial portion of the U.S. sugar quota. Since the preferential trade agreement with the U.S. expired in 1974, the managers of the sugar monopoly virtually ignored the U.S. market. According to the critics, such lack of foresight was the biggest blunder in the marketing of Philippine sugar. Because Philippine sugar exports to the United States were allowed to drop drastically after 1975, the Philippines was allotted a substantially reduced amount when the U.S. restored its country-by-country sugar quota in May 1982. Although errors in judgment are not in themselves evidence of incompetence, the critics feel that if the Philsucom and Nasutra had allowed the planters, millers, and traders to participate more in the management, such a disastrous blunder could have been avoided.

Then there was the monopsonization of the coconut industry when, in 1979, funds from a levy imposed on coconut products were utilized to establish the United Coconut Oil Mills, Inc. (UNICOM), a private milling and marketing company controlled by one of the closest associates of President Marcos (the only one, in fact, who proudly admits to being a crony of Marcos). The UNICOM controlled over 75 percent of the coconut oil milling capacity of the country after an aggressive campaign of purchasing distressed firms with the use of the levy funds. This monopsony has been severely criticized as prejudicing the coconut farmers (whose households represent almost one-third of the Philippine population) on two counts: UNICOM paid farmers 9-15 percent below the price it would have paid under more competitive conditions, and the levy funds were utilized in a way that the farmers could not control since there was very little public accountability of the managers of UNICOM.

This was another case of an attempt to "rationalize" a strategic industry affecting the lives of more than 15 million people that became counterproductive because market forces were negated and public accountability was not enforced. As I have personally communicated to the UNICOM managers, the laudable objective of market rationalization (that is, the prevention of such ruinous competition for copra among mills as prevailed in the seventies) could have been attained if UNICOM had been satisfied with only 20-30 percent of total milling capacity. Four or five other independent groups (including the subsidiaries of Procter and Gamble and Unilever) could have been allowed to compete with one another, following the model of the petroleum industry. Complemented by public accountability, such a move would have been much more politically palatable to the coconut farmers.

Finally, let the former minister of economic planning and director general of the National Economic and Development Authority himself speak about the grains monopoly. In a "valedictory address" to the Philippine Economic Society (he was leaving the country to join the World Bank as policy research director), Dr. Gerardo Sicat severely criticized the government for mandating monopolies in grain trade. The target of his attack was the National Food Authority (NFA), which had a monopoly of the wheat trade. NFA's predecessor was the National Grains Authority (NGA), which had done an effective job of rationalizing rice and corn marketing by controlling a little over 10 percent of the trade, allowing private traders to compete for the other 90 percent.

Unfortunately, NGA was merged with the bureaucracy of the powerful Ministry of Human Settlements, which under the leadership of the first lady has given the Philippines the image of extreme profligacy before the whole world. When NGA became NFA in 1981, the lessons of NGA were lost to the managers. There was literally an obsession to monopolize the trading in grains. As Dr. Sicat himself lamented, the result was disastrous to the industry and to the general consuming public it was supposed to serve. With the setting up of what were called *kadiwa* centers (distribution outlets run by the government), NFA took over not only wholesale distribution but also the retail trade, competing directly with the very last bastion of private enterprise in the country—the family-run *sari-sari* store. Dr. Sicat was quick to point out that the public might have been deceived into believing that *kadiwa* goods were cheaper. When expenses on buildings, equipment, and personnel are reckoned with, one realizes the heavy subsidies granted to these stores. Where did these subsidies come from? Obviously, from the taxpayers.

There is, in fact, a common defense of these agricultural monopolies that runs as follows: clandestine profits had to be made in, say, sugar trading because there was pressure on the government to incur expenses indispensable to national stability that could not be covered by the meager tax revenues. Specific reference is usually made to the military expenditures in strife-torn Mindanao. Such an argument should not be taken seriously by anyone who holds the principle that a good end does not justify an unlawful means. Any attempt to make profits through unfair trade practices is sure to backfire in the form of a debilitated private sector and a disillusioned public.

The Foreign Borrowing Binge

If the misallocation of resources resulting from flawed economic policies and political interference had been largely financed by domestic savings, the Philippine economy might still have had sufficient flexibility to bounce back within a relatively short period of time. Unfortunately, the Philippines went on a borrowing spree, especially during the 1979-1983 period, and now has to face the harsh reality of paying back its loans from the resources of an economy that is hardly growing.

In 1984, the total foreign debt of the country of $26 billion was about equal to its gross national product. This staggering level of debt was the culmination of a series of years of large current accounts deficits that were increasingly financed by high-interest loans. The Philippine foreign debt of the non-monetary sector alone increased 8.6 times, from $1.9 billion in 1969 to $16.5 billion in 1983. During the thirteen-year period 1969 to 1982, total foreign debt increased by 19 percent annually.

The piling up of Philippine foreign debt was largely due to increases in government borrowings. During the same thirteen-year period, public sector debt increased by 25 percent per year, whereas borrowings of the private sector expanded by 17 percent annually. Growing especially fast was the government's share of total fixed-term external debt, which jumped from 47 percent in 1976 to 77 percent by the end of 1983. It was quite evident that the government was taking a more dominant role in the economy during the years immediately preceding the economic crisis.

The government was lulled into complacency and a false sense of security because it was relatively easy to obtain foreign loans during the years of petro-dollar recycling. The Philippines also had the continued support of official lenders. Besides, export growth was robust, with growth in nontraditional items galloping at 25-30 percent per annum from 1973-78.

However, the second oil shock in 1979 ushered in a world recession that was to last till 1983. Interest rates rose to very high levels, and banks became more wary about lending to Third World countries. Instead of adapting to the new international financial conditions, the Philippine government continued its aggressive spending. It may be recalled that it was in 1979 that President Marcos and his newly appointed minister of trade and industry announced the launching of eleven major industrial projects (petrochemicals, an aluminum smelter, a copper smelter, an integrated steel mill, pulp and paper manufacture, etc.) that would have involved $4 billion more of capital spending, most of which was to be borrowed from abroad. Fortunately, loud protests from the private sector forced the government to scale down drastically these ill-advised projects that would have pulled the country even deeper into a financial quagmire.

In the early 1980s, the government resorted to larger amounts of short-term borrowings, which reflected not only the rise in the current account deficits but also less favorable conditions in financial markets. Between 1978 and 1982, the Philippine foreign debt rose from the equivalent of 2.2 times the exports of goods and services to 3.1, and the share of short-term liabilities of total debt rose from 35 to 47 percent. By 1982, the Philippine ratios of external liabilities in relation to export earnings were already as bad as or worse than the corresponding ones of the so-called basket cases of Argentina, Chile, Brazil, and Mexico. Its debt structure was the worst, since its 47 percent (short-term to total debt) was extremely high compared to the 16.4 percent of Brazil, 19.2 percent of Chile, 21.2 percent of Argentina, and 27.2 percent of Mexico.

As discussed above, the mounting external debt was increasingly utilized to finance public sector activities. With the rising foreign debt and higher rates of interest, debt service payments by the Philippines increased to dangerously high levels during the late 1970s. Total debt service payments, excluding rollover of short-term debt, rose by 45 percent between 1978 and 1980, and by 80 percent between 1980 and 1982. As measured against exports of goods and services, the debt service (interest on all maturities and amortization of medium- and long-term debt) rose from 19 percent in 1980 to 36.5 percent in 1982.

By the end of 1982, the international financial community was concerned about the precarious situation of the Philippine economy. The country found it increasingly difficult to raise additional loans. Any hope for an orderly and relatively rapid debt restructuring vanished altogether when the country was thrown into pandemonium by the Aquino assassination. There was massive flight of capital during the last quarter of 1983. The first debt moratorium was declared in October of 1983.

It may be noted at this point that the over-reliance of the Philippines on foreign debt contrasts with the experience of other ASEAN countries that have been more successful in attracting foreign investments. The Philippines had the lowest level of foreign investment inflows during the period 1974-1981. The contribution of net foreign investments to the capital account balance averaged only 9 percent for the period. In Malaysia and Singapore, net foreign investments contributed the largest share to the capital account. Despite higher levels of current accounts deficits, these two countries have maintained an admirably stable foreign exchange rate because of significant inflows of equity financing. Attracting more foreign investments may have to constitute an important ingredient of the Philippine recovery program for the remaining years of the eighties.

The Economic Recovery Program

The severe economic crisis produced a considerable consensus among people in government about the stabilization measures and structural reforms needed in the economy. Given appropriate political leadership, the recovery program that was a result of internal soul-searching and consultation with foreign creditors could lead the country back to economic normalcy. The Economic Memorandum used in the negotiations for debt rescheduling has outlined the commitments of the government to specific reforms.[5]

In the medium term (1985-1990), the government committed itself to further reduce the public sector deficit, strengthen the domestic financial system, and maintain monetary aggregates at levels that support price stability and balance of payments objectives. The main goal of fiscal policy was to improve the structure of expenditures and resource mobilization. There was a commitment to improve the efficiency of recurrent government expenditures. Investment programming was to be streamlined so as to focus on new and ongoing projects with high economic rates of return.

Public corporations were to be sold, where possible, to the

[5] Republic of the Philippines, *Economic Memorandum*, November 1984.

private sector, and those retained would have to rely more on internal cash generation for funding requirements. The tax base would be broadened, the tax system made more cost effective, and tax collection and administration more efficient. The financial system would be rationalized under closer supervision by the Central Bank so as to improve its operating efficiency. Government-owned financial institutions would be required to maintain portfolios that could be supported by nonbudgetary sources.

Structural adjustment efforts would be geared toward balanced agro-industrial development, the Memorandum said. To make up for the negligence of the past, the government intended to place greater emphasis on agriculture and agri-based industries. The agricultural sector, for the first time in postwar history, was expected to be the leading sector of the economy. Agricultural reforms would focus on production, pricing and marketing, credit, and institutional arrangements. Market-oriented reforms would be introduced into the sugar and coconut industries so as to undo the harm done by agricultural monopolies during the late seventies.

In the manufacturing sector, according to the Memorandum, the main objective was to establish world-competitive industries. There would be complementary measures to: increase foreign exchange earnings and savings, mainly through export promotion, especially of nontraditional manufactured and agri-based exports, and through reduced dependence on imported oil; generate employment opportunities through the development and promotion of labor-intensive, resource-based, small- and medium-scale industries; distribute equitably the benefits of industrialization through the regional dispersal of industries.

In November 1984, the government laid out a revised development strategy in its updated Five-Year Plan for the period 1984-1987.[6] The major features of the recovery program were:

[6] Ibid.

a. an economic stabilization program aimed at improving the balance of payments position, reducing the budget deficit, and bringing down inflation through appropriate demand management measures;

b. an external financing program that included rescheduling external debt maturities falling due from October 17, 1983, to the end of 1985, new loans, and extension of credit lines;

c. a refocusing of priorities, which would include a reduction in the public investment program, increased emphasis on completion of ongoing projects, and rehabilitation of existing infrastructure;

d. the continuation of the structural adjustment program that started in 1980. Reforms in trade liberalization, industrial development/restructuring programs, and in the investment incentive regime will be reinforced. The structural adjustment program will be expanded to include agriculture, with emphasis on productivity improvement, reforms in pricing and marketing, and sectoral planning and management;

e. programs to achieve social equity, including improvements in health care, education, and housing.

Prospects for Recovery

The question still remains: when can the Philippines expect to recover? Assuming a minimum of political stability, the Philippine economy can resume its normal rate of growth (6 percent or more) only in the 1990s. Even the optimistic projections contained in the Economic Memorandum assumed that GNP growth would remain at 4 percent per annum till 1990.

The World Bank was even less optimistic. In a document analyzing the ongoing economic crisis, the World Bank saw the medium-term outlook for the Philippine economy as "highly uncertain."[7] This uncertainty was attributed to the unclear future of the international trade and financing environ-

[7] World Bank, *The Philippines: An Agenda for Adjustment and Growth.* Report No. 5258-PH, November 30, 1984.

ment, volatile commodity prices, the prospect for the implementation of stabilization measures and continuation of
structural reforms domestically, and private-sector responses
to government policies and political developments.

The World Bank presented two possible scenarios for 1985-
1990: a high-case or optimistic one and a low-case or pessimistic one. Under the high-case scenario, which assumed that
the stabilization program was fully implemented in a timely
fashion and structural reforms were adopted, annual GDP
growth rate would average 4 percent during the 1985-1990
period, reaching 6 percent only by 1990. Even this already optimistic scenario did not augur well for the masses. Personal
consumption expenditures would grow at a rate slightly lower
than the 2.4 percent population growth rate; per capita income would be 9 percent lower in 1990 than it was in 1983.
The growth in employment would be insufficient to create
enough productive jobs for the additional 700,000 that would
join the labor force every year.

The low-case scenario could be frightening. Assuming that
the stabilization program and structural adjustment were less
successful, GNP growth would average 1.1 percent in 1985-
1990, reaching only 3.0 percent by 1990. Per capita consumption in 1990 would be 21 percent below the 1983 level. There
would be growing under- and unemployment in the economy,
and significant declines in living standards for the majority of
the population, declining real wages, and increasing proportions of people living below the poverty line. Such a prospect
was so unpalatable that it should be enough to convince Philippine political leaders to do everything possible to succeed in
the stabilization and structural adjustment programs.

A Sanguine View of the Philippines

Despite the murky medium-term outlook, there were some exceptional investors (mainly from Asia Pacific and Western European countries) who were shopping for good investment
buys in the Philippines, especially in resource-based industries
such as wood processing and agro-processing, and in labor-in-

tensive, export-oriented industries such as semiconductor components, garments, finished wood products, houseware and giftware.

The Philippines has a highly literate population that can provide reasonably productive manpower at wage levels anywhere from one-fourth to one-third of those prevailing in the "tiger economies." One often hears the leaders of such multinational corporations as Motorola, TMX, Fairchild, and Matsushita praising their Philippine workers as among the most productive in Asia Pacific.

The agricultural resources of the country have the potential to enable the Philippines to follow the paths trodden by Malaysia and Thailand in agribusiness development. In fact, because of acute labor shortages in Malaysia, such companies as Sime Darby and Guthrie are already investing in palm oil and rubber plantations in the Philippines. Similarly, Thai investors are looking for joint ventures with Filipino entrepreneurs in poultry, tapioca, aquaculture, and food processing.

If the new political leaders are able to restore peace and order in both the rural and urban areas—still a big "if"—it is possible for the country to attain rates of growth in nontraditional exports of 20-30 percent per annum. Such growth rates would enable the country's GNP to expand at 6 percent per annum even earlier than 1990. What is needed is greater investor confidence. Filipinos alone are estimated to own at least $10 billion of assets abroad. They could be the first ones to reinvest part of this money in the country if there is a significant improvement in the investment climate. Will the political leaders meet the challenge implied in this more sanguine view of Philippine economic prospects during this very turbulent era? Only time will tell.

CHAPTER VII

RECONSTITUTING THE POLITICAL ORDER

CAROLINA G. HERNANDEZ

On February 25, 1986, Corazon Aquino was acclaimed president of the Philippines. Her accession to power had the support of an extraordinary coalition of forces. She quite evidently was the choice of a large majority of the citizens who voted or tried to vote in the election of February 7. She had the support of the citizen's watchdog group, the National Movement for Free Elections NAMFREL, led by business executives and Catholic clergy, who mobilized 400,000 volunteers to police the voting and who found the official count in favor of Ferdinand Marcos patently and massively fraudulent. She had the support of the Catholic bishops, led by Jaime Cardinal Sin, the archbishop of Manila; as a body the bishops called on the people to demonstrate their rejection of the official election count by engaging in nonviolent civil disobedience. She had the support of Juan Ponce Enrile and Fidel V. Ramos, the former defense minister and armed forces deputy chief, who, facing arrest, and knowing they had the support of reform-minded officers in key military units, declared for Mrs. Aquino. And finally, she had the support of tens of thousands of ordinary citizens of Manila who answered the Cardinal's radio appeal, went into the streets, and halted the armed units of the presidential guard—the "people power" that assured Mrs. Aquino a victory that was among the most peaceful revolutions of the century.

The massive support for Mrs. Aquino, in the face of physical danger and threats of every kind, was a clear indication of the confidence the Filipino people had in her personal qualities and in her program, as well as their opposition to a family obsessed with power and wealth. The events before, during, and after the election also were an extraordinary testimonial to the attachment of the Filipino people to the democratic ethic. Had any people ever demonstrated more clearly their attachment to the central idea that leadership is accountable, when all else fails, to the people themselves? Or their adherence to the equally central belief that, in deciding on a leader's steward- ship, there is a sacred quality to a free and fair election in which each citizen has an equal voice?

Nevertheless, as the euphoria of the popular victory began to subside, it was recognized that the new government faced gargantuan tasks. National reconciliation with the commu- nist-led insurgency had to be pursued. The economy had to be started moving again. Social services had to be restored. Each of these tasks was urgent and complex. But central to all of them were questions of how the old political regime was to be replaced by a new political order. In part what was required was the dismantling of a system of laws, institutions, and prac- tices in which absolute power had become centered in the hands of a single individual, a system that had not only failed to resolve the country's problems but had actually contributed greatly to them. At the same time, decisions had to be made as to how the new order was to be constituted—how, drawing on the lessons the country had learned at great cost, a new begin- ning was to be made in building a political system that would be recognized by both the supporters and the opponents of the new government as legitimate, that would be subject to checks and balances and to continuing accountability, and that would be restructured and reformed in ways that were responsive to the evident desire of the people to have a voice in public affairs.

Not since Ramon Magsaysay had a Philippine leader had the popular support which Corazon Aquino enjoyed as she and her associates set about this task of political reconstitu- tion. She had strong support in the capital city for her initial cabinet appointments. Her decisions to disband key elements of the Marcos machine, including the Office of Media Affairs, the Presidential Security Command, and the National Intelli- gence Security Authority, and to retire many "overstaying" generals, were widely expected and applauded. So also was her action, over some opposition, to meet her campaign pledge to release all political prisoners, including the reputed founders of the Communist Party of the Philippines (CPP) and of its military arm, the New People's Army (NPA). These and other steps of dismantling could be achieved with relative speed.

At the same time, however, President Aquino and the Philippine people faced a wide array of complex issues in rebuilding a new political order. Some involved the constitution, how laws were to be made, and how authority and accountability were to be balanced to create a government that was both effective in addressing problems and responsive to social needs. Others had to do with the future roles of political parties, of the media of mass communication, and of the bar. There also was the question of how "people power" was to be institutionalized, so that the popular forces which helped to propel Mrs. Aquino to the presidency might continue to have an influence on future events.

Not all these issues could be resolved in a short period of time, or by decision of the new government alone. Some issues were urgent. Others would need to be worked out in the behavior of many individuals over a period of years. The fundamental question was, on the basis of what principles would the issues be addressed? Would the Philippines return to the traditional political culture that produced and sustained Ferdinand Marcos? Or did Corazon Aquino's victory signal the beginning of a new political culture?

It might be argued that, if many Filipinos were attached to liberal democracy, its disruption and decay from 1972 onward should not have been possible. Indeed, many Filipinos took the imposition of martial law in stride; many even viewed the event with favor, putting an end as it did to the lawlessness and violence that characterized the period just before martial law was imposed. However, the progressive erosion of democratic political institutions, values, and practices, and the steady institutionalization of authoritarian rule reached such alarming proportions that eventually only a catalyst was needed for protest to erupt. Having lived with such a rule for thirteen years, many Filipinos learned, as other peoples had from the time of the ancient Greeks, that unbridled power in the hands of a single individual can be extremely dangerous to human welfare.

Moreover, the liberal democratic ethic also was a part of Philippine tradition. Its roots could be traced to the nineteenth-century reform movement in Hispanic Philippines. And the tradition was established by the political order founded under American tutelage before 1946. Mrs. Aquino appealed to this element of Philippine tradition in the course of her campaign. She would delegate authority to her cabinet colleagues, she had said. As chief executive, she would share power with the legislature. She would restore the independence of the judiciary, return local government to local leaders, and reaffirm the professional role of the armed forces under civilian leadership.

The main hope for the liberal democratic ethic in the Philippines rested, nevertheless, in the common sense and sentiment of the Philippine people. Constitutional authoritarianism simply did not work for them. It polarized the society, hastened the exodus of Filipinos of every class from the country, and made a radical option attractive to ever more people. A liberal democratic future, though fraught with many problems and handicapped by an unhappy democratic past, seemed clearly preferable to the bulk of the population.

Would liberal democracy work better in the period ahead? Would it produce a society that was more equitable? The events of February 1986 surely demonstrated that revolutionary change is possible, and that it is possible by peaceful means.

The Constitution and Legitimacy

The Constitution of 1973 was surrounded with controversy from the time of its creation by the Constitutional Convention of 1971-1972. Charges that the Marcos government was paying delegates to the Convention, to assure that its preferred provisions were written into the draft, temporarily disrupted the proceedings of the constituent body. After the declaration of martial law, a further controversy arose over the manner in which ratification of the constitution was sought. Special "citizens' assemblies" were convened by Marcos as martial law administrator, and these, by a show of hands, reportedly ratified the instrument. This procedure was not provided for by the old constitution. Amendments proposed either by a constituent assembly, such as the Constitutional Convention, or by the legislature sitting as a constituent assembly were to be ratified by the electorate through a plebiscite called for the purpose. Nevertheless, the Supreme Court ruled that there was no legal impediment to the new constitution's coming into full force and effect.

This alleged unconstitutionality of the ratification of the new constitution led many in the opposition to view Marcos' rule after 1973 as itself illegitimate. The same grounds were cited by some who refused to participate in any of the referenda or elections held after the declaration of martial law. The reasoning went that their participation would serve only to legitimize Marcos' "illegitimate" rule.

The 1973 constitution also was seen as legitimizing some of the most objectionable features of constitutional authoritarianism. The most controversial of these was Amendment No. 6. This amendment, introduced in 1976, provided for the president to rule by decree. It remained in force after the election of the "interim" National Assembly in 1978, and indeed even after the election of the "regular" National Assembly in 1984. Amendment No. 6 thus permitted the president to preempt the proper function of the legislature. It also assured Marcos of a winning hand in any political controversy, since he could change the rules of the game at will.

The extent of the abuse that the presidential decree-making power invited was demonstrated by the phenomenon known as "secret decrees." These were decrees known only to the president and a few associates until the appropriate time arrived to announce their existence. As their very existence was not known, the real dates of their signing was not known, either. The most notorious example was undoubtedly Presidential Decree No. 1952. This decree became known only weeks after a number of attorneys had challenged the grant of jurisdiction over the Aquino assassination case to the Tanodbayan. The Tanodbayan was the ombudsman of the Philippines, designed to handle complaints against the government; in practice it had dealt with cases of petty corruption. Existing laws provided that military personnel accused of crimes would be tried by military courts. PD 1952, alledgedly signed in September 1984, authorized the waiver of courts martial jurisdiction by the president in selected cases "in the interest of justice." Many believe that PD 1952 was not actually signed before the Agrava Fact-Finding Board submitted its reports to Marcos in October 1984, but only afterwards, and possibly only after the Tanodbayan's jurisdiction was challenged.

The 1973 Constitution was thus seen by many Filipinos as tailor-made for Marcos. In its thirteen years of operation, it underwent an unusual number of amendments, and there were few Filipinos who mastered its intricacies, thanks to the rapidity with which amendments were proposed and predictably ratified. It was therefore argued that the constitution had no place in the post-Marcos era. The United Nationalist Democratic Organization (UNIDO), the umbrella political organization of Vice President Salvador H. Laurel, at one point indicated a preference for the restoration of the 1935 constitution. Many others, however, thought it unrealistic or undesirable to scrap the 1973 constitution in its entirety. Its Bill of Rights needed not scrapping so much as implementing. Its provision for a unicameral legislature also was a feature many would want to see preserved. Some revision of the 1973 constitution, however, seemed assured as President Aquino prepared for the convening of a constitutional body to draft a new constitution.

On April 23, 1986, Mrs. Aquino issued the Constitutional Commission Law of 1986 (Proclamation No. 9), providing for the appointment and operation of a body that would be responsible for the drafting of a new constitution for the country. The constitution was expected to be "truly reflective of the ideals and aspirations of the Filipino people." The Constitutional Commission would be composed of thirty to fifty national, regional, and sectoral representatives appointed by the president on May 25, 1986. The Commission would then have up to ninety days in which to draw up a new constitution, after which the draft instrument would be submitted to the people for approval in a plebescite within sixty days from its submission to the president. All told, the exercise was expected to produce a new constitution before the end of 1986 and to make possible parliamentary and local elections soon thereafter.

Meanwhile, a provisional government under a Freedom Constitution governed the Philippines. While this constitution granted full and plenary powers to the president, it enshrined the Bill of Rights of the 1973 Constitution, securing that as a guarantee and constraint against dictatorial and repressive rule and as a source of public accountability. Freedom to dissent was upheld, even as some dissenters tended to push the practice of that freedom beyond reasonable and justifiable limits. It was expected, nevertheless, that before 1986 was over, the provisional Freedom Constitution would give way to a new, reformed, and permanent one.

A reformed constitution would help restore legitimacy to government to the extent that it reflected the recent history of the Philippines. But a constitution is more than legal formulas. It becomes institutionalized only through practice and observance. So it would be up to many public officials and private citizens to contribute to the legitimacy of any new constitution by their adherence to it and their readiness to protect it over the years to come.

Constitutional reform, it was assumed, would remove the objectionable features of the 1973 constitution. A reformed constitution also had to provide for a satisfactory mechanism for presidential succession. Prior to January 1984, it was not clear how succession was going to occur in the event of a vacancy in the presidency. A constitutional amendment of January 1984 restored the position of vice president, and the election of February 1986 filled the office. However, the law remained unsatisfactory because it did not provide for succession if the unexpired portion of the president's term was less than eighteen months. If Marcos had died in office with less than eighteen months left in his term, given the likely state of affairs in the country, a political conflict of chaotic proportions could have ensued. The competition for power might well have encouraged military intervention, if only to restore order, and in the absence of alternative leadership the military might have stayed on in power indefinitely.

Another weakness of the mechanism for succession was its failure to provide for situations in which the president became incapacitated, either temporarily or permanently. The constitution had no provision at all for this eventuality. The need for it was most evident in November 1984, when Marcos was rumored to require hospitalization, and indeed disappeared from public view for nearly two weeks. Public apprehension was exacerbated by the allegation made by an opposition assemblyman that Marcos was going to the United States for medical treatment, and that a junta of two senior military officers and two civilian leaders was going to run the country in his absence. The arrangement was irregular, but entirely conceivable under the prevailing constitutional provisions.

Thus one of the priorities of constitutional reform was the adoption of a stable, precise, and reliable mechanism for presidential succession, leaving no room for doubt or diversity of interpretation.

Authority and Accountability

Constitutional reform also had to address the need for a balance between authority and accountability in the post-Marcos period. We have seen how too much authority led to massive abuse and national crisis. But governmental effectiveness would not be served by too little authority, either.

Without question, a strong executive would be required in a reconstituted political order because of the magnitude of the problems with which future governments would have to deal. At the same time, Filipinos now had a better sense than before of what a strong, centralized executive authority could and could not achieve. In the Philippines between 1973 and 1986, it was not effective in promoting social justice, national integration, or even economic development. And as we have seen, political development actually retrogressed. It seemed that one could not live in the best of all possible worlds. Somehow men must choose. After the experience of the previous thirteen years, the choice for the Philippines seemed obvious: authority must be made much more accountable to the people, even if that meant a decrease in government effectiveness.

The first step was to reduce the primacy of the presidency. This meant more than shearing the presidency of decree-making powers. The executive role in lawmaking also had to be limited to making proposals to the legislature, and to a power of veto that could be overridden by a significant legislative majority.

The locus of appointive authority also had to be diffused. One or more independent bodies were needed with power to review presidential appointments at policy levels. One possibility was to create bipartisan bodies within the legislature that would be empowered to review appointments to the cabinet, to the high ranks of the military, and to the highest courts in the land.

Limiting executive authority also required fixed and restricted terms of office for all elective officials, and this applied especially to the presidency. A reformed constitution would need to make it extremely difficult to circumvent fixed terms of presidential office, in light of the Philippine experience. Marcos was able to rule beyond the two terms allowed by the 1935 Constitution by exercising emergency powers and then altering the constitutional system. Had the declaration of an emergency in 1972 required the participation of either the legislature or the judiciary, it would not have been so easy for him to place the country under martial law. Had the duration of the exercise of emergency powers been limited, martial law might not have made possible the altering of the constitution.

It was for such reasons that President Aquino was under immediate pressure to declare how long she intended her provisional government to last, and to declare her intentions with regard to constitutional reform.

In ancient times, the Greeks valued the principle of rotation of office, ruling and being ruled by turns, because they believed this would discourage rulers from becoming arbitrary, disregarding the interests of the ruled, and putting the life of the *polis* in jeopardy. There is great wisdom in this view. Human history has shown that those who rule indefinitely often come to forget the limits of their moral authority. They come to see themselves as infallible, possessing a monopoly on wisdom and righteousness. Like the Marcos family, they also might come to view the country as their own private preserve, to direct and exploit as they see fit. A people could not be more sensitive to these dangers than the Filipino people were in the early part of 1986.

A reordering of power among the branches of government in the Philippines also seemed likely to give a high priority to the restoration of judicial independence. It is difficult to describe in a few words how deeply the legal system had fallen into disrepute as a result of abuse and corruption. The decision of the nation's highest court in the Aquino assassination case was notorious; the court not only found the defendants not guilty, but went on to say that the government had established that Benigno Aquino was killed by a lone gunman, a known criminal, while in the custody of government security personnel. That finding was met with widespread disbelief. The court's ruling on challenges to the procedures governing the 1986 election also could only be described as craven. Yet what could one expect when the appointive authority to all judicial posts was in the hands of one person? It was clearly essential that the constitution should provide for the independent review of judicial appointments, at least at the highest level.

An independent judiciary also was needed to provide a means of defining the circumstances under which authority could be lawfully exercised under any future constitution. It was yet another deficiency of the 1973 constitution that it did not spell out the authority of the courts to pass on the constitutionality of laws, decrees, orders, and other official acts of public officials to ensure the rightful exercise of authority.

A clearer separation of powers between the executive and

the legislative branches of government also could serve to put to rest the confusion between presidential and parliamentary systems of government that has existed in the Philippines. The much-amended constitution of 1973 created the confusion by assuming a dominant president and providing for a presidentially appointed prime minister. But Philippine political parties have not developed an ethos supportive of parliamentary government. Parties have been organized along personal lines, and politicians have changed parties freely. "Turn-coatism" has been institutionalized in the Philippines and continues to be practiced to this day by disgruntled or opportunity-seeking legislators who bolt their party and call themselves "independents" or, even worse, simply shift to the party in power. A parliamentary system requires party loyalty and support for the party's programs, regardless of personal considerations. This ethos has simply not developed among Filipino politicians.

Marcos made things worse by appointing a weak prime minister who was not a parliamentary leader at all, but merely a reliable technocrat in his bureaucracy. This choice affected the problem of succession as well, because neither the prime minister nor any of the other Marcos appointees in the line of succession was a credible national leader. These circumstances led, under considerable pressure, to the restoration of the vice presidency, which was to be filled by direct election and whose incumbent was to succeed to the presidency in the event of a vacancy. In early 1986, as a result, the Philippines had a president, a vice president, *and* a prime minister. The anomaly was only temporarily addressed by the appointment of the elected vice president to the office of prime minister.

President Aquino and Vice President Laurel entered office in February 1986 committed to restoring the checks and balances that a separation of powers would provide. It remained to be seen whether a less personal and more professional style of politics could be developed. This seemed essential if the work of the three branches of government was to proceed without being unduly hampered by obstructionism and unwarranted delays. The new government leaders realized that the "old politics" could work against the kind of decision making that was needed to reverse the downward course of the economy and to institute other reforms. But the history of autocratic rule could not be ignored, and the risk inherent in a separation of powers appeared to be one that the new political leadership seemed prepared to take.

The Role of Political Parties

The revival of political parties in 1978, after an interruption of almost six years, enabled Philippine opposition groups to have some impact on Philippine politics. That year, when elections were held to choose the members of an interim legislature, opposition parties were able to win a handful of seats. In 1984, when elections to a regular legislature were held, they were able to win about 32 percent of the elective seats. Although they were unable to influence legislative outcomes significantly, they were at least able to bring issues before the legislature, to publicize them outside of the legislature, and to debate them on the floor. Their ultimate powerlessness, however, was starkly demonstrated by their inability to keep the Assembly, dominated by the government party, from proclaiming Marcos the winner of the February 1986 election, in spite of the widespread fraud that occurred.

The moderate opposition parties were brought into a united front to contest the February 1986 elections, but even then only with great difficulty. A series of efforts under the sponsorship of several prominent individuals known as the Convenor's Group and later under that of a National Unification Committee failed. Cause-oriented groups representing a wide spectrum of political attachments also aspired for unity under the Bagong Alyansang Makabayan (BAYAN or New Nationalist Alliance), but several prominent nationalists pulled out of the alliance, charging that the Communist party was manipulating its affairs, and BAYAN ended up boycotting the elections along with the rest of the far left.

In the end, the Aquino-Laurel partnership was created only after the personal intervention of Jaime Cardinal Sin. In party terms, this meant a coalition between the Philippine Democratic Party and the Lakas ng Bayan (PDP-LABAN), which were joined in support of Mrs. Aquino, and the UNIDO, which was supporting Mr. Laurel. Both groups had contested the Assembly elections in 1984, and had some experience at that time in developing working agreements to avoid splitting the opposition vote. The united Aquino-Laurel slate in February 1986 enabled the coalition to deliver a lead of more than 800,000 votes among the twenty-odd million that NAMFREL was able to count. Several million more votes were not counted at all, particularly in areas in which Mrs. Aquino was known to enjoy great popularity, because of fraudulent practices. It was clear that the Aquino-Laurel slate had a substantial majority of the nation behind it.

How this would be translated into a working political coalition for other purposes remained to be seen. The elections to the Assembly and to local posts, expected sometime in 1987, would provide a serious test of how lasting the coalition might be. It also was unclear whether Mrs. Aquino intended to weaken the role of the coalition, and enhance her own independence, by moving to create a new set of institutions through which "people power" could make itself felt in political affairs.

At the outset, the coalition seemed to hold fast in the face of highly divisive and politically sensitive issues like the release of political prisoners, prosecution of human rights violators among military and police personnel, and selective payment of foreign loans. In confronting all of these issues it appeared that Mrs. Aquino's influence was sufficiently strong to keep the coalition together. Other divisive issues were bound to surface in the future. Whether her ability to hold the coalition together would continue remained to be seen.

The future of the party of Marcos, the Kilusang Bagong Lipunan (KBL), was also unclear. The party remained loyal to Marcos to the bitter end. It seemed likely to suffer from the stigma of his repression and corruption for some time to come, if indeed it continued to exist at all. Some of its most ambitious members had been removed from its ranks; the flight of Imelda Marcos from the country and of Juan Ponce Enrile to the

Aquino camp deprived it of potential leadership but also of potential rivals for leadership. Former Labor Minister Blas P. Ople proposed to lead the party in the Assembly as a loyal opposition, and this was a function that needed to be performed. The ability of the KBL to attract much support in future elections, however, in the absence of the Marcos machine and its patronage, was in serious doubt.

The Aquino-Laurel group was divided before the election over how to deal with the Communist Party of the Philippines (CCP), and its military arm, the New People's Army (NPA); the issue remained after the new leaders took office. Views among Mrs. Aquino's advisers were wide-ranging. Former Senator Jose W. Diokno at one point had suggested permitting the CPP to keep its arms as a demonstration of the government's sincerity in welcoming it back into the political mainstream. The Convenors Group had proposed that the CPP should be legalized, one of the points in its proposed manifesto that had led Salvador Laurel to withdraw from its proceedings. Defense Minister Enrile was opposed to the post-election release of any political prisoners who had been among the founders of the CPP and NPA.

The CPP itself was opposed before the election to participation in any activity that would imply approval of the regime. With its insurgency growing dramatically, and with its own timetable calling for a stalemate with the armed forces in three to five years, the CPP had little reason to change course. It boycotted the February 1986 presidential election, declaring that dictators could not be defeated in elections, and that, in any event, Mrs. Aquino was no real alternative to Marcos. After the election, some CPP members further alienated popular opinion by attributing the downfall of Marcos to a plot by the U.S. Central Intelligence Agency—no doubt a surprise to those Filipinos who had redeemed the nation through their own courageous action.

It seemed clear that the February 1986 "revolution" had set back the CPP-NPA timetable, perhaps substantially. The "revolution" also demonstrated, dramatically, the ability of the Catholic hierarchy to influence public opinion and action. Indeed, the determination of so many people from all social classes to fight Marcos at the polls had to be seen as an unambiguous sign of their dedication to a third way, to an alternative to both the Marcos dictatorship and the proposed communist "dictatorship of the people."

Mrs. Aquino characteristically took a position spanning that of most of her advisers. She said that national reconciliation was her highest priority. She said that she intended to deal energetically with the economic, social, and political grievances that had led young men and women to take up arms against the Marcos government. She asked them to appreciate that she too had been a victim of that regime. She said that she was prepared, if they would give up their arms, to grant them amnesty from future prosecution for any actions they had taken while they were members of the NPA. She left open the possibility of permitting the CPP to participate in national affairs as a legally recognized political party. She also said that, if her offer of reconciliation was rejected, and if insurgents continued to use force of arms to impose their will on others, she was prepared as commander in chief to use the full power of the reformed Armed Forces of the Philippines to defend the government and civil society.

One could only hope that the CPP leadership, as well as its followers, would give the proposals of President Aquino serious consideration. The leadership had to recognize that they had played no part in the downfall of the Marcos dictatorship, and now had little claim to popular support. Moreover, the fall of that dictatorship through militant nonviolence by people of all social classes did not at all fit the communist theoretical mold, so that a rethinking of ideology seemed to be in order. The presence in President Aquino's cabinet of many individuals entirely new to politics, many of whom were closely identified with populist interests and concerns, was also a potential source of encouragement to members and supporters of the CPP that social reform could be pressed without the tragic and wasteful destruction of more lives and property. If it were willing to engage in mainstream politics, the CPP could help these cabinet members to press for the people-oriented programs to which President Aquino herself was committed. There had never been a better time for the CPP to rethink its whole approach to the issue of social change.

Whatever the particular array and alignment of political parties that might claim a legitimate role in the affairs of the Philippines in the future, it would be significant to the political system as a whole how each performed the classic functions of recruitment, organization, and education. No party performed, or was able to perform, these functions adequately in the recent past. Nevertheless, the limited practical experience from 1983 on was modestly encouraging. The PDP-LABAN had been recruiting, organizing, and conducting political education since that time. So also had UNIDO. The present position of these two groups, allied to the nationally elected leaders of the country, materially enhanced their prospects for success in the future. Within a short time of the election, they were able to begin to build local bases of support through the appointment of local executives, pending the holding of local elections. The KBL also retained a good deal of its local machinery, although this was likely to suffer the same stigma as that of Marcos's former party at the national level.

Given the nature of party competition, it seemed likely that political parties would continue to play their usual—and necessary—roles in the political system, if only out of self-interest. It also was likely in the new Aquino era that the electorate would demand more from the parties in the way of results on behalf of their constituents. The discovery by the people of the immense power in their hands seemed bound to have a lasting impact on Philippine politics. Performance seemed likely to be a much more important test of whether parties would attract and hold the loyalty of citizens in the future.

The Mass Media and the Bar

The mass media also played a role in the fall of Ferdinand Marcos from power—a role that in the final hours was crucial. The issues of ownership, allegiance, and accountability of the media thus seemed likely to figure prominently in debates about the reconstitution of the political order.

The mass media had been placed under close government supervision with the imposition of martial law. Control over television and radio stations and over daily newspapers was transferred in time to hands friendly to the Marcos government. They remained there for a decade. During the 1986 presidential campaign, Marcos enjoyed a near-monopoly of the electronic media, and had the uncritical support of most newspapers as well.

With the Aquino assassination, however, serious efforts to break the government monopoly began. The Church obtained rights to establish a radio station. Numerous new publications sprouted up, and although some were shut down, others managed to survive and prosper. Media coverage influenced the membership of the Fact Finding Board that was appointed to investigate the assassination, and coverage of its proceedings facilitated its independence of action.

Foreign media coverage of the election was intense, and its focus on irregularities, most dramatically represented by the walk-out of computer operators at the official election commission headquarters, was a major factor in turning international opinion against the Marcos regime. In the final days of the regime, control of television and radio stations in Manila was fiercely contested. Armed units fought over the major television station in the capital, and the strength of the military dissidents was demonstrated by their ability to take the station and cut off the broadcast of Marcos' inauguration before he could take the oath of office. Pro-government units blew up the Church's principal radio transmitter, but the Cardinal was nevertheless able to broadcast to the citizens of Manila his appeal to take to the streets and halt the armor of the presidential guard.

It was thus amply demonstrated that the mass media were critical to the mobilization of people power. Their significance was underscored by the appointment by President Aquino of a minister of information to her cabinet—and by the immediate criticism which greeted that appointment. The government's announced intention to inquire into the ownership of several television channels was reasonable enough. But how ownership and control were to be dispersed, and by what means the media were to be held accountable to the public, were issues that remained to be resolved.

The role of the bar in a reconstituted political order was also of much interest in the early days of the Aquino government. That the reputation of the bar had been badly tarnished along with that of many other institutions of society was sadly true. Reports of attorneys bribing judges on behalf of their clients were widespread; it had become the only way to protect them. One of the results was that many of the country's best legal minds had withdrawn from the practice of civil and criminal law and taken refuge in the legal staffs of large corporations. To say there was disillusionment with the corruption of the judicial system would be an understatement.

Nevertheless, not all lawyers had lost courage. At least a few had been indefatigable in their defense of political detainees. Others had dedicated themselves to defending the rights of the underprivileged. Such individuals were rare, but they helped to suggest to many of their fellow citizens that the profession was not beyond redemption.

It seemed assured that in the new political order there would be ample opportunity for the best of the legal profession to carry on and augment this tradition of a few. Even under a government with the best of intentions, ordinary citizens would need to be assured that infractions of the law and violations of their rights would not go unchallenged. This was especially so if the Aquino government was to succeed in its announced intention of bringing about social change as significant as the political change of February 1986.

The bar also faced a large task in reviewing and upgrading the quality of the law. The entire body of decrees that had emanated from the Office of the President during the Marcos dictatorship, for example, needed to be examined. It seemed certain that some would be found to be unjust, onerous, or at least undesirable in the light of contemporary realities. Consciously working to rationalize the country's legal system more generally was a long-term task, and one of the responsibilities of the bar to the society.

The bar also faced the task of providing legal education to the population at large, instructing men and women in their rights and duties as citizens. The poor and the uneducated were the primary group in need of such instruction. The foundations for a large-scale program of legal education were already in place in some law schools and in some chapters of the Integrated Bar of the Philippines.

People Power and National Leadership

The Aquino government owed its position to many developments, but especially to two fundamental elements: the person of Corazon Aquino and the unparalleled support she had among the people. The leadership of the Church was alert to the significance of both. So also were the leaders of the armed forces who came to her support. It is doubtful that either group would have reached the decisions they did if Mrs. Aquino had not demonstrated a potential for leadership in the course of the campaign, and if that potential had not been widely recognized among the population.

It was of great importance to Mrs. Aquino that she should develop some means of continuing to communicate with this base of her support. The enthusiasm generated by her revolutionary victory would last only so long. Some means of continuing to mobilize popular opinion was likely to be needed if Mrs. Aquino was to press ahead with her programs. She faced possible opposition from several quarters. Some of her programs, such as land reform, faced opposition from the established elite. She also faced likely obstruction from the bureaucracy, dominated as it was at the outset by Marcos appointees. There also was the danger that some of her own cabinet colleagues and advisers, who gained their political experience in the pre-1972 period, would too readily fall back into the old political habits that gave democracy a bad name and made martial law a not unthinkable alternative. If Mrs. Aquino was going to change the political culture of the country, she was going to need to continue to tap the support of all those citizens who became politically conscious and active, many for the first time, in the course of her campaign.

The mass media provided one available means, and it seemed likely that Mrs. Aquino would come to depend on them more than any of her predecessors had. But she also was in need of a means of communication that could work in both directions. She needed a means of keeping informed of popular sentiment if she was to remain independent of the old political parties, all of which had their own leaders, and independent of the government bureaucracy, which she could not trust. The credibility of her government also seemed likely to be better assured if her supporters had some confidence that their opinions were being taken into account as the government set policies and made decisions, especially in matters of obvious interest to them.

One possible means of meeting this latter need was the institution of new community-based councils at the local level. One concrete instance in which such consultative bodies could be immediately useful was in regard to revising the constitution. Well before proposals were ready to be submitted to a plebiscite for ratification, a process of widespread consultation would help to educate both the public and the government about what was most in need of attention. Community councils might also have a role to play in examining projected policies of the government that were likely to have a local impact, such as those affecting education and other social services. Such councils also could in time provide President Aquino with an organized power base of her own, and one which might be more suited to her needs than a political party in the traditional mold.

In addition to her widespread popular support, President Aquino had the asset of her own personality. The loss of integrity and moral authority in the presidency of the country had been extremely costly to the nation. It was not only that the moral bankruptcy of the Marcos regime had led to economic decline and social polarization. The Filipino people suffered national humiliation. They lost their pride, their sense of dignity as a people. What first brought people to Mrs. Aquino's support was the perception that she was a person of integrity and of upright moral character. In the course of her campaign, she also came to be seen as a credible leader who could restore confidence in government and bring together causes and movements that tended to fragment and polarize the nation.

Former Minister Vicente Paterno once spoke of the need of the Filipino people for "a national dream." They need a vision of the future, he said, that could motivate them to action and achievement, provide them with an incentive to make sacrifices they would not otherwise make, and give them an objective toward which their collective efforts could be directed. The Filipino people found that vision and acted on it in four climactic days in February 1986. Amorphous and independent groups disciplined themselves to act in unison. They acted peaceably and with enormous courage. And they stopped what looked like certain bloodshed and mob rule. The future demanded that they not lose sight of what they gained in those days.

The Future of the Democratic Ethic

The Philippines had a democratic government before 1972. It was imperfect, slow, inadequate, and inefficient. And it was lost in September 1972. In the long dark night of dictatorship that followed, the Filipino people learned the value of what they had had. If only because of the years of authoritarian rule, the democratic ethic has a future in the Philippines.

It has already been noted that this ethic had its foundations in the Spanish era in the Philippines. The Propaganda Movement of the nineteenth century espoused the liberal democratic values its leaders imbided in Europe. The political writings of Apolinario Mabini, Jose Rizal, and other Filipino heroes were strongly rooted in these values. So also was the Malolos Constitution. American tutelage, from early in the present century, contributed further to the development of this tradition. Even the 1973 Constitution, which imposed authoritarianism on the Philippines, paid lip service to the values of liberal democracy.

It is sometimes argued that Filipino culture is basically authoritarian, but the democratic ethic remains a strong competitor within that culture. Even during the years of authoritarian government, democratic values retained a powerful hold on the Filipino imagination. There was a persistent clamor for a restoration of democratic institutions from the mid-1970s on, and a spontaneous and continuing outpouring of democratic sentiment after August 1983. Even the boycott movement was an indication of the struggle of the democratic ethic for recognition, as the movement asserted the right of citizens to demand conditions that would make elections meaningful.

The emergence of numerous new parapolitical groups after August 1983 was a further assertion of the democratic ethic. Many were involved in voluntary self-help projects to aid the poor in society—feeding them, educating them, trying to help them become self-reliant. Many also were soon participating in the political process—organizing, socializing, articulating, and processing demands, and representing opinions and interests before decision-making authorities.

The performance of the electorate during the 1984 elections to the national assembly also was an indication of the prospects for the democratic ethic in the country. Despite well-recognized odds, many opposition candidates participated, and did better than their own best expectations. They also made a point to those who had boycotted the voting, obliging them to reexamine their position when the "snap" presidential election was called for early 1986. They had shown that, with determination and vigilance, their sentiments could be registered and could make a difference. Another factor, of course, was the difference between electing a superfluous institution, which is what the legislature was in 1984, and electing a chief executive with real political authority in 1986.

The assertion by the mass media, particularly radio and the press, of the right of expression and the right of the people to know, was also a positive development that contributed to a better prospect for the survival of the democratic ethic in the

Philippines. The press and radio both made significant advances toward liberalization after 1983. Even the mysterious killings and disappearances of media people throughout the country did not erode the determination of many of their colleagues.

The reform movement within the armed forces, and the behavior of the military leadership during and immediately after the downfall of the Marcos regime, also demonstrated that there were forces for democracy within the armed services. The armed forces had often been viewed as a monolithic organization, blindly committed to the security of Marcos and the support of his programs. The reform movement demonstrated that members of these services were capable of asserting their own professional values. These were values that had been seriously compromised during the Marcos years. If the aims of the reform movement could be achieved, the probability of continuing civilian control of the armed forces was high—and the prospect of a military takeover in the immediate post-Marcos era was considerably diminished.

The full restoration of the democratic ethic, however, could come only with constitutional reform and the building of democratic institutions of government. The Philippines was on the threshold of this reform in the early part of 1986. In the light of the daily discovery of what seemed to be an endless trail of Marcos corruption and decadence, it appeared certain that the principles of government responsibility, public accountability, separation of powers, and respect for the sovereign will of the people would find their way into the new fundamental law.

A peaceful resolution of the communist and Muslim insurgencies also needed to be diligently sought, even as structural reforms were planned with the aim of dealing with their root causes. The positive response of leaders of both groups was initially encouraging. They seemed prepared to give President Aquino a chance to resolve matters in a peaceful manner. With parallel reforms in the military, these developments suggested it might be possible to see the end of the insurgencies within a few years.

Finally, the survival of Mrs. Aquino as president was centrally important to the democratic future. This was not only because of her commitment to peaceful democratic restoration, but also because of the high level of public credibility and trust that she enjoyed. Any effort to remove her from the leadership would have to be resisted by the citizenry. On that condition might well rest the survival of the democratic ethic in the Philippines.

CHAPTER VIII

ECONOMIC RELATIONS

JESUS P. ESTANISLAO

Economic relations between the Philippines and the United States, like those between most peoples, have been dynamic and changing over time. They transcend simple models of exploitation of the weak by the strong. American motives have often been less than idealistic. But there has been ample self-interest displayed on the Philippine side as well. Moreover, the wider environment has changed over the decades, so that neither party could claim all the bargaining chips all the time. There has often been an imperative for some give and take. It has been a process that has produced results that are at best only mixed from the point of view of either side.

For the Philippine economy there have been important gains. A great deal of progress has been achieved, in part because of the dynamic relationship with the United States. But there is no hiding the structural difficulties bedeviling the Philippine economy either. And at least some of these can be traced to the special features of the U.S. relationship.

Changes in a Dynamic World

The economic facet has, of course, been only one of several in a wide-ranging relationship between the two peoples. And the relative importance of the economic element has not always been the same. In the space of less than a century, the United States has metamorphosed from potential friend to actual foe; from absolute colonial master to guide and guardian of an independent, democratic future; from ally and savior to grantor of independence and aid; from natural scapegoat for many of the country's ills to banker lending recycled funds to one more developing country. There have been several distinct periods in

Philippine-American relations from an economic point of view, and quite different features have characterized each.

The period of initial experimentation saw the entry of American merchants, contractors, bar and restaurant keepers, newspaper owners, and bicycle shop and livery stable proprietors. These were the pioneers, men who had visions of private fortunes to be made for themselves by providing services to the growing American community of soldiers and government officials. Their investments were small. They banked on quick returns. They were mainly in trading and services. It was only after the Cooper Act of 1905, which carried an assurance that the United States would remain in the Philippines for at least twenty years, that bigger investments in infrastructure and public utilities were undertaken. Since mass education, already pursued by the Spanish regime, was continued and even expanded, investments in the manufacture of school supplies and of school buildings were also made. Indeed, the first American corporations in the Philippines reflected the character of the initial economic thrust: the Manila Electric Company, the Manila-Dagupan Railroad, International Harvester, the Philippine Education Company, and Atlantic Gulf and Pacific, a corporate contractor.

The second period covered most of the colonial era. In 1909, free trade was introduced on a duty-free quota basis. In 1913, complete reciprocal free trade was established. Philippine objections to such provisions, which Philippine leaders had the foresight to see as molding the economy into a colonial dependency, were given short shrift. As feared, the pattern of Philippine exports shifted toward one of predominant concentration on the American market; a similar shift occurred in the pattern of imports. Two export crops became the engine of the Philippine economy: export earnings from sugar and coconut determined overall Philippine economic performance. Although a few other exports, such as tobacco and Manila hemp (abaca), were considered traditional and received some attention in the formulation of American protectionist bills during the depression years, they were relatively unimportant. Gold mining and log processing were important when taken by themselves, but in the context of the whole economy they were leagues behind sugar and coconut.

The third period covered the Second World War and its immediate aftermath. The destruction of the Philippine economy during the war took specific form in the abandonment of sugar mills and coconut oil mills. But the toll was much wider. After the war, the country was in no position to resume normal economic life as before. Reconstruction was the first economic priority, and independence on schedule remained the first political priority. The pent-up demand of a population deprived of consumer goods for years was high. Spending by the re-occupation army and aid provided by the Bell Trade Act provided temporary resources, but the country's reserves were draining rapidly, and import controls had to be imposed in 1949. Despite assertions of economic independence, the shadow of past colonial trading ties still loomed large; the Bell Trading Act had to give way to the Laurel-Langley Agreement, which stretched the period of economic readjustment to 1974 and conferred continuing privileged access of a few Philippine exports to the U.S. market.

The fourth period took shape during the 1970s, when Philippine external borrowings soared dramatically, in part because of the oil crisis. Previous to the 1970s, both the Philippine government and the Philippine private sector had already been tapping the credit resources of American lending institutions. The indebtedness to such institutions was not relatively significant, however, until the end of the 1970s. By this time, of all fixed-term external debts of the Philippines, 40 percent was owed to U.S.-controlled or dominated financial institutions. As foreign borrowing became an increasingly critical need for the Philippines, the influence of U.S. financial institutions on the Philippine economy through the creditor-debtor network became impossible to disregard.

All through these different phases, one observes a gradual evolution that has followed an almost natural, understandable pattern. The age of the pioneering merchant with no long-term commitment to developing the economy was to be expected in the generally unsettled conditions of that time. The age of the colonizer with its own structure of dependence and its strict fiscal and financial discipline followed the decision to retain the Philippines as a colony. The age of the grantor came as a result of a promise enshrined in law and the devastation wrought by a war in which the Philippines took sides firmly and clearly and fought for the eventual military victor. The age of the banker was set in train as trade held only limited prospects as a way for the Philippines to balance its external accounts, and as aid was mutually held to be an inappropriate basis for furthering economic relations.

While structural changes occurred as a result of changes in policy regimes and of economic growth in general, there have been no abrupt turns in the structure of the Philippine economy except for the period of Japanese occupation. Indeed, changes in the economic structure of the Philippines over time have been gradual, and although they have been influenced by changes in policy, they occurred largely in a continuous, secular manner.[1]

Costs and Benefits

Economic relationships between the Philippines and the United States were struck and fashioned after the perceived self-interest of both countries. Following the initial flush of taking possession over the islands, the United States recognized that it had administrative responsibilities to get economic and social life going. After free access to each other's market was established, sugar and coconut oil mills had to be set up so the Philippines could earn the foreign exchange needed to import goods from the United States. And after the continuing demand for independence had been met, some temporary concessions had to be provided to enable a colonially dependent economy to readjust to its new status. Especially after the oil shocks, which made it imperative for U.S. financial

---

[1] J. P. Estanislao, E. M. Ocol, and F. E. Agdamag, *Broad Dimensions of Long-Term Economic Growth in the Philippines, 1908-1978* (Manila: Center for Research and Communication, 1982).

institutions to recycle funds from dollar surplus countries to dollar deficit countries, short-term loans had to be extended to a number of developing countries; a few of these became the top borrowers, and to this league the Philippines belonged.

Thus, Philippine-American economic relations have been responsive to the varying needs of the time. Although American economic interests were far from disregarded, and guided decisions as they were taken, still Philippine economic needs also had to be accommodated. It is not possible to gloss over the behavior of American vested interests as they lobbied in the U.S. Congress when economic bills affecting the Philippines were being framed. But given the objective economic record of the past eight decades, it also is impossible to deny that some progress has been achieved by the Philippine economy as a result of its relationship with that of the United States.

As this economic relationship evolved over the decades, one characteristic feature stands out. For the United States, Philippine matters have generally been a minor distraction. For the Philippines, economic relations with the United States have been almost an obsession. Too much of the economy depended on this relationship, and for too many sectors of the economy it constituted the dividing line between progress and mere survival.

Thus, in deciding on various economic issues arising in their relations with the Philippines, Americans could afford to be guided by their own prevailing intellectual and economic moods. The late empire-building moves of the European countries helped goad the United States to acquire a colony of its own. The need to show that a colony should not be a drain on the U.S. Treasury, and devotion to the discipline of the gold standard, imposed an overly conservative fiscal and financial mechanism on the Philippines. The Great Depression and the protectionist virus led to the imposition of quotas on Philippine exports to the United States. The grant of political independence and eventually of credits through the international financial system coincided with the mores generally accepted in the United States at the time. For the United States as a large and, after 1945, global power, the Philippines was merely one more country that had to be dealt with, one whose degree of importance to the core interests of the United States was limited.

But for the Philippines, the position was different. The country's economic fortunes, through no choice of its own, were tied up with those of the American market. The industries to be developed were dictated by the free-trading relations with an industrial power. The economy had to be readjusted to conform with a new political status. It is not surprising that different viewpoints should arise from such unequal bargaining positions. It was only to be expected that nationalism would be equated in some quarters in the Philippines with anti-Americanism.

Even though economic issues tended to be decided by reference to prevailing American moods and the more narrow interests of American lobby groups, still a number of developments occurred which, although not within the immediate ambit of economics, nonetheless affected the long-term economic position of the Philippines. The attempts to develop the physical infrastructure; to raise the already high levels of literacy and to universalize the already widespread educational opportunities; to improve standards of public health and sanitation, which gradually reduced mortality rates and raised life expectancy; to introduce experiments in American democracy with its stress on election to positions of power and glory: all these could not fail to have a deep influence on the economic foundations of Philippine society. The rise of transport and communication, the spread of high consumer expectations, the export of manpower, rising population growth rates, an eloquent political leadership, and a dispirited, loosely organized bureaucracy—all these have helped to set the potentials and problems for long-term economic growth in the Philippines.

The Philippine economy during these eight decades has not been catapulted from a relatively undeveloped state to one that is acceptably developed. On the other hand, in real terms, it has managed to grow at an annual average rate of 3.5 percent. Partly because of such long-term growth, developmental patterns have emerged: the economy is less agricultural and more industrialized; investment and savings rates have risen to beyond 20 percent; exports are more diversified; the government has become a more active agent for the management of economic development; a domestic mass consumer market has been tended as a base for local industry.

At the same time, however, the Philippines has not been free of problems arising from its relations with the United States. With the baggage of its colonial past, the Philippines has shown an ambivalence that has brought it to a muddle. Fearing foreign competition, the country has tended to be overly protective of its domestic industries, which has meant that it has wanted to avoid free trading rules with respect to its imports. But hoping for the benefits of freer trade, it has continued to expect relatively free access in the United States, Japan, and the EEC for its exports. As a consequence, the country has hung on to an inward-looking, import-substituting path of industrialization, while leaving untended the equally important task of continuing to export under competitive conditions in foreign markets.

Current Economic Relations

However one assesses the U.S. economic relationship, a new reality has been evolving in recent years.

The Philippines has been developing economic ties with a widening circle of countries; Philippine trade flows now go in important directions other than the United States. Both Japan and the EEC have become important destinations and sources of Philippine external trade. The Middle East cannot be disregarded as a source of oil and as a temporary haven of Philippine construction workers. China, the Soviet Union, and the socialist bloc also add a new dimension to Philippine trade relations. Thus, while Philippine economic relations with the United States are still important for the Philippines, the degree of their importance has been cut by half.

This development has come about both by the conscious design of Philippine national policy and by the broader imperatives of international trade. It is a trend that can prove healthy

Relative Importance of Trading Partners
in Philippine Exports and Imports:
1970 and 1980

| | *Percent of Total* | | |
	Japan	*U.S.*	*Others*
Exports			
1968-1970	36.5	40.1	23.4
1978-1980	24.9	29.7	45.4
Imports			
1968-1970	28.9	33.3	37.8
1978-1980	20.8	22.6	56.6

Source: Basic data from the IMF Direction of Trade Yearbook, various issues.

for economic relations between the Philippines and United States. For the former, it is the only trade pattern consistent with its truly independent status. For the latter, it means that the U.S. need not be the scapegoat for whatever problems the Philippine economy may be confronted with in the future.

A large percentage of Philippine borrowings from external sources and of foreign investments in the Philippines now comes from Japan as well as the United States. Philippine economic issues that touch on external trade balances, on technology transfer, on industrial restructuring, and on capital flows must now be discussed in reference to these two countries. Indeed, international economic issues brought out at UNCTAD, at North-South seminars, and at other world conferences or meetings find their concrete specification for the Philippines in its economic relations with not only the United States but also Japan and the other more developed countries in the Pacific Basin.

Indeed, the region of the Pacific Basin may well be the most appropriate context in which to consider Philippine-American economic relations in the future. Bilateralism does not fit the emerging multipolar world that even the Philippines has entered. Complete universalism is an ideal that practical men of affairs may yet be unprepared to turn into a reality. But regionalism—which enables the Philippines to reach out and relate much more substantially with its neighbors in Southeast Asia, and together with its partners in ASEAN to work out practical arrangements for economic interaction with the United States, Japan, and the other developed countries in the Pacific Basin—may well be the trend of the present decade and the next.

But the current economic crisis in the Philippines strains any hope for the future. Internal reforms are needed, and needed immediately. Yet the danger is that the focus might be instead on cosmetic assistance that the United States might be called upon to render to an old ally and friend. It would be tragic if the present opportunity for establishing a new basis for an altogether different economic order in the Philippines is let pass without instituting the internal substantive reforms that are required. The long-term needs of the Philippines will best be served if Filipinos are left largely on their own, with their own resources, to confront the basic choices they must make if they are to effect a much needed transformation in their economy and society.

Past Romanticism

Romanticism can weaken any nation's capacity to face facts. It can moor policy to a past whose relevance has waned, and bedevil it with fears and complexes that should no longer have a place in the circumstances of a significantly altered present.

Philippine economic policy sentiment has in large measure been entrapped by the past. Its main dynamic can be traced to the felt imperative of increasing the nation's relative economic independence. This was further specified as the ability to produce locally most, if not all, of the goods that used to be imported. Plants for textiles, cement, food processing, and the assembly of consumer durables such as radios, TVs, refrigerators, and automobiles were quickly set up. Indeed, the poten-

higher, because relocation to Japan or Guam or Hawaii would require using higher-paid Japanese or American workers for maintenance and repairs. It would also require considerably more ships and men to retain the same military capability in the area because more time would be needed to get there from bases so far away. Nevertheless, according to Admiral Long, the U.S. could maintain its present military capabilities in the region if it were willing to pay the price.

The value of the bases is enhanced by two additional facts regarding their location. First, the proximity of Subic Bay and Clark Field to each other increases the usefulness of each beyond what it would be if they were, say, a thousand miles or more apart; with the two so close together, services and training activities can be performed jointly. Second, because the mission of the bases is to support operations both to the north (the western Pacific) and to the west and south (mainland Southeast Asia and the Indian Ocean to the west; Indonesia, Australia, and New Zealand to the south) moving the bases in any direction would weaken their ability to perform some part of their mission. A major study done by the Congressional Research Service of the Library of Congress in 1977 also concluded that relocating the bases in any single direction would detract more from their capabilities in the areas that became more distant than it would enhance their capabilities in the areas that became closer.

Many Filipinos see the bases from quite a different perspective from that of most Americans, and object to their continued presence in the Philippines. The objection that they leave the Philippines less than fully sovereign has already been mentioned. The changes made in the 1979 revision to the bases agreement reduced the intensity of, but did not eliminate, such feelings. Other Filipinos object to the bases on the ground that their principal use is to support America's grand strategy rather than to defend the Philippines. Others go further, arguing that in a U.S.-Soviet conflict the bases would make the Philippines a target of Soviet nuclear missiles, whereas the Soviets would have no reason to attack the Philippines if the bases were not there. Still other objections are that the Philippines is not adequately compensated by the United States for the bases, although this objection appears to have diminished as U.S. aid has increased. Finally, some Filipinos object to the impact of the bases on the areas surrounding them, where bars and brothels have turned some nearby towns into unsavory places.

It is difficult to tell how widespread Filipino objections to the bases are outside political and intellectual circles in Manila. Most observers have found little anti-base sentiment in other parts of the country. Moreover, the history of recent decades has included examples of Filipino leaders who voiced anti-base sentiments while they were in the political opposition, and reversed their positions when they came to power, both because of the economic benefits the country derived from the bases and because the bases were a major reason for the U.S. security guarantee.

U.S.-Philippines Relations: The 1980s

The Nixon administration's lack of concern for advancing the cause of democracy and promoting human rights was reversed by the Carter administration, especially in its early years. Carter's emphasis on human rights did not lead to any fundamental change in U.S. policy toward the Philippines because of U.S. security concerns, although U.S.-Philippines relations were somewhat tense during the Carter years. Nixon's neglect of human rights had had another effect, however, and that was to cause Congress to become increasingly interested in the subject.

Laws were enacted forbidding most types of economic and military assistance—as well as military sales—to countries judged guilty of "gross violations of internationally recognized human rights." This standard left considerable latitude of interpretation to whatever administration was currently in office. It did make a concern for human rights a part of the law of the land, however, and thus an element of U.S. foreign policy. It also provided an aura of legitimacy whenever an administration wished to apply strict standards. That this has seldom occurred should not cause us to overlook the value of what has been accomplished. The fact that the laws are on the books, the possibility that more rigorous standards might be applied, and the holding of periodic hearings by Congressional committees, taken together, have given U.S. political leaders a useful lever for diplomacy involving human rights. This leverage is rarely so great that the government can force an authoritarian regime to adopt democracy, or even allow political opponents or groups the freedom to organize and carry out activities that actually threaten the regime. U.S. leverage has often been sufficient, however, to save individual lives, to cause a regime to exert less control of the press, or to allow a somewhat greater degree of political freedom for opposition groups than would have existed without U.S. pressure. By the beginning of the 1980s, rights advocates in the U.S. were focusing increased attention on the Philippines and on allegations of widening abuses there.

Although martial law had been welcomed by many Filipinos and accepted by nearly all in the early 1970s, the end of the decade found the country's mood changing. Neglect of agriculture, increasing government mismanagement of the economy, and adverse international economic trends began to weaken Marcos' support. The pervasive corruption, the politicization of the armed forces, and the grants of special economic favors to the relatives and friends of the president and his wife aroused increasing criticism. As the rate of economic growth slowed, the maldistribution of income worsened. By the early 1980s, real wages for most workers were lower than they had been a decade earlier.

Marcos attempted to defuse the growing opposition by ending martial law in January of 1981, but only after constitutional changes that left his basic powers intact. Under these circumstances, few Filipinos accepted his claim to have secured a new popular mandate in the elections held that year. Marcos held the levers of power, and there was little his opponents could do. Yet popular opposition to the regime was increasing, and the country was simmering with discontent. This situation boiled over with the August 1983 assassination of Benigno Aquino.

The assassination brought a change in the U.S. stance toward Marcos. The Reagan administration had showered Marcos with praise in the previous years. At Marcos' inauguration in June 1981, Vice President George Bush had toasted him: "We love your adherence to democratic principles and to democratic processes." President Reagan gave President Marcos a lavish welcome when he visited Washington in 1982. And in early 1983, the administration concluded a review of the bases agreement and promised Marcos it would make a "best effort" attempt to persuade Congress to provide $900 million in aid for the bases between 1984 and 1989—an 80 percent increase over the previous level. During this period, more and more Filipinos came to view the U.S. as a major prop of the Marcos regime, and anti-Americanism increased.

After Aquino's assassination, the administration began to distance itself from Marcos and to expand its contacts with the opposition. The U.S. House of Representatives on October 25, 1983, voted 413 to 3 for a resolution calling for an impartial investigation of Aquino's murder and for free and fair elections to the national assembly in May 1984. Administration spokesmen also began to speak out on the need for democracy in the Philippines, and President Reagan canceled a visit to the Philippines scheduled for November 1983.

During 1984, the U.S. government gradually became aware that Marcos was not the only threat to democracy and, over the long term, to U.S. interests in the Philippines. By mid-1984, U.S. officials had taken a fresh look at the Communist Party of the Philippines (CPP), its New People's Army (NPA), and its united front organization, the National Democratic Front. What these officials saw was a communist-led insurgency that had made rapid gains since 1980, especially in the year after Aquino's assassination. The economy had gone into a serious recession, providing new grievances for communist-led groups to exploit. Moreover, the Philippine government had not developed, much less begun to implement, a strategy to halt and eventually reverse the NPA's gains. By 1984, the NPA was operating in more than two-thirds of the country's provinces and had some degree of influence in as many as 20 percent of the nation's barrios, its smallest administrative units. Indeed, only at the end of 1984 did Marcos acknowledge that the NPA had become a significant threat; he admitted then that the NPA had caused the death of 4,922 soldiers and civilians in the three years ending the previous August. But Marcos undertook none of the political, economic, or military reforms that might have checked the growth of the NPA or of the Communist-dominated National Democratic Front. During 1985, the NPA experienced some difficulties when it tried to conduct larger-scale operations than the small raids it had concentrated on previously, but its strength nonetheless steadily increased. If the growth of the NPA continued at its recent rate, it would be able to establish secure bases and challenge government control of many towns within a few years and could take over the country by the end of the decade.

The situation in the Philippines thus bore a certain resemblance to Nicaragua in the late 1970s, with the United States again appearing to be linked to a corrupt and ineffective government that had lost the confidence of its people. There were, it should be noted, important differences between the two situations. The New People's Army, unlike the Sandinistas, was not receiving any outside support. And it had to contend with the democratic tradition of the Philippines. Yet the CPP's program made clear that, if it won power, the Philippines would be ruled by a communist dictatorship. The party's orientation and policies, as well as its propaganda against "the Marcos-U.S. dictatorship," indicated that it would be an avowed enemy of the United States, and would force the United States out of its military bases in the country.

The year 1985 was a difficult one for U.S. policymakers, who saw themselves confronted by an impossible dilemma. Most of them not only recognized that basic reforms were necessary if the NPA was to be checked, but also stated such convictions quite openly in testimony before Congress. Throughout the year they also stated publicly, though in a somewhat more muted fashion, in testimony before the Senate Foreign Relations Committee and the House Foreign Affairs Committee, that Marcos was doing little to carry out such reforms. Off the record, they expressed the fear that Marcos was stonewalling the United States, and conceded that they saw less and less likelihood of his changing course. The tone of Congressmen from both parties became steadily more critical of Marcos. But Administration officials also feared that strong anti-Marcos action, such as curtailing or halting aid, might precipitate an economic or military collapse or lead Marcos to threaten the U.S. bases. This led them to urge continued economic and military support to the Philippines government, and at the same time, support for domestic Filipino pressures for a restoration of democratic institutions. The dismissal of charges against General Fabian Ver, who had been implicated in the Aquino murder, and his immediate reinstatement as chief of staff, seriously disappointed American officials. They saw these developments as dooming any hope for meaningful military reform. But no significant U.S. policy change followed, in part because Marcos announced a few days later that he would stand for re-election in early 1986, more than a year ahead of schedule, and attention was quickly diverted to the forthcoming election.

Those officials who were inclined to adopt a stronger anti-Marcos stance also had to contend with President Reagan's continued attachment to Marcos as a friend of the United States. During his 1984 election debate with Walter Mondale, the president had characterized the choice facing the United States as one between Marcos and the communists, a view that dismayed the democratic opposition in the Philippines. Although administration spokesmen subsequently modified the president's position, there was little doubt that his statement reflected his basic feeling. Indeed, when the full story of the evolution of U.S. policy during 1985 and early 1986 finally comes to light, it is likely to revolve around the struggle of Marcos critics in the Congress and of foreign policy and defense specialists in the Administration to convince the top political leadership, and especially President Reagan, that Marcos had become so much of the problem that he could no longer be a significant part of any solution. Congressman Stephen Solarz, chairman of the Subcommittee on Asian and Pacific Affairs of the House Foreign Affairs Committee, who had long been a Marcos critic, was by late 1985 joined by men such as Senator David Durenberger, chairman of the Senate Select Committee on Intelligence, in calling on Marcos to resign. Yet for the leaders of the Administration, who had attacked President Carter for abandoning Somoza of Nicaragua and the Shah of Iran only to see them replaced by worse regimes, walking away from Marcos was psychologically and politically difficult—even though the major opposition forces in the Philippines were clearly democratic in outlook.

The United States was saved from its dilemma when President Marcos made the fatal mistake of calling the early presidential election. Marcos compounded his error by inviting foreign observers and media to observe the election, thereby focusing international attention on the contest. Marcos' misjudgment probably reflected a basic conviction that he could not lose to a divided opposition because he controlled the traditional sources of power; that an election victory would give him a fresh mandate and renewed legitimacy; and that it would silence his critics in the United States. Yet all of his calculations were proven wrong. Most of his opponents united behind Mrs. Aquino, who proved a remarkably able candidate. His years of misrule had so alienated public-spirited citizens, modern-minded businessmen, and the Catholic bishops that they gave dedicated support to Mrs. Aquino's candidacy, seeing it as the last chance for democracy and decency in the country. Moreover, Marcos' popular support had so eroded that it was impossible for him to win the February 7 election with a little bribery here and a little cheating there. The cheating required was vast, and the means available crude and obvious, particularly in key urban areas, and were widely detected and reported on by aroused citizens and by outside observers and media. American conservatives as well as liberals were shocked. In this atmosphere, when Senator Richard Lugar, chairman of the Senate Foreign Relations Committee, proclaimed the election a fraud, the remaining U.S. supporters of Marcos dwindled in number and credibility. President Reagan's statement that there had been cheating on both sides sent shock waves through both the Philippines and the United States, and was quickly retracted.

The climax of these events occurred with the February 22 revolt of Defense Minister Juan Ponce Enrile and Deputy Chief of Staff General Fidel Ramos, who were apparently targeted for arrest by General Ver because of their contact with the military reform group that had arisen in the officer corps—a group of men seeking not a military coup but a return to professionalism. Although Enrile and Ramos initially had only a limited amount of active military support, the Cardinal Archbishop of Manila—who with his fellow bishops on February 13 had declared the election fraudulent and stated that Marcos had lost all moral claim to the people's loyalty—now urged the citizenry of Manila to protect the rebels, and large numbers placed themselves between the rebels and the government forces sent to arrest them. When key government units refused to fire and then defected, the tide began to turn. The United States publicly stated it would halt all military aid to the government if it attacked the rebels, thereby signaling to the Philippine military—and to the Philippine people—that it was in effect supporting the rebellion. When Marcos was told by President Reagan's close friend Senator Paul Laxalt that he should resign, Marcos realistically saw that he had little choice but to surrender power, a decision made easier by a U.S. offer of asylum.

Marcos' downfall was overwhelmingly due to the courage and dedication of vast numbers of the Filipino people, many of whom took great risks to bring about a new order in their country. For all of its earlier support of Marcos and later equivocation about him, however, the United States—even if it did no more than is described here—played an important and constructive role at the crucial moment, and thereby increased its responsibility to help the country overcome the legacy of Marcos' misrule.

Policy Issues Facing the United States

The collapse of the Marcos dictatorship freed the United States from having to deal with a regime so repressive, corrupt, and inefficient that it was leading the country toward disaster. The triumph of Mrs. Aquino offers the United States a far better chance of protecting its interests while simultaneously helping the Philippines build a better life for its people. Yet if the policy issues before the United States have changed dramatically and the outlook for the country has improved substantially, our optimism needs to be tempered by two considerations: an awareness of the magnitude of the tasks facing the new Philippine government, and an appreciation of the limits on American ability to influence or contribute to a resolution of many of the problems facing the country.

Except in the wake of a major war—either foreign or civil— few countries have faced as many serious problems as now confront the Philippines. A new constitution must be drafted and elections held before a stronger and more democratic political system can take root. The drastic overcentralization of power in Manila (chiefly in Marcos himself), which emasculated the institutions of regional and local government, must be reversed if these governmental units are to become responsive to regional and local needs. President Aquino has no institutionalized political base of her own, since she heads no political party. The present government is not only untested, but is composed of disparate elements and rival parties, some of them long-time opponents of Marcos and some collaborators until the last days of his regime. Its ability to maintain enough unity to adopt and implement a cohesive set of policies remains uncertain. Military reform measures and a return to professionalism are essential if the armed forces are to regain the self-confidence and popular support necessary to check the NPA. An independent judiciary must be reestablished so that citizens will see the courts as instruments of justice rather than as tools of the presidency. And at some point the government must seriously address the issue of the future of the U.S. military bases.

Moreover, the economy is in shambles, with gross national product down over 10 percent in the past few years, and per capita incomes more than 15 percent below 1982 levels. This trend must be reversed quickly if the government is to retain popular support, even though it will take several years under the best of circumstances to regain the ground lost in recent years. The government must provide basic economic guidelines while withdrawing from detailed management of the economy, and simultaneously dispose of hundreds of bankrupt companies. The country has approximately $26 billion in foreign debts, much of which was incurred for economically dubious projects for which large "commissions" were charged by Marcos' cronies. Over 40 percent of Filipino exports are currently required to service this debt, and the level could rise to 50 percent if a rescheduling of payments is not worked out.

In short, a society that still has many feudal elements must undergo a major political, social, economic, and military transformation if it is to meet the heightened expectations and demands of the populace. The people do not expect miracles, but they will insist on discernable progress. Can the Filipino "elite"—which includes the present Aquino government—reform the system it has long dominated to its own benefit? There are few examples of such behavior, but it would be a serious mistake to conclude that it is impossible. There is a widespread awareness among much of the elite and the middle class that Marcos was leading the country to ruin, and a strong conviction that massive changes are essential if the country is to have a better future. The country has a well-educated and talented populace, which will respond if a proper political and economic environment is created. A few developments, such as falling interest rates and oil prices in international markets, will ease the country's economic burdens. A start has been made in the area of military reform by the retirement of over-age and incompetent senior officers. And Mrs. Aquino, though untested as a government leader, proved herself to be an unexpectedly able campaigner who set forth—in general terms, to be sure—a sensible set of policies in her campaign.

Under these circumstances, it is not possible to propose detailed U.S. policy positions, or even to forecast with confidence the particular policy issues that the United States will face. It is conceivable, for example, that the Aquino government will falter so badly that the NPA will continue to make steady gains, and the Philippine military will at some point decide it must seize power. Yet despite the present strains between the Aquino forces and the military over the issues of amnesty for NPA rebels and investigations of past military abuses, any open military challenge to the government probably is too far in the future for the United States to plan how it would respond. U.S. actions would depend heavily on the unpredictable specifics of the situation.

In broader terms, however, the United States must deal with two general issues as well as formulate several specific policies toward the Philippines in the next few years. The first task is to decide which of the many problems facing the Philippines are matters that the United States can appropriately and effectively influence. Some, such as the drafting of a new constitution, the holding of elections, and the establishment of an independent judiciary, are matters best left to the Philippines. The United States can certainly express its support for an early return to full democracy, but unless there is a prolonged delay in the process, our approach should be to keep a low profile. The same approach should govern the U.S. stance on the issue of strategy and tactics for negotiating with—and fighting—the NPA. More U.S. military assistance and training for the Philippine military forces are desirable, but we must recognize that U.S. involvement beyond such measures probably would be counterproductive. The United States can, on the other hand, play an active and useful role in helping revive the economy of the Philippines, although certain types of support are likely to be both more feasible and more effective than others.

The second general task is to decide what the general posture and stance of the U.S. government toward the Philippines should be on those issues where U.S. involvement is appropriate. Several points are important in this respect. Given the U.S. government's recent role in the demise of the Marcos regime, its earlier backing of Marcos, and the long history of close Filipino-American ties, the United States should be as supportive as possible of the Aquino government. However, U.S. support should be largely responsive to Philippine requests rather than take the form of an American program or blueprint for the Philippines to follow. The United States can hardly be expected to provide significant resources to the Philippines without any advice or conditions, but since the basic goals of the two governments are the same, the United States should proceed in a low-key manner.

The United States should continue to provide as much of its support as possible in a multilateral context—through international institutions such as the International Monetary Fund, the World Bank, and the Asian Development Bank—and in concert with other donor countries, particularly Japan, in order to increase the level of resources available to the Philippines. Although reforms urged by international institutions can generate nationalist resistance, they are less likely to do so than direct pressures from the United States, and thus those Filipino officials who favor such reforms will be in a stronger position. Finally, although U.S. policy must be flexible enough to deal with unforeseen events, we should accord a high priority to policy stability, which is not always an American strong suit. The task of national reconstruction will fall mainly on Filipino shoulders, and the Philippines will be better served by the predictability of a U.S. policy that consistently provides 75 percent of what they want from us rather than one that gives them 90 percent one year and 50 percent the next.

It is also important for the United States to increase its bilateral aid to the Philippines. The Reagan Administration has announced it will seek an additional $100 million in economic assistance and $50 million in military aid. However, U.S. resources are limited, especially in a time of fiscal stringency, as are the Philippine government's peso resources. One useful method to surmount these problems might be to provide foodstuffs to be used in a food-for-work program to improve both nutritional levels and the infrastructure, especially in rural areas.

There are several ways the United States can help provide larger and more effective amounts of resources than through direct financial assistance. The first, and probably the most important in terms of political symbolism, is to do everything possible under American law to help the Aquino government recover the large sums that Marcos appropriated for his personal use. An American administration that even appears to be shielding Marcos' huge fortune will alienate many Filipinos, as well as find it difficult to persuade Congress to provide increased resources. This need not mean harassing or impoverishing Marcos. Perhaps an arrangement could be reached under which Marcos would return most of his assets while being allowed to keep enough to provide for a comfortable retirement and a haven secure from law suits by the Philippine government.

A second avenue of U.S. support is in the area of debt rescheduling. There are limits to how much more flexible the United States can be in dealing with the Philippines—and can urge other countries and commercial banks to be—relative to other debtor countries. However, given the importance of the Philippines and the history of U.S.-Philippine relations, the United States should be as supportive as it can in order to free up as large a proportion of Philippine export earnings as possible for economic growth. Reducing debt payments is likely to be more valuable, dollar for dollar, than direct aid, since the funds released can be used more flexibly than can government-to-government assistance.

If the United States provides a moderately higher level of bilateral aid, helps arrange the return of Marcos' wealth, and promotes increased multilateral assistance and significant debt relief, these measures could well have a multiplier effect by reviving confidence in the country's future and spurring a return of a sizable part of the billions of dollars of private Filipino capital that fled the country over the past several years. Although the size of these holdings is unknown, and some will remain outside the country in the best of circumstances, the return of such capital from abroad could provide a major stimulus to private investment and economic growth.

Many Filipinos are also urging that the United States provide special treatment for Philippine exports, and some regard this as more important to the country's economic future than U.S. aid. Economic growth is essential if the country's situation is to improve, and the country's economic progress will be heavily dependent upon the growth of exports. Export growth is also essential if the foreign debt burden is to be reduced. Moreover, export earnings would help revitalize the private sector and quickly translate into increased employment and investment. Yet if the importance of export growth is clear, the appropriate and feasible U.S. response is much less so. Many actual and potential Filipino exports are agricultural and light industrial products in competition with U.S. goods already battered by imports, and the rising forces of protectionism suggest the United States may find itself unable to do more than prevent new restrictions on foreign goods. In addition, U.S. trade policy has generally been formulated on a multilateral rather than a bilateral basis, and this basic policy line should be continued. Yet given the importance of the Philippines, and of exports to its future, the United States should make a special effort to provide greater access for at least a few types of goods the Philippines produces, as well as offer some American aid to provide marketing advice and assistance to firms that lack the expertise necessary to sell their goods in the U.S. market.

Another area in which the United States may be able to assist is in combatting the NPA. The armed forces (and police) face two separate but interrelated tasks before they can check the growth of the NPA rather than contribute to the insurgency's expansion by their own corruption, brutality, and inefficiency. One is to foster a return to professionalism, discipline, and honesty in their conduct and their relations with the people. The second is to secure the resources necessary to provide adequate pay, logistics, and weapons to improve their morale and efficiency. The task of reform rests largely in Filipino hands, and the government and the present military leaders have made a promising start. The United States should not become involved in providing resources for improved pay scales for the military and police forces, except indirectly through the contribution we can make to spurring economic growth. But the United States can and should be prepared to undertake a substantial and sustained program of supplying the armed forces with the simple but essential types of equipment needed to fight an insurgency, for even if some NPA guerrillas accept an amnesty offer, large NPA forces are likely to continue their struggle. Uniforms, trucks, radios, simple weapons, and adequate maintenance facilities are what is required by a military establishment whose budget has declined in real terms over the past ten years. Perhaps surplus U.S. stocks can be used to provide some of the necessary items. Although no amount of resources allocated to the military will be adequate to check and then defeat the NPA in the absence of economic growth and economic justice, the armed forces must have the resources to stop the growth of the NPA until improved economic conditions reduce its basic appeal. In thinking of the levels of both military and economic aid, the United States would do well to keep in mind the cost it would face in relocating its military bases if the NPA were to come to power.

The future of the U.S. military bases at Clark Field and Subic Bay will have to be dealt with in the next few years, because the current five-year aid agreement linked to the bases expires in 1989, and the present base agreement can be terminated by either party after a year's notice beginning in 1991. At present, Filipino attitudes toward the bases are divided. In one recent survey, 43 percent of those polled favored continuation of the bases, 23 percent favored their removal, and the rest had no clear position. Another survey found approximately one-third of those polled for the bases, one-third opposed, and one-third without an opinion. Perhaps equally important are the reports of many knowledgeable observers that the bases are not a high priority issue to most Filipinos at this time, although both noncommunist and procommunist leftist forces that oppose the bases are trying to make them such an issue. These facts suggest two points: first, the U.S. should keep a low profile on the bases for the next year or so, with as little public reference to them as is feasible as long as the Philippine government is preoccupied with other issues; and second, the U.S. should study carefully which Filipino concerns about the bases can be accommodated when negotiations do begin, while recognizing that Filipino demands for U.S. concessions will be determined in part by how responsive the U.S. is to other Filipino needs in the next few years. At the same time, we should take at least the initial steps toward preparing the best possible alternatives to the bases, not only in case agreement cannot be reached, but because our bargaining position will improve somewhat if we do so. (Such actions will also strengthen the positions of those Filipinos who want the bases to remain.)

Mrs. Aquino, in a speech just before the February election, set forth a position that provides an insight into her thinking as well as leaving her considerable negotiating leeway. She said:

> Concerning the military bases, let me simply reiterate the assurance I have already given, that we do not propose to renounce the existing Military Bases Agreement or the Treaty of Mutual Defense with the United States. At the same time, however, I must state with candor that no sovereign nation should consent that a portion of its territory be a perpetual possession of a foreign power. The Bases Agreement expires in 1991. Before such date, a process of consultation will be undertaken—with the United States, with neighboring states, but, above all, with the Filipino people—so that an arrangement that will serve the best interest of the entire free world, but especially of the Filipino people, can be reached.

Among the issues likely to arise in the next set of negotiations are: the level of "aid" or "rent" which the Philippines will receive; the possibility of changing the bases agreement from an executive agreement to a full-scale treaty ratified by the U.S. Senate and the Philippine legislature; the "unhampered use" clause, which many Filipinos see as an infringement on sovereignty as well as a possible danger in terms of drawing the Philippines into a war in which the United States might become involved; and the extent of the U.S. obligation to consult with the Philippines regarding its use of the bases. There also may be Filipino pressures to reduce the size of the bases once again.

Although it is unlikely that the United States will have to accede to all the proposals by the Philippines for changes, we clearly must be prepared to meet some of them. We should be as willing as we are able to meet Filipino requests for increased aid, to the extent that U.S. flexibility on this issue is likely to increase Filipino flexibility on other key issues. Such a stance would not only provide resources the Philippines will need, but would also maintain the utility of the bases to the United States. Yet we should recognize that no amount of aid is likely to eliminate the need to be at least partially responsive to some of the other Philippine proposals for changes. Since we still do not know what the specific content of such proposals will be— or what possible trade-offs can be arranged—it is impossible to set forth what our response should be. One useful guideline can be set out, however, namely, that we be particularly responsive to Filipino proposals that would make the bases, both symbolically and actually, a manifestation of a more equal Filipino-American partnership. Such a stance is not easy for a great power to adopt toward a small nation. But we should be aware that in the post-colonial era it is not easy for a small nation to remain close to a major power unless the latter demonstrates in tangible ways that its policies reflect a true concern for the needs of its ally as well as the pursuit of its own national interests.

In sum, the United States must do all that it can to help the Philippines meet the many challenges its faces, while recognizing the limits of American influence in many areas. In post-war Germany and Japan, the United States was able to promote far-reaching reforms—but there it was the occupying power. Less dramatic but still substantial reforms were successfully fostered by the United States in Greece, Taiwan, South Korea, and a few other countries by the combination of skillful use of American resources and influence, supporting local forces interested in bringing about change. Fortunately, there is a democratic if not a strong reform tradition in the Philippines, and there are grounds for hope that, now that democracy has been restored, the Filipino people themselves will insist upon the necessary reforms.

SELECTED READINGS

I. Friend, Tensions in History

Agoncillo, Teodoro. *The Fateful Years: Japan's Adventure in the Philippines, 1941-1945.* 2 vols. Quezon City: R. P. Garcia, 1965.

Bernad, Miguel A. *Tradition and Discontinuity: Essays on Philippine History and Culture.* Manila: National Book Store, 1983.

Constantino, Renato. *Insight and Foresight.* Quezon City: Foundation for Nationalist Studies, 1977.

Friend, Theodore. *Between Two Empires: The Ordeal of the Philippines, 1926-1946.* New Haven: Yale University Press, 1965.

Halle, Louis J. *The United States Acquires the Philippines: Consensus vs. Reality.* Lanham, Md.: University Press of America, 1985.

Joaquin, Nick. *The Aquinos of Tarlac.* Manila: Cacho Hermanos, 1983.

Kerkvliet, Benedict J. *The Huk Revolt in the Philippines.* Berkeley and Los Angeles: University of California Press, 1977.

Lachica, Eduardo. *Huk: Philippine Agrarian Society in Revolt.* Manila: Solidaridad, 1971.

Pringle, Robert. *Indonesia and the Philippines: American Interests in Island Southeast Asia.* New York: Columbia University Press, 1980.

Stanley, Peter W. *A Nation in the Making: The Philippines and the United States, 1899-1921.* Cambridge: Harvard University Press, 1974.

———, ed. *Reappraising an Empire: New Perspectives on Philippine-American History.* Cambridge: Harvard University Press, 1984.

Steinberg, David Joel. *Philippine Collaboration in World War II.* Ann Arbor: University of Michigan Press, 1967.

Steinberg, David Joel. *The Philippines: A Singular and a Plural Place.* Boulder: Westview Press, 1982.

Sturtevant, David. *Popular Uprisings in the Philippines, 1840-1940.* Ithaca: Cornell University Press, 1976.

II. Steinberg, Tradition and Response

Cushner, Nicholas P. *Spain in the Philippines: From Conquest to Revolution,* Quezon City: Ateneo de Manila University, in cooperation with Charles E. Tuttle Co., Rutland, Vermont, 1971.

Edgerton, Ronald K. "The Politics of Reconstruction in the Philippines, 1945-1948." Ph.D. dissertation, University of Michigan, 1975.

Friend, Theodore. *Between Two Empires: The Ordeal of the Philippines, 1929-1946.* New Haven: Yale University Press, 1965.

Guerrero, Leon Ma. *The First Filipino.* Manila: National Heroes Commission Benipayo Press, 1963.

Ileto, Renaldo C. *Pasyon and Revolution: Popular Movements in the Philippines, 1840-1910.* Quezon City: Ateneo de Manila University, 1979.

Kerkvliet, Benedict J. *The Huk Rebellion: A Study of Peasant Revolt in the Philippines.* Berkeley and Los Angeles: University of California Press, 1977.

Larkin, John A. *The Pampangans: Colonial Society in a Philippine Province.* Berkeley and Los Angeles: University of California Press, 1972.

Majul, Cesar A. *Political and Constitutional Ideas of the Philippine Revolution.* Quezon City: University of the Philippines Press, 1967.

Owen, Norman G. "Kabikolan in the 19th Century: Socioeconomic change in the Provincial Philippines." Ph.D. dissertation, University of Michigan, 1976.

Salamanca, Bonifacio S. *The Filipino Reaction to American Rule, 1901-1913.* New Haven: Shoe String Press, 1968.

Schumacher, John N., ed. *Readings in Philippine Church His-*

tory. Quezon City: Ateneo de Manilia University, Loyola School of Theology, 1979.

Schurz, William L. *The Manila Galleon.* Reprint ed., New York: E. P. Dutton & Co., 1959.

Stanley, Peter W. *A Nation in the Making: The Philippines and the United States, 1899-1921.* Cambridge: Harvard University Press, 1974.

Steinberg, David J. *Philippine Collaboration in World War II.* Ann Arbor: University of Michigan Press, 1967.

Wickberg, Edgar. *The Chinese in Philippine Life, 1850-1898.* New Haven: Yale University Press, 1965.

III. Arce and Abad, The Social Situation

Canlas, Dante B. et al. "An Analysis of the Philippine Economic Crisis: A Workshop Report." Mimeographed. Quezon City: University of the Philippines School of Economics, June 1984.

Carroll, John J. "Social Theory and Social Change in the Philippines." *Pulse,* 1:1 (1984).

Castillo, Gelia T. "Beyond Manila: Philippine Rural Problems in Perspective." Ottawa: International Development Research Center, 1979.

————. "Has Bayanihan Gone Out of Style?" *Daluyan,* May-August 1981, pp. 12-29.

————. "How Participatory is Participatory Development? A Review of the Philippine Experience." Makati: Philippine Institute for Development Studies, 1983.

Garner, George. "Interdependence and Competition among the Philippine Rural Poor." In *People Centered Development,* edited by David C. Korten and Rudi Klauss. West Hartford, Ct.: Kumarian Press, 1984.

Hollnsteiner, Mary Racelis. "Confronting Urban Poverty." Working paper prepared for UNICEF Philippines, typescript, 1977.

————. "Mobilizing the Rural Poor through Community Organization." *Philippine Studies* 27:4 (1979), 387-416.

Lynch, Frank. "Perspectives on Filipino Clannishness." *Philippine Sociological Review*, 21:1 (1973).

———. "Social Class in a Bikol Town." Chicago: University of Chicago Philippine Studies Program, 1959.

———. "Trends Report of Studies in Social Stratification and Social Mobility in the Philippines." *East Asian Cultural Studies* 4:1-4 (1965), 164-165.

Makil, Perla Q. "Mobility by Decree: The Rise and Fall of Philippine Influentials since Martial Law." Final Report, Volume 1. Quezon City: Ateneo de Manila Institute of Philippine Culture, 1975.

———. "PAASCU/IPC Study of Schools and Influentials 1969-70." Final Report, Part 1. Quezon City: Ateneo de Manila Institute of Philippine Culture, 1970.

Po, Blondie. "Policies and Implementation of Land Reform in the Philippines, A Documentary Study." Final Report. Quezon City: Ateneo de Manila Institute of Philippine Culture, 1981.

———. "Rural Organizations and Rural Development in the Philippines, A Documentary Study." In *Rural Organizations in the Philippines*, edited by Marie S. Fernandez. Quezon City: Ateneo de Manila Institute of Philippine Culture, 1980, pp. 1-123.

Umehara, Hiromitsu. "Green Revolution for Whom? (An Inquiry into its Beneficiaries in a Central Luzon Village, Philippines)." In *Second View from the Paddy*, edited by Antonio J. Ledesma, Perla Q. Makil, and Virginia A. Miralao. Quezon City: Ateneo de Manila Institute of Philippine Culture, 1983, pp. 24-40.

IV. Noble, Politics in the Marcos Era

Bello, Walden; David Kinley; and Elaine Elinson. *Development Debacle: The World Bank in the Philippines*. San Francisco: Institute for Food Development Policy, 1982.

Harkin, Duncan A. "Philippine Agrarian Reform in the Perspective of Three Years of Martial Law." Madison: University of Wisconsin, Land Tenure Center, 1976.

Majul, Cesar Adib. *The Contemporary Muslim Movement in the Philippines.* Berkeley: Mizan Press, 1985.

McCoy, Alfred W. *Priests on Trial.* Victoria: Penguin Books Australia, 1984.

Mijares, Primitivo. *The Conjugal Dictatorship of Ferdinand and Imelda Marcos.* San Francisco: Union Square Publishers, 1976.

Poole, Fred, and Max Vanzi. *Revolution in the Philippines: The United States in a Hall of Cracked Mirrors.* New York: McGraw-Hill, 1984.

Rosenberg, David A., ed. *Marcos and Martial Law in the Philippines.* Ithaca: Cornell University Press, 1979.

Steinberg, David Joel. *The Philippines: A Singular and Plural Place.* Boulder: Westview Press, 1982.

Youngblood, Robert, "Church Opposition to Martial Law in the Philippines," *Asian Survey*, 18 (May 1978), 505-520.

———, "Structural Imperialism: An Analysis of the Catholic Bishops' Conference of the Philippines." *Comparative Political Studies*, 15 (April 1982), 29-56.

V. Lande, The Political Crisis

Alburo, Florian A. et al. "Towards Recovery and Sustainable Growth." Mimeographed. Quezon City: University of the Philippines, School of Economics, September 1985.

Canlas, Dante B. et al. "An Analysis of the Philippine Economic Crisis: A Workshop Report." Mimeographed. Quezon City: University of the Philippines School of Economics, June 1984.

Hernandez, Carolina G. "The Philippine Military and Civilian Control: Under Marcos and Beyond." *Third World Quarterly*, 7:4 (October 1985), 907-923.

Lande, Carl H., and Richard Hooley. "Aquino Takes Charge." *Foreign Affairs*, 64:5 (1986), 1087-1107.

Marlay, Ross. "Is Ferdinand Marcos a Political Genius?" *Pilipinas. A Journal of Philippine Studies*, 5 (Fall 1985), 1-26.

Munro, Ross. "The New Khmer Rouge." *Commentary*, December 1985, pp. 19-38.

Niksch, Larry A. "The Armed Forces of the Asia-Pacific Region. The Philippines: Uncertainties after the Aquino Assassination." *Pacific Defence Reporter*, February 1984, pp. 21-30.

Rosenberg, David A. "Communism in the Philippines." *Problems of Communism*, September-October 1984.

——. *Marcos and Martial Law in the Philippines*. Ithaca: Cornell University Press, 1979.

Steinberg, David Joel. *The Philippines: A Singular and Plural Place*. Boulder: Westview Press, 1982.

VI. Villegas, The Economic Crisis

Center for Research and Communication. "1985: More of the Same." Monograph, December 1984.

Governor of the Central Bank. "Report to the President: First Quarter 1984." Mimeographed.

National Economic and Development Authority. "Updated Philippine Development Plan, 1984-1987." September 1984.

Republic of the Philippines. "Economic Memorandum." November 1984.

Canlas, Dante B. et al. "An Analysis of the Philippine Economic Crisis: A Workshop Report." Mimeographed. Quezon City: University of the Philippines School of Economics, June 1984.

World Bank. *Annual Report: 1983*.

World Bank. *The Philippines: An Agenda for Adjustment and Growth*. November 30, 1984.

VII. Hernandez, Reconstituting Political Order

Bacungan, Froilan M., ed. *The Powers of the Philippine Executive*. Quezon City: University of the Philippines Law Center, 1983.

Hernandez, Carolina G. "Constitutional Authoritarianism and the Prospects of Democracy in the Philippines." *Journal of International Affairs*, 38:2 (Winter 1985).

————. "The Philippine Military: Under Marcos and Beyond." *Third World Quarterly*, October 1985.

Magno, Alexander R. "Technocratic Authoritarianism and the Dilemmas of Dependent Development." In Godfrey Gunatilleke, Neelan Tiruchelram, and Radhika Coomaraswamy, eds., *Ethical Dilemmas of Development in Asia.* Lexington, Massachusetts: Lexington Books, D. C. Heath and Company, 1983.

————, ed. *The Nation in Crisis: A University Inquires into the Present.* Quezon City: University of the Philippines Press, 1984.

————. "The Succession Crisis; An Artificial Order Disintegration." *Diliman Review*, March-April 1984.

Miranda, Felipe B. "The Future of Government in Developing Countries." *Futuristics*, 1, July 1983.

Nemenzo, Francisco. "The Current Philippine Crisis." *Arena*, 65, December 1983.

————, and R. J. May, eds. *The Philippines after Marcos.* London: Croom-Helm, and New York: St. Martin's, 1985.

Rivera, Temario C., ed. *Feudalism and Capitalism in the Philippines: Trends and Implications.* Quezon City: Foundation for Nationalist Studies, 1982.

VIII. Estanislao, Economic Relations

Estanislao, J. P. "On to Financial Reforms." *Business Day* (Manila), January 1985.

————. "A View on Further Financial Reforms." Paper given at Council of Financial Associations, Manila, April 1985.

————, E. M. Ocol, and F. E. Agdamag. *Broad Dimensions of Long-Term Economic Growth in the Philippines, 1908-1978.* Manila: Center for Research and Communication, 1982.

Gleek, L., Jr. *American Business and Philippine Economic Development.* Manila: Carmelo & Bauermann, 1975.

Hartendorp, A. V. *History of Industry and Trade.* Manila: McCullough Printing Company, 1958.

Legarda, B., Jr., and R. Garcia, "Economic Collaboration: The

Trading Relationship." In Frank Golay, ed., *Philippine-American Relations*. Manila: Solidaridad House, 1966.

Patrick, H., and D. Cole, "Financial Development in the Pacific Basin Market Economies." HIID Development Discussion Paper, 182. Cambridge: Harvard Institute for International Development, 1984.

Ranis, G. "Economic Development and Financial Institutions." Economic Growth Center Discussion Paper. New Haven: Yale University, 1977.

―――. Prepared Statement before the Sub-committee on Asian and Pacific Affairs, Committee on Foreign Affairs, U.S. House of Representatives, Washington, D.C. Mimeograph, 1984.

Sicat, G., and J. Power. *Industrialization in the Philippines*. Manila: University of the Philippines, IEDR, School of Economics, 1970.

Valdepeñas, V., and G. Bautista. *The Emergence of the Philippine Economy*. Manila: Papyrus Press, 1977.

IX. Barnds, Political and Security Relations

Bowen, Alva. *Philippine Bases: U.S. Redeployment Options*. Congressional Research Service Report 86-44F, February 1986.

Buss, Claude. *The United States and the Philippines*. Washington, D.C.: American Enterprise Institute, 1977.

House Foreign Affairs Committee, Subcommittee on Asian and Pacific Affairs. *Situation and Outlook in the Philippines*. Print 39-479-0, 98th Congress, 2nd Session, October 1984.

House Foreign Affairs Committee, Subcommittee on Asian and Pacific Affairs. *U.S.-Philippines Relations and the New Base and Aid Agreement*. Print 23-754-0, 98th Congress, 1st Session, June 1983.

Manning, Robert. "The Philippines in Crisis." *Foreign Affairs*, 63:2 (Winter 1984/85), 392-410.

Meyer, Milton W. *Diplomatic History of the Philippine Republic*. Honolulu: University of Hawaii Press, 1965.

Munro, Ross. "Dateline Manila: Moscow's Next Win?" *Foreign Policy*, 56 (Fall 1984), 173-190.

Pelaez, Emmanuel. "The Military Bases Issue." *Foreign Relations Journal*, 1:1 (January 1986), 1-39.

The Philippines: Facing the Future. An Assessment of the Prospects for the Philippines and for Philippine-American Relations. New York: The Asia Society, 1986.

Senate Foreign Relations Committee. *Insurgency and Counterinsurgency in the Philippines.* Print 99-99, 99th Congress, 1st Session, November 1985.

Senate Foreign Relations Committee. *"The Situation in the Philippines."* Print 98-237, 98th Congress, 2nd Session, October 1984.

Senate Select Committee on Intelligence. *The Philippines: A Situation Report.* Print 99-96, 99th Congress, 1st Session, November 1985.

ABOUT THE AUTHORS

RICARDO G. ABAD is Professor and Chairman of the Department of Sociology and Anthropology as well as Research Associate at the Institute of Philippine Culture, Ateneo de Manila University.

WILFREDO F. ARCE is currently Director of the Institute of Philippine Culture and Professor in the Department of Sociology and Anthropology, Ateneo de Manila University.

WILLIAM J. BARNDS is President of the Japan Economic Institute of America. He was Staff Director of the Subcommittee on Asian and Pacific Affairs of the House Foreign Affairs Committee from 1981 to 1985

JOHN BRESNAN is Senior Research Fellow and Director, Pacific Basin Studies Program, East Asian Institute, Columbia University; and Senior Program Associate and Staff Director, Williamsburg Conferences, The Asia Society.

JESUS P. ESTANISLAO is Chairman of The Development Bank of the Philippines. He has been President of Associated Bank and Executive Director of the Center for Research and Communications in Manila.

THEODORE FRIEND is President of Eisenhower Exchange Fellowships, Inc., based in Philadelphia. He was previously President of Swarthmore College.

CAROLINA G. HERNANDEZ is Professor and Chairperson of the Department of Political Science at the University of the Philippines.

CARL H. LANDE is Professor of Political Science and Asian Studies at the University of Kansas.

DAVID D. NEWSOM is Associate Dean of the School of Foreign Service and Director of the Institute for the Study of Diplomacy at Georgetown University. He was Ambassador to the Philippines in 1977-1978.

LELA GARNER NOBLE is Professor of Political Science and Associate Academic Vice President for Faculty Affairs, San Jose State University.

DAVID STEINBERG is President of Long Island University. He has been consultant to the U.S. government, agencies of the United Nations, and the Ford Foundation.

BERNARDO VILLEGAS is Chief Economist and Senior Vice President of the Center for Research and Communication in Manila. He is also a member of the board of directors of numerous national and multinational firms.

INDEX

Aglipay, Gregorio, 9
Agoncillo, Teodoro, 127
Agrava Commission, 24, 115, 181
Agriculture: American influence on, 10; economic situation and, 151-52; foreign domination of, 60-61; Japanese influence on, 153; monopolies, 164-68; plantation, 44, 99; problems of, 92-94; productivity of, 90-91, 99; reform of, 90-94, 99, 160-61, 172, 175; rice self-sufficiency and, 99, 160-61; sugar as product of, 44, 93; trade and, 213. *See also* Hukbalahap rebellion; Land reform; Rural population
Aguinaldo, Emilio, 4, 6, 7, 9, 47
Aguinaldo, Leopoldo, 10-11
Alliance of Multi Sectoral Organizations (AMA), 123
Amendment No. 6, 180
American colonization of the Philippines, 8-9, 17, 26, 47-49, 119, 152-53, 201-204, 206, 232
Aquino, Agapito, 124, 125
Aquino, Belinda, 89-90
Aquino, Benigno, Jr.: arrest of, 23; background of, 24, 114-15; blamed for Plaza Miranda bombing, 83; blames Marcos for unrest, 84, 87; exile of, 113, 115; attitude about Interim National Assembly, 123; as a martyr, 24, 31; protests suspension of writ of habeas corpus, 82; television appearance from prison of, 97; testifies at U.S. Congressional hearings, 70-71; U.S. secures release from prison of, 104. *See also* Aquino, Benigno, Jr., assassination of

Aquino, Benigno, Jr., assassination of: demonstrations and, 116, 117, 139; economic situation and, 145, 147-49, 151, 170; elections and, 139-42; politics and, 114-18, 121-24, 129, 139-42; Presidential Decree No. 1952 and, 180-81; United States reaction to, 244, 246
Aquino, Corazon: Catholic church helps, 31; military base views of, 256; personal popularity of, 195-96; supporters of, 176-78. *See also* Aquino-Laurel government; Election of 1986; PDP-Laban; Philippine Democratic Party; UNIDO, PDP-Laban
Aquino-Laurel government: armed forces and, 251; communism and, 144, 178, 189-91, 250-51; democracy and, 198-99; dismantling Marcos' machine by, 177-78; inexperience of, 249-50; mass media and, 195; military base position of, 256; potential of, 29, 198-99; problems of, 28, 177-79, 249; recovery of Marcos' fortune by, 252-53; separation of powers in, 186; support for, 25, 142, 187-88, 194-96, 251-52; two-party system and, 142; United States support for, 251-52. *See also* Election of 1986; PDP-Laban; People power; UNIDO; UNIDO, PDP-Laban
Armed forces: Aquino-Laurel government and, 251; corruption in, 137; election of 1986 and, 142; economic situation and, 110-11; expenditures of, 168; Ilocanization of, 135, 136, 138; increased

LIBRARY OF CONGRESS CATALOGING-IN-PUBLICATION DATA

Crisis in the Philippines.

Bibliography: p.   Includes index.
1. Philippines—History—1946-   . 2. United
States—Relations—Philippines.   3. Philippines—
Relations—United States.   4. Marcos, Ferdinand E.
(Ferdinand Edralin), 1917-   . I. Bresnan, John, 1927-
DS686.5.C75 1986   959.9′046   86-91448
ISBN 0-691-05490-8
ISBN 0-691-00810-8 (pbk.)